W9-BEF-516

LONDON 200

AN ILLUSTRATED HISTORY

LONDON
200

AN ILLUSTRATED HISTORY

ORLO MILLER

With Miriam Wright, Edward Phelps *and* Glen C. Phillips

© Copyright Orlo Miller, London, Ontario 1988 (text of *This Was London*)
© Copyright 1992 by London Chamber of Commerce: Corporate Profiles, historical additions, captions, etc.

All rights reserved. The use of any part of this publication reproduced, transmitted in any form or by any means, electronic, mechanical, photo-copying, recorded, or otherwise, or stored in a retrieval system, without the prior consent of the publisher, is an infringement of copyright law.

Canadian Cataloguing in Publication Data

Miller, Orlo, 1911-
   London 200: An Illustrated History

Rev. ed.
Previously published under title: This was London.
Includes bibliographical references and index.
ISBN 0-920298-98-2

1. London (Ont.) - History.   1. Title.   II. Title:
This was London.

FC3099.L65M54 1992   971.3'26   C92-095340-9
F1059.5.L65M54 1992

Published 1992 by London Chamber of Commerce
Printed and bound in Canada

IN RECOGNITION OF THE 200TH ANNIVERSARY
OF THE CITY OF LONDON

A LONDON CHAMBER OF COMMERCE PROJECT with the authorization of the London 200 Committee.

EDITORIAL ADVISORY COMMITTEE

Chairman
Jack Mann
   London Chamber of Commerce

Members
Jim Etherington
   London Life Insurance Co.

Duncan Callam
   Coopers & Lybrand

Kay McLaughlin

Pat Betteridge
   London Chamber of Commerce

Karen Hueston
   The Aylmer Express Ltd.

Greg Salmela
   Thomas Watt Cohen McCall

Edward Phelps
   University of Western Ontario Library

Glen C. Phillips

Miriam Wright

Marisa Zammit

Project Manager
Jack Mann
   London Chamber of Commerce

Associate Editor
Edward Phelps

Layout & Design
Greg Salmela
   Thomas Watt Cohen McCall

Business Profiles
Marisa Zammit
   London Chamber of Commerce

Editorial Assistant
Miriam Wright

Photo Editor & Researcher
Glen C. Phillips

Printing & Publication
Karen Hueston
   The Aylmer Express Ltd.

Proof Reader
Alice M. Gibb

Contents

Please note: Chapter 12 has been revised and updated by Miriam Wright and Edward Phelps in collaboration with Orlo Miller.
Chapters 13 and 14 have been compiled and written by Miriam Wright and Edward Phelps.
Chapter 15 has been provided by the London Chamber of Commerce.

Foreword

Michael Ondaatje wrote in the preface to *The Faber Book of Contemporary Canadian Stories* that "The past is still, for us, a place that is not safely settled." That's an interesting thought for you as you read your way through Orlo Miller's re-published history of London, Ontario. This is not an ordinary history book as it is not only enjoyable but also highly readable. In Canada we just don't think about our past in that way. Unless it's complicated, slightly boring, and difficult to follow, it can't be Canadian history, safely settled or not.

Orlo Miller must have missed those lessons on how to write history. He positively revels in the stories of London from its almost accidental founding, through the turbulent years when far-away wars dictated the strength of our local economy, to a host of interesting characters that we wish we had met.

London has always been "the city" for me, growing up as I did on a farm near Exeter. As a child I loved to hear the story of one of my great-grandparents who walked through the woods down the Huron Tract to London to acquire a hoe so he could put in the spring crop in frontier Exeter. He didn't have enough pennies to buy the hoe, so he walked home and planted the crop with an axe.

For one fascinating decade I was a news reporter with the London *Free Press* and that gave me an opportunity to meet many interesting people including Orlo Miller. Before I knew him as a writer and eminent historian, I knew him as a "good interview". He seemed to know everything there was about London and that isn't surprising when you learn he was a leader in reorganizing the London and Middlesex Historical Society in 1936.

In 1988 he wrote and had published *This Was London*, a book packed solid with the anecdotes, the events, and the people who were part of London's history since March 2, 1793. That was the date when John Graves Simcoe gazed on the forks of the Thames River and pronounced it a fitting site for the capital of Upper Canada. Now, most people recognize that some place called York, and later Toronto, ended up as the capital, but that hasn't really bothered the people of London very much. We just went on chopping down trees and paving muddy streets for a couple of hundred years and now it's time to look back two centuries and celebrate a bit.

Thus, when a group of dedicated citizens formed the London 200 Committee and asked for ideas on how to make 1993 a special year, the London Chamber of Commerce began thinking about publishing a suitable history book. The Chamber had had some experience in publishing with *The Forest City, An Illustrated History of London* produced in 1986.

History is philosophy by examples.
Dionysius of Halicarnassus
(c. 40-8 BC)

Historian Edward Phelps brought to the Chamber's attention the now out-of-print Miller book *This Was London* and offered to oversee the updating and reprinting of 200 years of London's history in this book. Ed Phelps and I go back more than 30 years when he was a student councillor and I was the editor of the University of Western Ontario *Gazette*.

An interesting addition to the original book are the stories of 44 London businesses and organizations and the roles that they have played in the history of our community. Many of the companies, of course, are mentioned in Orlo Miller's narrative as they have been part of the fabric of the city for a century or more. But the book's heart and soul is pure Orlo. In many ways he "owns" a large piece of the history of London. We at the Chamber of Commerce are proud to be a part of Orlo's legacy to the community.

We are also pleased to be a part of the 1993 celebrations and authorized to produce this, the official history book for London 200. The Chamber's roots go back to 1857 when the city was working its way through a major depression. Thus it is both appropriate and coincidental that we join today with Orlo Miller to mark a new beginning from an old past.

Jim Etherington

Nearly all our best men are dead! Carlyle, Tennyson, Browning, George Eliot! — I'm not feeling very well myself. Punch, 104 (1893), 210

Preface
to the first edition, 1988

This is a social history of a middle-sized Canadian City.

It covers a period of 195 years, from the time it emerged as a concept in the mind of John Graves Simcoe, the first lieutenant- governor of Upper Canada, to the present year.

It may justifiably be called an "anecdotal history." It is meant to be read, not grappled with. An attempt has been made in this history to present as fair a picture as possible of the various strata of London society over the 162 years of its official existence.

Much space has been devoted in the past to the story of London's Establishment — the community leaders, the wealthy and the influential. The middle classes — the artisans, the small merchant and businessmen, the professionals — have received a lesser amount of attention. The poor, the disadvantaged, the visible and invisible minorities have been largely ignored. What is here written about then can in no sense be construed as the last word on the subject. One can only hope it may be the first.

No city, not even one as prideful and insular as London, Ontario, exists in a vacuum. Inevitably its history is influenced by events occurring far outside its boundaries. Marshall McLuhan did not invent the global village. He merely gave it definition.

To demonstrate this linkage between urbs et orbis, a timetable is appended at the bottom of each page. These entries illustrate what events were taking place in the contemporary world outside the Forks.

Finally, I would ask the reader to remember that the people who inhabit these pages were real people. They were not statistics or mere dates on cemetery headstones. They did brave things. They did stupid things, just like us.

However, it must always be remembered that they obeyed standards and reacted to stimuli that were much different from ours. Failure to recognize this basic fact has resulted in much distortion of historical evidence. As the American writer Gerald W. Johnson wrote in 1943:

> Nothing changes more constantly than the past; for the past that influences our lives does not consist of what happened but of what men believe happened.

This present book purports to be a record of some of the things that actually happened in London, Canada, between 1793 and 1988.

History is bunk.
Henry Ford
(1863-1947)

Acknowledgements

It was Major Hume Blake Cronyn who first aroused my interest in the general subject of history. It was Dr. Fred Landon who directed my attention to the history of my own community. It was Dr. Edwin Seaborn who helped me unearth previously unknown collections of original source material. It was Dr. Richard E. Crouch who provided me with quarters to use as a centre for historical and genealogical research. I am deeply indebted to the memory of those dear friends of many years ago.

Since 1926, the year of the centennial of London's founding, I have relied heavily on the resources and assistance of the London Public Library and the library of the University of Western Ontario.

Over the years the staff of the municipally-operated library have given me generous help under a succession of librarians, beginning with Fred Landon and continuing with his successors, Richard Crouch, Deane Kent, Stanley Beacock, and the present director, Reid Osborne. Staff members to whom I am especially obliged include Miss Eleanor Shaw, Miss Elizabeth Spicer, and the present custodian of the London Room, Glen Curnoe.

At the University of Western Ontario I have enjoyed the academic assistance and personal friendship of Dr. James J. Talman, Dr. Landon's successor as Librarian. I owe an enormous debt of gratitude and affection to the indefatigable director of the Regional Collection, Edward Phelps, whose skill in finding and annexing source material is legendary. I am grateful to many of his colleagues at the D.B. Weldon Library, including John Lutman, Guy St.-Denis, Stephen Harding, and Alan Noon.

Many individuals have provided help. Martha Blackburn who, like her late father, Walter J. Blackburn, is a good friend, has graciously given permission for the use of material from *A Century of Western Ontario*, a history of the London *Free Press*. Janet Hunten has brought many pictures and articles to my attention. Nancy Poole, director of the London Regional Art Gallery, has always been a tower of strength, academically and personally.

Above and beyond all these friends of history, I submit my heartfelt thanks to my wife, collaborator, editor, critic, and CEO (Chief Encouraging Officer) Maridon, who has shared in, and suffered from, my obsession with the past.

Finally I must acknowledge the city of London itself, my joy and my despair.

May it someday grow up and take its place among other gracious cities of the world.

Orlo Miller, March, 1988

Mad from life's history, Glad to death's mystery, Swift to be hurl'd Anywhere, anywhere, Out of the world!
Thomas Hood
(1799-1845)

CHAPTER ONE

Beginnings

FROM ADAM TO JOSHUA

*It is a place with only one post a day ... In the country
I always fear that creation will expire before tea-time.*
— Reverend Sydney Smith

When Queen Victoria reigned over the world, many village antiquarians began the history of their community with the creation of the world. In that most stable of Western societies, in Victoria's empire of certainty, that precise date was registered on the first page of many popular Bibles. It had been established by an eminent Irish cleric, Archbishop James Ussher (1581-1656) that this event occurred on a certain day in October, 4004 B.C.

Well!

The bishop's painstaking research served Christendom well for a couple of centuries. Then, in the nineteenth century Charles Darwin's epic voyage in the *Beagle* and the discovery of an ancient skull in the Neanderthal in Germany destroyed that comfortable image of time, the ever-rolling Anglican stream.

According to the new dispensation, we now know that on the date laboriously worked on by James Ussher, the hill of Jericho, in the Holy Land, had been home to a community of human beings for more than five thousand years.

About that same time, say 9000 B.C. a party of Paleo-Indians were enjoying a fish fry on Manitoulin Island in Lake Huron. Soon after Ussher's creation date of 4004 B.C., the descendants of the fish-eaters were mining flint at what is now Port Franks on Lake Huron and selling the weapons made from the stone to both sides in a continuing war between divisions of the Iroquois people.

Geologically speaking, the history of the site of the city of London begins somewhat earlier than all of the dates so far mentioned. It begins with the retreat of the massive glacier that covered the northern half of North America during the last of the enigmatic Ice Ages. At the height of the glaciation, the ice was over one mile thick above the site of London's city hall. Most of it has now melted.

The melting ice sheet spawned a great Niagara of water which formed the giant ancestor of the Thames River. When it, over the millennia, shrank to something like its present dimensions, it left piles of debris and puddles of stagnant water behind. The hillocks of gravel mark the course of

JOHN GRAVES SIMCOE
John Graves Simcoe, Upper Canada's first lieutenant-governor, embraced the future site of London as the location for his provincial capital. His plans, however, were dashed and York (Toronto) was selected as the seat of government.

1789
George Washington elected first US President.

LAWSON SITE, 1986

Paleo-Indian peoples came to the London area upon the retreat of the last glacier some 15,000 years ago. In the 1400s, a thriving village of nearly 1,000 Neutral Indians existed at what is now known as the Lawson Site at the London Museum of Archaeology. The longhouse, a reconstruction of which is pictured, was central to the Neutral's civilization.

1793

York (renamed Toronto in 1834) is founded by Governor John Graves Simcoe and becomes the Upper Canada capital.

the retreat of the ice. The puddles are now very old swamps. At least one — the Sifton Bog — lies within the city limits of the modern city.

From these remote stations in the corridors of time we must leap a dozen millennia before we come to anything of interest to our T.V.-weary eyes. Native Indian peoples, from time to time, set up farming villages, but mysteriously abandon the area sometime in the sixteenth century. The "distinct society" of the French period made very little impression on the site of London. Some unknown traveller christened the river *La Tranche* and an unknown French gentleman left his bones and a dress sword in a grave in a knoll in what is now downtown London.

We must move forward still in time before we find the beginnings of the present city. The future City of London takes its shape in the mind of a man with a military map of Upper Canada and a vision.

MONDAY, 4 FEBRUARY 1793

The Gov. set off from hence (Niagara-on-the-Lake) in a sleigh with 6 officers & 20 soldiers for the Mohawk Village on the Grand River where Capt. Brant & 20 Indians are to join him & guide him by the La Tranche River to Detroit, no European having gone that track & the Indians are to carry provisions.

The Gov. wore a fur Cap tippet & Gloves & Maucassins but no Great Coat. His servant carried two Blankets & linen. The other Gentlemen carried their Blankets in a pack on their Back.

Mrs. Simcoe's Diary, ed. Mary Quayle Innis (Toronto: Macmillan of Canada, 1965).

By an act of Parliament of Great Britain, the western portion of the old Province of Quebec, from the Ottawa River to the Detroit, has been set up as a separate British colony under the name Upper Canada. The appointee of King George III to the governorship of the new province is Lieutenant-Colonel John Graves Simcoe, a veteran of the late war with the rebellious American colonies, which have now been transformed into a republic under the presidency of General George Washington.

Along the banks of the St. Lawrence and Niagara rivers and the north shore of Lake Ontario, smoke rises from the chimneys of the log-cabin homes of thousands of dispossessed persons made homeless by the revolution, heroes by act of parliament. The United Empire Loyalists are settling into their new homes, preparing to establish a tradition, a way of life, a national mythology.

Westward of these pioneer encroachments, there is little but wilderness and wolves. Here and there along the waterways — at Brantford on the Grand River, at Delaware on what is now the Thames, and at Sandwich on the Detroit River — an occasional plume of smoke unfurls in the damp spring air from the clearing of a solitary settler. Between these lonely shielings, nothing but the leafy hush of the nearly impenetrable forest. This is the Western District of the Province of Upper Canada. Its southern limit is Lake Erie, its northern (by statute), Rupert's Land.

In the heart of this huge administrative district, the capital of which is Detroit, on a high, pine-crowned bluff overlooking the confluence of the two branches of the river known to the courieur de bois as *La Tranche,* a group of men in military uniforms stands surveying the scene. The envoy of King George III is inspecting his royal master's western dominion.

Accompanying Simcoe are his aides-de-campe, Lieutenants Thomas Talbot, Thomas Grey, James Givins and surveyor David William Smith. The governor's secretary Major Edward Baker Littlehales is taking careful notes, for this is a special stop on the vice-regal tour. He notes the reason later, in his journal:

> We struck the Thames at one end of a low, flat Island, enveloped with shrubs and trees. The rapidity and strength of the current were such as to have forced a channel through the mainland, being a peninsula, and formed this Island. We walked over a rich meadow, and at its extremity came to the forks of the River. The Gov'r wished to examine this situation and its environs, therefore we remained here all the day. He judged it to be a situation eminently calculated for the metropolis of all Canada. ...

In this manner a dream was born. Say, rather, still-born, for Simcoe's plan was not viewed with favour in the places where such decisions were made, in Quebec City or London, England. A site known by the Indians and the French as Toronto was renamed York and established by Simcoe, however reluctantly, as the capital of the province.

Besides selecting the site for the future city of London, the Simcoe party also managed to sample some exotic cuisine:

> The young Indians, who had chased a herd of deer in company with Lt. Givins, returned unsuccessful, and brought with them a large porcupine, which was very seasonable, as our provisions were nearly expended. This animal afford-

COUNTIES OF UPPER CANADA, 1793
Based primarily on various French explorations, this map, dated 1793 and registered with the Colonial Office in London, England, depicts the temporary electoral counties established by John Graves Simcoe in what would become present-day Southwestern Ontario. Simcoe's Upper Canada, especially its western reaches, was largely an unsettled wilderness.

1793
Slavery abolished in Upper Canada by an act of the first Parliament, at Niagara.

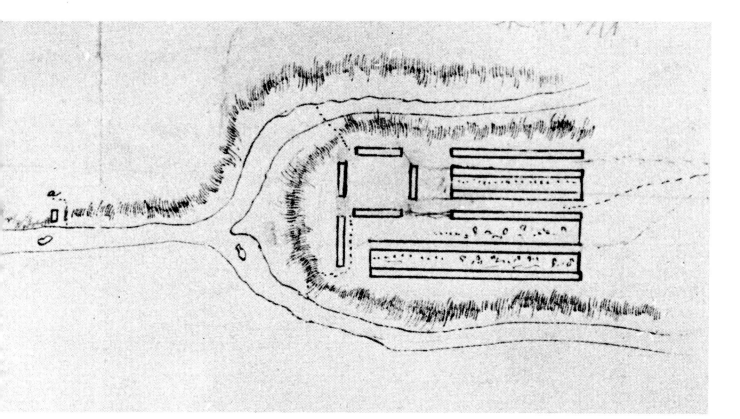

**"THE FORKS"
TOWNSITE, 1793**
*Upon his arrival at
"The Forks" on
March 2, 1793, John
Graves Simcoe em-
braced the future site
of London as his
choice for the capital
of Upper Canada.
His wife, Elizabeth
Postuma Gwillim
Simcoe, sketched this
somewhat ambitious
townsite for "The
Forks". Among other
features, Mrs. Sim-
coe's plan called for
her own villa (indi-
cated by the letter
"a" to the left).*

1793
*Alexander Macken-
zie reaches the
Pacific Ocean from
Montreal, by land.*

ed us a very good repast and tasted like a pig. The Newfoundland dog attempting to bite the porcupine, his mouth was filled with the barbed quills and
gave him exquisite pain. An Indian undertook to extract them and, with much
perseverance, plucked them out one by one, and carefully applied a root or
decoction, which speedily healed the wounds.

And, they stumbled across London's first art gallery:

Various figures were delineated on trees at the forks of the River Thames, done
with charcoal and vermillion; the most remarkable were the imitation of men
with deer's heads.

Promising beginnings indeed!

From the coming of the Loyalists in 1784 until the War of 1812,
immigration into Upper Canada flowed from south to north — from the
New England states, New York, and the adjacent Northwest Territory into
the Canadas. After the war the direction changed. The next great tide of
immigration flowed from east to west. Building to a crest in 1832, the year
that saw 92,000 migrants reach British North America, this movement originated in the United Kingdom. Dispossessed Scottish crofters, famine-
weakened Irish peasants, land-hungry English tenant farmers — all saw
Canada as a land of promise, a new Canaan overflowing with milk and
honey. Land in this new dominion of trees was free for the asking. Every
man could become a land-owner in his own right. In the Old Country a
single freehold acre made a man a proprietor. Here, every Tom O'Brien,
Dick Brown, and Harry MacKenzie could have a fifty-, one hundred-, or
two hundred-acre *estate*, by simply asking for it.

Thus, in the course of a single generation, from this tattered collection of beggars, thieves, rogues, failed merchants, tax evaders, shepherds,
and little people, there emerged a Canadian middle class.

In hundreds of clearings throughout the length and breadth of the peninsula, smoke is rising from the settlers' chimneys. In the last thirty years the population of the western section of the province has increased tenfold. From the older settled areas in the east the tide of immigration has been flowing steadily westward. A decade ago, in 1816, the vanguard has surged to and past the Long Point district on Lake Erie. The high-water mark of this period was the little village of Vittoria. As a centre of population, it became the administrative capital of the huge District of London. A courthouse was built here that also housed the District grammar school.

Now, in 1826, the centre of population has shifted. It may now be placed at the geographical centre of the district that bears the name placed upon it by the late Governor Simcoe — London — at approximately the forks of the River Thames. North and south of the Forks are two rapidly growing settlements.

South, in the Township of Westminster, a mix of Scots and New Englanders, with the Americans predominating numerically. North, in the Township of London, a growing settlement of Tipperary Irish Protestants, awaiting the arrival of their Roman Catholic compatriots to renew old feuds and shed new blood.

Squarely between these two thriving groups, at the Forks itself — almost nothing. From time to time, since 1807, the land here has been involved in paper transactions of licences of occupation, squatters have squatted, shacks have been built and most have fallen down, speculators have gambled, lost, and moved on. But, in early 1826, at Simcoe's chosen dream-city, not a smoking chimney was to be seen.

The governor's phantom community is still part of the twilight zone, even though it appears, firmly marked in its proper place, in a geography textbook printed in England, in 1824.

Why?

How is it that with settlements springing up on all sides, with the strategic location of the site so apparent, how is it that this splendid, pine crowned bluff overlooking the fertile forks of the Thames stands bare and lifeless? Quite simply, the government at York has still not opened Simcoe's reserve to permanent settlement.

But, let us look at the site more closely. For clarity, we will use the modern street grid. First, the bluff itself, an elevation that falls steeply from its crest to the west and north. The pitch is still evident today from the west, but the declivity to the north is camouflaged by 150 years of road-building. The original surface of the ground at the corner of Dundas and Ridout streets is nearly twenty feet below the modern roadway.

Directly to the east of the bluff is a swamp that covers half the area of a city block, fed by a meandering, marshy stream. Tradition claims that an early resident lost a wagon to the gluey depths of the bog, which was apparently filled in by the 1840s. Southward, a second creek, its bed marked by two more miasmic marshes, wanders down to the south branch of the Thames, in the general vicinity of the former Hay Stationery building on York Street. Nearly a kilometre to the north, a third stream, much larger than the other two, but just as swampy, feeds into the north branch

1806
Death of Governor Simcoe (served in Upper Canada 1791-1796), at his home in Exeter, England.

Arrangement For 1831.

Niagara Falls, Oswego, Montreal and Quebec.

THE SPLENDID NEW STEAM-BOAT

Great Britain
CAPT. JOS. WHITNEY,

PROPELLED by two Low Pressure Engines, 90 Horse power each, *Boilers on the Guards.*   Will leave Niagara, at 4 o'clock, P. M. every fifth day, viz:

JULY, 5th, 10th, 15th, 20th, 25th, 30th.
AUG.   5th, 10th, 15th, 20th, 25th, 30th.
SEPT. 5th, 10th, 15th, 20th, 25th, 30th.

Calling at *Oswego* on the following morning, (previous to the departure of the Canal Packet Boats for Syracuse,) also Kingston and Brockville, and arrive at Prescott the same evening ; at which place Stages are always in readiness to convey Passengers to Montreal.

Will leave Prescott, at 1 o'clock, A. M. every 5th day:

JULY, 3d, 8th, 13th, 18th, 23d, 28th.
AUG.   3d, 8th, 13th, 18th, 23d, 28th.
SEPT. 3d, 8th, 13th, 18th, 23d, 28th.

Calling at Brockville, Kingston, and at *Oswego* on the evening of the same day, also at York and Niagara.   The GREAT BRITAIN was built in the Fall of 1830, by Messrs. Brown & Bell, of New-York, is 162 feet in length, Promenade Deck 148 feet, extreme breadth 60 feet.

The Ladies' and Gentlemen's Cabins are finished in the same manner as the New-York and Liverpool Packet ships, with State Rooms.   No expense has been spared in furnishing the Boat in the most comfortable manner, and every endeavour will be used to accommodate Passengers and ensure regularity.

By this conveyance Passengers from Buffalo can arrive at Oswego in 24 hours.   Passage including fare from Niagara to Oswego $6.

JULY 1, 1831.

David M. Day, Printer, Buffalo, N. Y.

STEAMBOAT BROADSIDE, 1831
For the newly arrived immigrant, during the 1830s, the fastest trip from Quebec City to London was best accomplished through a combined series of water and land routes. The steamboat Great Britain *carried the new arrival from the St. Lawrence River port of Prescott to the western head of Lake Ontario. From either York (Toronto) or Niagara, the traveller then proceeded to London by stagecoach or on foot.*

1824
William Lyon Mackenzie starts his Colonial Advocate *newspaper in Queenston, U.C., soon moves to York (Toronto).*

of the Thames, south of Oxford Street.

Between the two southern streams and the northern watercourse there is a tall gravelly knoll, roughly located on the present street allowance between St. Paul's Cathedral and the London Club. At the foot of this knoll, extending from Queens Avenue to Dundas Street, a quicksand bog. The Dominion Public Building at the corner of Queens Avenue and Richmond Street, the former press room of the London *Free Press* on the east side of Richmond Street, and the Canadian Imperial Bank of Commerce building at the northeast corner of Dundas and Richmond streets — all have their footings in this ancient Ice Age bog.

South of the quicksand trap is another gravelly knoll. Where this hillock was, on the east side of Richmond Street, between Dundas and King streets, there stands today one half of a major commercial building erected in the year London became a city. The fire that destroyed part of the structure left the datestone intact — The Victoria Block 1855. In clearing this site for the building the contractors of 138 years ago found the grave of the unknown French gentleman, dress-sword at his side.

This then was the site of London in the year 1826 — sand, gravel, trees, marshy streams, the debris of the great glaciers of the Ice Age.

To Simcoe's military mind, the physical conditions of the site in no way detracted from its strategic importance. Those same conditions, however, rendered it inappropriate for farming and so the Forks remained unoccupied.

Now, a generation after the governor's visit, Simcoe's dream-capital has been given a second chance. In November, 1825, the London District courthouse and gaol at Vittoria were heavily damaged by fire. This gave the authorities an opportunity to choose a more central location for the administrative capital. A principal factor in the eventual choice of the Forks of the Thames was undoubtedly the influence of Simcoe's former aide-de-campe Thomas Talbot on the members of the commission appointed to determine where the new courthouse was to be built.

It has fallen to Talbot's right-hand supporter, the dour New Jersey native Colonel Mahlon Burwell, to lay out the new townsite. Among his helpers, all anxious to pick up a few much-needed government shillings, is a local tavern keeper, a Highlander named Peter MacGregor, who is serving as a chain bearer.

By late summer, the plan of the new town is complete — on paper.

The plan is much more modest than the sketched outline of Simcoe's city, which is to be found in the National Archives at Ottawa. As defined in Burwell's work the site was bounded on the south and west by the Thames River. The northern boundary is a street allowance appropriately called North Street. This street jogs to the south around the southern boundary of the farm owned by John Kent since 1824. The jogged portion of the street is now called Carling, the eastern section is Queens Avenue.

The eastern border of the town plot is a street named in honour of Thomas Talbot's boyhood friend, Arthur Wellesley, Duke of Wellington. Between Wellington Street and the Forks, one north-south thoroughfare is named for the Duke of Clarence, card-playing regal roisterer, third son of the third George and drinking companion in the days of the Regency of the same Thomas Talbot. Another bears the name of the Duke of Richmond, governor-general of Canada, which country he made famous in 1819 by dying of hydrophobia in what were then its western wilds. One is named for Talbot himself and one for Thomas Ridout, surveyor-general of Upper Canada, to whom presumably Mahlon Burwell was indebted for this and other surveying commissions. Ridout Street, following an ancient Indian trail, is the community's principal north-south artery.

The major east-west street is Dundas, a road built by order of Governor Simcoe to connect the village of Dundas, on Lake Ontario, with his phantom city of London. Both the road and the village were named for the Right Honourable Henry Dundas, secretary of state for the Home Department from 1791 to 1801. Another east-west street is named after His Majesty King George IV (King Street); another for Frederick Augustus,

1825
Erie Canal completed between Albany and Buffalo, N.Y., a boon to immigrants and travellers to Upper Canada.

Duke of York, second son of George III, who was Thomas Talbot's commander in the ill-fated invasion of Holland by the British Army in 1799; one bears the name of Wilmot Horton, under-secretary of state for the colonies, and the last honours Henry, third Earl of Bathurst, colonial secretary and secretary for war from 1812 to 1827.

The names are grandiose. The markers are wooden stakes pounded into gravel, sand, and mud.

MONDAY, 2 OCTOBER 1826

In the bogs, the bullfrogs are croaking. Overhead, a flock of geese honks mournfully, southbound over the scarlet and yellow forest.

On the main branch of the Thames, below the Forks, a river ferryman, pole poised in midstream, stops. Struck by something unusual in the well-known scene, he looks upriver. With his ague-stricken forefinger he draws his passengers' attention to a slow stream of smoke, crawling into the upper air from a hidden chimney behind the bluff that crowns the Forks.

It's the smoke of London's *first* chimney.

Eastward of the site, a seventeen-year-old resident of London Township, on his way to the grist mill at Byron, also notices the rising signal of human habitation. Many years later, when he is an internationally-renowned Methodist minister, author, and supporter of women's rights, the Reverend Doctor Thomas Webster will recall that autumn evening and identify the two participants in the domestic drama at the Forks. They were, according to him, Peter MacGregor and his friend John Woods.

The following morning, by the simple process of hanging a tin cup on the doorjamb, first settler Peter MacGregor becomes London's first hotel-and-tavern-keeper, its first businessman. He is soon joined by others. Abraham Carroll, a United Empire Loyalist from Westminster Township, opens a second hotel, grandly christened Mansion House, on Dundas Street. Work is done on a pretentious, Gothic-style courthouse, designed more or less in the fashion of Thomas Talbot's birthplace, Malahide Castle, Dublin, Ireland. The affable Dennis O'Brien, a former pedlar, opens the town's store, sells his first stock over a board suspended between two kegs. The Church of England sends a missionary priest, the Reverend Edward Jukes Boswell, to found a congregation and to build a church.

Meanwhile the tide of immigration continues to flow steadily westward; Highland Scots for Lobo Township, Tipperary Irish for London, Pennsylvania Dutch for Yarmouth. For Kent County, French Canadians, English, Irish, Scots, and refugee black slaves from the United States of America. Onward the tide sweeps, into Lambton and Essex counties, until it washes up in a polyglot surf on the east shores of the Detroit and St. Clair rivers' meeting, for the moment at least in amity, the almost forgotten backwater of the Sandwich settlement, established by the French nineteen years before the Battle of the Plains of Abraham.

From York to Sandwich are 250 miles of military highway, rough-hewn from the dense forest in 1811. From it, extending off in a dozen directions, new roads, new trails, leading into scores of new settlements.

Everywhere the ''plock-plock'' of the settler's axe, ripping into the

1826
Bytown (Ottawa) founded by Colonel John By.

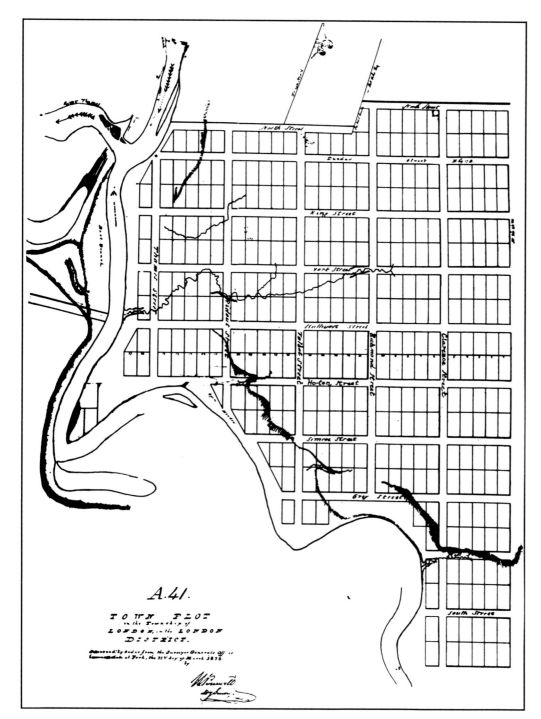

A.41.

TOWN PLOT
in the Township of
LONDON, in the LONDON
DISTRICT.

THE LONDON TOWNSITE, 1826
Under the direction of Thomas Ridout, the Surveyor-General of Upper Canada, Mahlon Burwell was instructed to survey the London townsite. Burwell, who was responsible for dozens of surveys throughout the London District and elsewhere, was able to produce this map in 1826. At the time, the majority of London's streets were named in commemoration of members of the English royal family, or in tribute to officials and men of influence found in the Upper Canadian establishment.

earth, thousand-year-old woody bulwark, tearing the roots from the yielding earth, building gigantic bonfires of walnut, oak, and hickory, whose smoke can be seen as far away as Chicago. The Western Ontario pioneer labours from dawn to dusk, industriously laying the groundwork for the twentieth century's ecological cataclysm.

Like the dissolving view in a motion picture, the trees are going, revealing the bare, rich soil beneath. In the next stage the pioneer, scratching the stump-strewn ground with a pine branch, will give way to the wheat farmer, roiling the soil with his iron plough, stripping it of its laboriously-accumulated humus, in a mad race for the gold in bread-hungry England's bulging coffers.

Almost imperceptibly, pre-history has become history.

1827
John James Audubon publishes his great book Birds of North America.

The first business of the new capital of the huge District of London is the law; the second is the lodging and entertainment of those whose business brings them to the courts.

The first court to meet in London is the court of general quarter sessions of the peace. The bench of magistrates combines to some degree the functions of a modern grand jury and a county council. Serious criminal charges like murder, manslaughter, and grand larceny are brought here first. If the magistrates, after due consideration, bring in a true bill, the case is passed on to the court of assizes for trial. In its civil capacity the bench is responsible for naming surveyors. It also allots licences for "houses of entertainment," taverns that have some rooms available for travellers.

Today's sessions are being held in a two-storey frame building standing on the southwest corner of Ridout and Dundas streets, on the public square. It is meant to serve as a temporary courthouse, gaol, and school, pending the construction of the permanent courthouse. Its timbers are still fresh from the axe and adze, for the building has been rushed to completion in time for the sittings of the hamlet's first court.

Almost the entire population took part in the erection of this structure. The contractor — if such a grand term may be used for a functionary more accurately described as an amateur foreman — was Peter MacGregor. Since there were prisoners who had to be housed during the pleasure of the magistrates, someone had to look after them. The most suitable person to do this was also the most conveniently located for the purpose — Peter MacGregor, host of the village's first inn.

Since many of the magistrates came from the remote regions of the District, accommodation had to be provided for them. For the first session, that meant Peter's so-far-unnamed hostelry.

Finally, both the visiting magistrates and the prisoners had to be fed. The obvious person to look after this responsibility was also, naturally, Peter MacGregor. Here then, was a classic case of conflict of interest. In the result, Peter chose to feed the prisoners first, in order to get them out of the way. This led to vociferous complaints by the hungry magistrates, some of whom remembered a similar incident some three years previously.

It had happened at a banquet of the Fourth Militia Regiment following Militia Training Day, regularly held annually on the birthday of King George III 4 June. The affair, in 1824, was being held at Peter MacGregor's inn, in London Township, across the river from Byron. As the party was about to be seated, an officer announced: "I do not want any common men, but we officers, to sit at this table."

The "common men" responded to the challenge by attacking indiscriminately the food and their officers. The incident was in no way Peter MacGregor's fault; but it, and his tender treatment of the London prisoners, gave additional emphasis to his reputation as a democrat.

Such clashes between classes were perhaps amusing at the time, but there was a darker side to them; in another ten years such differences would lead to bloodshed. In January 1827 MacGregor's error of judgment was not seen as a serious threat to civil order, but certainly as injurious to the dignity of the law, of which the magistrates, regardless of background, were

1827
Karl Baedeker begins publishing his travel guides.

all conscious. After all, these justices of the peace were men of substance. Some of them had had considerable experience in the development of the area: for instance, Joseph Ryerson, father of the renowned clergyman and educator Egerton Ryerson, was a United Empire Loyalist who had settled in Norfolk County, the eastern edge of the District, in 1799. In 1800 he was named first Sheriff of the London District, a post which he held for several years.

The agenda for this first London session of the court was heavily engaged with housekeeping matters. Among other items, Peter Van Every was appointed gaoler, thus relieving Peter MacGregor of one of his constellation of functions. A rash of minor assault cases followed, after which the court stood adjourned.

SATURDAY, 24 NOVEMBER 1827

News of the new community on the Thames has reached the people of Ancaster, Dundas, and Hamilton through the medium of the Gore Gazette. There was an advertisement and what in modern newspaper parlance would be termed "reader copy" — a sort of bonus to the advertiser, who in this instance was Peter MacGregor's principal rival, Abraham Carroll:

HOTEL in the New Town of LONDON. — The subscriber having erected, and licensed as an INN, a commodious two-story Frame Building, on Dundas Street in the Town or Village of LONDON, commonly called the Forks of the Thames, begs leave to apprise the Public thereof. The Hotel is within a few rods of the superb Building now erecting in the Town as a Jail & Court-house for the respect, well qualified to afford comfort and convenience to the Public who may have occasion to resort to the County Town of the London District.
London, Nov. 24, 1827

The accompanying news story is one of the earliest extant accounts of the infant community. It is generous in its description, which includes a subtle reference to the paper's new client, obviously the proprietor of the "very respectable Tavern."

NEW TOWN OF LONDON. Almost as long ago as we can remember, a Town of the above name was laid down on the Map of Upper Canada — and the people of Britain — with the exception of the very few, to whom actual observation had taught the fallacy of such an idea — were thence induced to believe that a young Metropolis was growing up on the banks of the Upper Canadian Thames. It will, therefore, be a matter of surprise to many, when they are informed that, until the last eighteen months, this Town had only an ideal existence, and that the spot upon which it was marked, was in the centre of an uncultivated forest. Within the period above mentioned, however, the spot in question has been fixed upon by Legislature, as the scite for the District Town, and in consequence here lately not a tree was felled all has now become bustle and activity. A considerable tract of country has been cleared — roads laid out — bridges built — and between 20 and 30 buildings, about half of Frame, have been erected — including a temporary Jail and Court House — a very respectable Tavern — a Blacksmith's Shop, a Brewery (erecting) — one or two small Merchants' Shops and some very good Dwelling Houses. The scite is a very handsome one, at the Forks of the Thames, on an elevated piece of table land, commanding an extensive view of Forests and cultivated Farms on the opposite banks of the River, to the South & the west,

1828
Catholic Emancipation Act allows Roman Catholics in Great Britain to sit in Parliament.

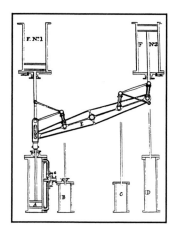

UPPER CANADA PATENT NO. 150
On July 18, 1834, Edward Allen Talbot, one of London's most enterprising citizens of the day, was granted Upper Canada Patent No. 150 for his invention of "a new mode of propelling Carriages, Ships, Boats, and other Water Craft". Designed to eliminate the need for paddle-wheels on river vessels, the device was driven by a single cylinder ("A") attached to a steam engine.

& thro' a fine avenue of trees on Dundas street, which has been opened from the Town for several miles. The Court House, which will be one of the most magnificent buildings of its kind in Upper Canada, is commenced, under the superintendence of a most respectable architect (Mr. Ewart) a great proportion of the bricks have already been made, the foundation dug, and preparations for actively carrying on the work, are in a forward state. The Town is favourably situated, and but for the state of the roads in its neighbourhood, which are at this time, scarcely passable, might soon become a place of some importance.

The correspondent for the *Gazette* gave the town "between 20 and 30 buildings." Another authority allots to these buildings a total population of 133. Some of them were destined to become permanent residents; others were just passing through.

Among the latter were adventurers like Thomas Fallon, a young Irishman who later recalled arriving in the village with a number of Irish families in this year of 1827:

> We were settled in London with about twenty other families by 1827. London was founded in that year in the crook in the river where the branches of the Thames meet, an east-facing "U" with the main building at its bottom. In those days the forest enclosed the village. ... Our home was a quarter mile down Rideout street and slightly east on the South Branch of the river. We had good land, and although we were in modest straits, my father took great consolation that we were "founders" of this place.

Some of those who arrived during London's first twelve months bore names that have become community fixtures. In the vanguard were the merchants, ready and eager to take advantage of a new and promising market. That is to say, they became merchants when they set up shop in the village. Previously most of them had been pedlars and tinkers, carrying their stock-in-trade or the tools of their profession on their backs, like George Jervis Goodhue, a pedlar, and the brothers John and Oliver McClary, who were tinkers. Most of them did very well indeed. When George Goodhue died a half-century after his arrival he was the richest man in the western portion of the province.

The McClary brothers did at least as well. They were New Englanders, sons of a former lumber merchant who had been bankrupted by the War of 1812-1814, subsequently settling in Westminster Township south of London. The brothers McClary were well-connected in the United States, being cousins of two presidents of the republic — John Adams (1735-1826), the second president, and John Quincy Adams (1767-1848), the sixth — a fact proudly proclaimed on a towering memorial in London's Mount Pleasant Cemetery. The brothers parleyed their tiny enterprise into one of the largest manufacturing concerns on the continent. The stoves fashioned by the McClarys became famous throughout the British Empire. Today the memorial in the cemetery, a city street, and a magnificent house on the southwest corner of McClary Avenue and High Street recall the name of the presidents' distant kin.

TUESDAY, 21 OCTOBER 1828

Under overcast skies, the tall, unsmiling, cold-eyed Yankee merchant George Jervis Goodhue follows the coffin of his beloved wife Maria Fullarton to her grave in the glebe land belonging to the Church of England at the northwest corner of Ridout and Dundas streets. The words of the Anglican service are spoken by the Reverend Alexander Macintosh, who has come up from his church at St. Thomas for the occasion. Most of London's population has turned out for the simple funeral and interment.

"Almighty God, with whom so live the spirits of those who depart hence in the Lord, and with whom the souls of the faithful are in joy and felicity. ..."

As the ancient words fall damply in the malarial mist arising from the river, the eyes of all turn on Goodhue. He has not many friends in this group; in the years to come he will have even fewer. How will he take the death of the girl he is said to have loved? His face tells nothing; it is not a face that speaks of what is behind it.

As the words of the final blessing fade away, Goodhue's principal rival, the Irish merchant Dennis O'Brien, steps forward to express his personal sorrow and regrets; but the Yankee, seeing nothing but his own grief, has already turned away to make his sad journey to his solitary bed.

"Unto Almighty God we commend the soul of our sister here departed. ..."

Shorty afterwards, when the land added to the north of the town is surveyed, the first of the new east-west streets is named Fullarton.

THURSDAY, 19 AUGUST 1830

They had been streaming into the village ever since the judge had spoken those awful words "and may God have mercy on your soul. ..."

It had been only three days since the verdict was delivered. Pioneer justice is swift. By the hour appointed the population of London had swollen temporarily to ten times its normal 300 souls. They came from all the surrounding townships; from Westminster, London, Lobo, Caradoc, Dorchester, Yarmouth, Bayham (where Constable Timothy Conklin Pomeroy had been shot and killed), Malahide, Southwold, Delaware, Nissouri, Zorra, and Oxford. They came from outside the sprawling District of London, from York (ne Toronto) and Hamilton. There was even at least one visitor from the United States, Orson Squire Fowler, a young student from Yale University.

The attraction?

It is Cornelius Burleigh's hanging day.

The sordid little story began on the morning of 16 September 1829. Constable Pomeroy, pursuing a suspect on a charge of "theft, burning property, destroying cattle, etc.," was ambushed by someone and fatally shot. A cap found at the scene was identified as belonging to the person Pomeroy was pursuing — Cornelius Alverson Burleigh (sometimes spelled Burley in later years). A reward of one hundred pounds offered by the District authorities speedily resulted in Burleigh's capture and confinement in the rude cells of the temporary courthouse.

Many people had doubts about Cornelius' guilt, fuelled by his odd behaviour during a jail-break in the long winter of his incarceration. Escaping from the primitive accommodations was no big deal. All the prisoners took advantage of the break for freedom, except Cornelius Burleigh.

1829
Sir Robert Peel (1788-1850) founds London England's modern police force; the moniker "Bobbies" catches on.

He, being certain, he said, of his own innocence, remained behind to await his acquittal.

Whatever the true facts of the case were, Burleigh's conviction of his innocence was not shared by others, including the witnesses who testified against him, the jury that found him guilty, and the judge who sentenced him.

Three men — two clergymen and a vacationing undergraduate — played leading roles in the last act of Cornelius Burleigh's pathetic little tragedy. The Reverend James Jackson, a Methodist circuit-rider said to have been distantly related to Andrew Jackson (1767-1845), seventh president of the United States, made Cornelius his particular charge, although "target" might have been a more accurate description of the object of his daily attendance. He was determined to elicit a confession; but owing to the "obduracy and insensibility" of the condemned man, it was not until forty-one hours before his execution that Burleigh "burst into a flood of tears" and "in the presence of the Revd. Messrs. Boswell, Smith and Jackson" made his "Dying Confession."

The wording of the confession, subsequently printed in handbill form at Hamilton, owes little to the prisoner and a great deal to his confessor-tormentor. Cornelius Burleigh could neither read nor write, yet in the confession this educational failure is acknowledged in these words:

> I was left to wander through the world, under the influence of depravity, without the advantages of education, or religious instruction, to counterbalance the influence of my natural propensities to evil, of various kinds, particularly that of frequenting all places of profane resort. I was often found in the merry dance, and lost no opportunity of inducing thoughtless and unguarded females to leave the paths of innocence and virtue. ...

These, of course, are the words and sentiments of a fundamentalist Methodist, not those of an uneducated farmer's son. The printed copy of this bogus production carried as well a multiple-verse piece of doggerel, also obviously the work of Mr. Jackson, based at least in part on a Methodist hymn dating from the early 1820s. The scansion is marvellously primitive.

The three ecclesiastical corbies, Jackson, Boswell, and Smith, are to share the religious functions surrounding the public death of Cornelius Burleigh. Jackson has top billing. He reads the "Dying Confession" from the scaffold "by Burley's request"; Mr. Smith, apparently a Baptist minister, gives the homily before the 3,000 witnesses, and the closing prayer; Edward Boswell, the Anglican missionary, has a less obvious role — he baptizes the young man "aged as he supposed about 26 or 27" and gives him Holy Communion.

Now at last it is time. In the presence of the multitude Cornelius is cast into eternity.

His time, however, is not yet. The official rope cannot bear the condemned man's weight. It snaps and he is deposited on the ground, dazed but alive. Someone is sent to fetch a new rope from Goodhue's store across the street. Burleigh's conversion is complete. He walks among the crowd with the tag-end of the broken rope dangling from his neck, his whole mind devoted to "prayer, prayer, praise, singing and thanksgiving."

Once more the condemned man is led on to the scaffold. The rope

1830
Simon Bolivar, warrior, writer and prophet, the liberator of numerous Hispanic-American countries, dies at age 48.

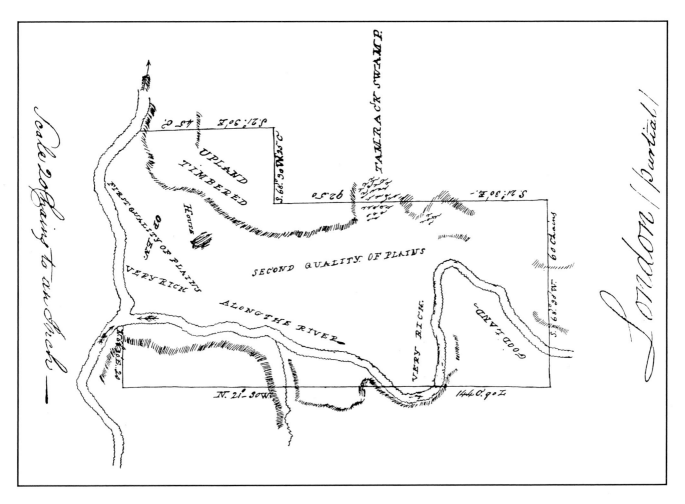

The map contains the following handwritten labels:

TAMARACK SWAMP.

UPLAND TIMBERED

FIRST QUALITY OF PLAINS

VERY RICH

House

SECOND QUALITY OF PLAINS

ALONG THE RIVER

VERY RICH.

GOOD LAND.

London (partial)

is adjusted and the trap sprung, to the sound of that peculiar and terrifying exhalation of breath from the crowd that seems to have been a feature of all public executions — a sound composed in part of civilized compassion, in part savage delight.

Some members of the crowd leave at this point, but most remain for the second act of the drama. The sentence of the court has only been half carried out; the corpse, by law, must now be "delivered to the Surgeons for dissection." This is the moment eagerly anticipated by the medical professionals of the District of London and their private students. Legally, the only corpses available for teaching purposes are those of condemned criminals. The British tradition said nothing about the place where the dissection was to be carried out. In Canada, lacking hospitals and operating theatres, it is carried out in public, in the open.

Scalpels at the ready, the physicians and their pupils crowd around the body, with the heavily-breathing audience peering over their shoulders. In short order, poor Cornelius' body is reduced to its basic components, some of which will find their way into specimen jars for later study.

A choice portion of the remains has been spoken for and promised to a lay student of another discipline: the pseudo-science of phrenology. Burleigh's skull, its contents removed, is cleaned, cured and presented to Orson Squire Fowler.

Fowler had been one of the many curious persons who had been allowed to visit Burleigh in his cell. There he had run his practised hands

MAP OF LONDON, 1808
Encompassing a healthy part of today's central London, this map represents the tract of land granted to Joshua Applegarth, the first European to settle London Township. Applegarth's licence of occupation stipulated that he cultivate an annual crop of hemp. Efforts in this pursuit failed miserably, and launched Applegarth into a lifetime of debt.

over the condemned man's cranium, indicating on a chart where the walls of the skull were thin, and where they were thick, and connecting these features with aspects, often of a contradictory nature, of Burleigh's personality.

After a short, indecent interval following the execution, Fowler conducted a lecture in a darkened hall, using the skull and a candle to prove the truth of his assertions. Sure enough, the geography of Burleigh's cranium bore out Fowler's predictions. Where he had said the skull walls were thin, the candlelight shone through; in other areas Cornelius' thick-headedness allowed no light to emerge.

How these facts could be said to "prove" the scientific accuracy of phrenology is difficult now to determine, but they actually did set the young man's feet on the road to phenomenal popular success and great riches.

In the 1880s, on a farewell lecture tour, Fowler returned to London and here left a portion of Cornelius Burleigh's skull with the Harris family of Eldon House, where it remains on public view to this day.

THURSDAY, 7 JULY 1831

The first issue of London's first newspaper, the London *Sun*, has appeared on the streets of the village. Its editor is Edward Allen Talbot, a native of Tipperary County, Ireland. Talbot and his father Richard Talbot were co-founders of an Irish settlement north of the Forks, in London Township, in 1818. E.A. Talbot was the author of *Five Years' Residence in the Canadas*, published in England in 1824. The book was subsequently translated into two or three European languages (without the author's permission) and had a perceptibly negative effect on emigration from the United Kingdom.

Talbot was considered a radical in politics and a visionary in everything else. Within the next handful of years, besides establishing London's first newspaper, he busied himself promoting a railway to link London and Hamilton, and obtaining letters patent for an "Atmospheric Propelling Engine"!

Such protean characters arise seldom in the life of any community, indeed of any nation or generation. They are often admired by their posterity but distrusted by their contemporaries.

Much of the four pages of Talbot's journal is given over to a description of the new District capital and the two adjacent townships of London and Westminster. Praise is heaped on the courthouse, just completed at a cost of 4,000 Provincial currency, equivalent to 16,000 American dollars:

> The Court House, which is allowed by strangers to be the finest building in the Province, stands within about twenty yards of the brink of the hill, which may be said to be the bank of the river. It is 100 feet long, 50 feet wide and 50 feet high. The building, although not strictly Gothic, is in that style, and with its Octagon towers has much the appearance of the ancient castles, so much admired in Great Britain and Ireland. ... The Court room is finished in a very superior manner. ... The prisoners are admitted into the dock from the jail beneath, by means of a trap door. ... The debtors prisons are in the upper part of the house, and are finished in a neat, convenient and comfortable man-

1830
Royal Arms painted for the Court House by an itinerant artist, Lefebvre.

ner. There has, however, been one great error committed in the erection of this building; it fronts the river instead of the town ... and exposes to the view of every person who enters the town the windows of the criminal cells; a sight at all times the least pleasing to the stranger or the citizen. ...

THURSDAY, 1 SEPTEMBER 1831

Edward Allen Talbot, London's chief and most eloquent promoter, continues his non-stop panegyric on the new village:

> As the rapid increase of this town is a subject which seems to excite very general astonishment, we shall from time to time lay before our readers, a brief statement of its population and improvements. About three months ago, we, in company with the Editor of the Western Mercury, counted the houses then built and building; the number was then about 70. To-day we again counted the number; and find it to be 96, viz: 22 story framed houses, 59 one and a half stories, also framed, and 15 hewd and other log houses one story high. ... In enumerating the houses we do not include the Court-house or places of public worship. There are building in the town a Protestant Episcopal Church, 80 by 40; a Methodist meeting house, and a Roman Catholic Chapel; and we understand the members of the Kirk of Scotland, residing in the town and its vicinity, have it in contemplation to build a Church so soon as they can obtain a Clergyman from Scotland.

As a further inducement to genteel settlement, the Irish statistician informs the world that males in the village outnumber females four to three. The precise figures are: twenty-six bachelors and fourteen spinsters. "It must therefore," says Mr. Talbot, "be a desirable situation for ladies of enterprise."

MONDAY, 23 JANUARY 1832

Dr. John Becker Crouse of Colborne, near Simcoe, Norfolk County, conducts an inquest on the bodies of Polly Sovereign (or Sovereene), wife of Henry Sovereign, and seven of their eleven children. The verdict is murder. Henry Sovereign is charged with the crime and committed to trial at the London assizes. The new year has begun badly. Worse is to come.

SATURDAY, 28 APRIL 1832

The *Constantine*, carrying Irish immigrants, docks at the quarantine station on Grosse Isle, near Quebec City. Of 179 passengers, twenty-nine have already died, the result of an epidemic of Asiatic cholera brought into England by refugees from the Polish rebellion of 1830-1831 and thence into Ireland, where it spread rapidly among the peasantry.

SUNDAY, 3 JUNE 1832

The *Carricks* from Ireland puts in at Grosse Isle; 145 passengers, forty-five deaths.

THURSDAY, 7 JUNE 1832

The *Voyageur*, a steamer plying the St. Lawrence River, makes an illegal stop at Grosse Isle, takes off some of the passengers from the *Carricks*, and lands some of them at Quebec.

1831
Archibald Ouray, a medical student with Dr. Elam Stinson, first London resident to drown in the Thames river.

THE COURT HOUSE AS VIEWED FROM KING STREET, c. 1870
Still proudly standing as the city's most prominent example of Gothic Revival architecture, the Court House was built in response to the transfer of the London District capital from Vittoria to London in 1826. The construction of the turreted building, which originally faced the river, spanned two years and was completed in 1829. The structure to the right was built about 1865 to serve the Middlesex County Council.

SUNDAY, 10 JUNE 1832

At Quebec, fifty-five cases of Asiatic cholera are reported, of whom forty-five have died.

FRIDAY, 15 JUNE 1832

The plague has reached York, following outbreaks in Montreal and Kingston. The lieutenant-governor of Upper Canada, Sir John Colborne, orders hospitals set up in the District of London at Turkey Point, Port Stanley, and London itself for the reception of sick immigrants.

SATURDAY, 30 JUNE 1832

Dr. John Patrick Donnelly, a retired Royal Navy surgeon, arrives in London on his way to the St. Clair River, where he intends taking up land. He appears before the board of health to offer his services, if needed. The board waives the rules governing the medical profession in the province, grants him an immediate licence to practice medicine, and asks him to assume charge of the cholera hospital on the Hamilton Road, some distance out of town. Later that night Donnelly writes to his family at St-Rock, Lower Canada:

London, U.C. 30th June, 1832
My dear Marie and little Family, I arrived here at 5 o'clock in good health, thank God, as I left you. It is now 1/2 past 6, I can say very little as I am in a hurry to post this, the post goes out tomorrow at 4 a.m. I'm certain you have been very anxious to hear an account of the ravages the cholera morbus made. Just as I was happening on my way through York, in this town, I attended two cases myself. I saved one by God's help. It happened in a home I lodged in. ... I am extremely anxious to hear from Edmund as he was in the

scene of the cholera. There is nothing of the kind here yet. ... I will go and see about my crown land on Monday 2nd, July, God willing. ...

THURSDAY, 12 JULY 1832

The London *Sun* reports that seven cases of cholera have been reported in the village; of these, three persons had died and one had recovered.

THURSDAY, 2 AUGUST 1832

The London *Sun* announces that the board of health has recorded forty-seven cases of cholera and thirteen deaths. The first victim of the disease was Eliza MacGregor, a sister of Peter MacGregor. Mrs. MacGregor mother of Peter and Eliza, prostrated herself on the damp earth of her daughter's grave and died the next morning. That was on 15 July. The following day, her son-in-law Richard Pullen, a coach-maker, died. Dr. John Patrick Donnelly died on 30 July. The wife of his colleague Dr. Elam Stimson died on 20 July, and their infant son five days later. The *Sun's* account concludes:

> The town is literally deserted by the inhabitants, there being now only about 27 men with their families remaining in it, there are on Dundas street alone upwards of 20 houses wholly shut up.

SATURDAY, 11 AUGUST 1832

Publication of the weekly newspaper, the London *Sun*, has been delayed two days in order to bring its readers the following report:

> Our Assizes which commenced on Tuesday morning, terminated at 11 o'clock to-day. And it is with ineffable pleasure that we announce the total disappearance of the Cholera in this town. On Tuesday morning such was the effect of public alarm that little hope was entertained that a sufficient number of Jurors, Grand or Petit, could be obtained to enable the Court to deliver the Gaol, but to the credit of the District a sense of public duty raised those called upon to perform it ... superior to personal fears. ... There were very few civil cases tried and those of an unimportant character. The following are the convictions which have taken place:
>
> Sovereign for the murder of his wife and 6 children. Sentenced to be hung on Friday; since reprieved until 11 o'clock on Monday.
> Michael Robins, Horse stealing, Sentence of death recorded.
> Alexander Root, Petit Larceny, Banished for 7 years.
> Andrew Root, do. [ditto] do.
> John White, grand do., do.
> Daniel Kemp, Stealing a yoke of oxen, sentence of death recorded.

The harsh sentences handed down by Judge James Buchanan Macaulay were mandatory under the old British criminal code, which decreed the death penalty for several hundred crimes, many of them having to do with offenses against property. By the early nineteenth century a popular reform movement had resulted in the commutation of most of these archaic sentences. Michael Robins and Daniel Kemp were not hanged at London; Henry Sovereign was. It was Sovereign's second date with the hangman. In 1819 he had appeared before the Judge William Campbell charged with horse-stealing and had received the mandatory sentence of death. Executive clemency spared his life on that occasion. This time no single

JOHN HARRIS
John Harris came to London in 1834. As a retired British naval officer, the Upper Canadian government considered his conservative politics ideally suited to check rising reform sentiments in the area. Harris remained a leading force in London's elite until his death in 1850.

1832
Immigration to Upper Canada reaches a peak with 66,000 arrivals this year.

voice was raised in protest. The evidence presented at his trial was overwhelming. By his wife, the long-suffering Polly, he had had eleven children. The youngest, Anna, aged two, somehow survived the savage bloodbath in the isolated cabin in Windham Township and died eighty-two years later, in 1914, a "tall, stately woman with beautiful white wavy hair." Three other children escaped the carnage by being away from home at the time.

The maniacal rage that had authored the tragedy filled the spectators at the trial with an almost supernatural dread, which was felt even by as sophisticated an observer as Edward Allen Talbot, who visited Sovereign's dungeon cell under the London courthouse on Sunday, 12 August 1832:

> I visited him, at his own request, on Sunday morning. ... he was confined in a cell about 10 feet square, perfectly dark and completely sheeted, floor, walls and ceiling with iron. As we entered this dark abode we found him reading the Church of England Litany. He sat on a rush bottomed chair holding the book in one hand and a candle in the other — as the Gaoler departed drawing upon us the massive door, I felt an indescribable thrill of horror pervade my whole frame. ... His beard, which was closely shaven the day of his trial, had grown considerably, and with the faint light which a single candle afforded in so black an abode, his countenance assumed the most terrific appearance.

If Talbot expected to elicit a confession from a convicted murderer, as the Reverend James Jackson had two years earlier, he was disappointed. Henry Sovereign continued to protest his innocence until the instant his body plunged through the trap in the presence of a mere three hundred spectators who had dared the pestilence of cholera to see justice done.

SUNDAY, 11 NOVEMBER 1832

A visiting Presbyterian missionary, the Reverend William Proudfoot, preaches in the temporary courthouse, which has now become a schoolhouse, on the morning of this day. The Methodist circuit-rider, the Reverend James Jackson, speaks in the building during the noon hour. At four o'clock a Church of England missionary, the Reverend Benjamin Cronyn, who arrived from Ireland the day before, conducts the Anglican service of Evensong. A delegation of local members of the Church of England appeals to Cronyn to remain in London instead of proceeding to his planned destination in the recently-settled Township of Adelaide. He will remain.

MONDAY, 31 DECEMBER 1832

"The Forks" has now been settled for a little more than six years. The population has grown to some 500, in spite of the ravages of the cholera epidemic. Few who passed through that terrifying time will ever forget it. London's first resident, Peter MacGregor, finding himself heavily in debt after operating an inn (the future Robinson Hall Hotel on the southeast corner of Ridout and Dundas streets), has removed to Westminster Township by May 1831. Dr. Elam Stimson, mourning his losses, has set off for Connecticut to find a new wife to mother his orphaned brood. He will not return to the village at the Forks. Nor will the Reverend Edward Jukes Boswell, off to a new charge in eastern Upper Canada, leaving the gaunt frame of an uncompleted church to his successor, young Benjamin Cro-

1832
The Great Reform Bill, a watershed in modern history, passed by the British Parliament.

nyn. Boswell will live on in local folklore as the minister who mounted guard at the northern entrance to London, at Blackfriar's Bridge, during the plague, warning travellers against entering the stricken town. He has sold his property to the treasurer of the District of London, Captain John Harris, RN, who has plans to build upon it a home that he will call "Eldon House."

The first of London's black settlers, refugee slaves who had heard rumours of freedom north of the American border, have begun to trickle into the community. A Quaker abolitionist, Benjamin Lundy, on passing through, notes that there are between twenty-five and thirty blacks living in the village.

Of the physical aspects of the village of 1832, little will survive the next 150 years — a part of the foundation of Eldon House and some unmarked graves on the courthouse square.

The courthouse, in spite of its ambiguous siting with its back to its constituents, is the most noteworthy feature of the village, commented upon by all visitors to the area. Otherwise, there is nothing to see; simply a straggling collection of log and frame buildings bordering the imaginary street allowances on which the major traffic is pedestrian, with an occasional ox-cart or even a patrician horseman. All, without exception, are obliged to weave their way in and out and around the ubiquitous tree stumps.

The little village has survived its first great test. It has beaten back the first of the many waves of pestilence to be brought by the European immigrants who will become its citizens. Still to come before its place in history is assured — rebellion, civic disorder, fire, financial panic, and poverty.

ELDON HOUSE, c. 1870
Built for John Harris in 1834, and modelled in the Regency style, Eldon House is one of the city's oldest surviving residential structures. Overlooking the banks of the Thames River, the residence played host to many of London's early balls and haughty social functions.

ST. PAUL'S EPISCOPAL CHURCH

St. Paul's Episcopal Church, when erected during 1844-46 dominated the skyline of the village of London. Now, as St. Paul's Cathedral, the seat of the Diocese of Huron in the Anglican Church of Canada, it remains as London's oldest church, centre of an oasis of dignity and calm surrounded by business towers and bustling streets of downtown.

W. THOMAS.ARC   F.C.LOWE.SC

CHAPTER TWO

Rebellion

To add some of my more personal recollections of these times, I will begin with the year of the Rebellion 1837. I was then in my fifth year. We resided on Lot 15, in the third concession of London, on the brow of the hill, over the north branch of the Thames. All male adults had been summoned to serve in the militia, and all firearms requisitioned for their use. My father was absent in Ireland, on urgent family affairs. My mother surrendered to the militia all firearms in her possession, with many musket bullets cast by herself. We lived in hourly apprehension of invasion, for rumours were rife of approaching bands of rebels, and it was thought that any night we might be burned in our beds.
— Verschoyle Cronyn, "The First Bishop of Huron," *Transactions* of the London and Middlesex Historical Society, Part III, 1911.

By 1836 the population of London had reached 1,246, according to Edward Allen Talbot. Of his fellow-townsfolk Talbot had this to say:

> Taking a view of the very great improvements made in this town and vicinity during the short period of settlement ... we think we may safely say that no town in British North America has advanced so rapidly, or can boast of a greater number of respectable families. ...

Many of the "respectable families" Talbot referred to were, like his own, parishioners of the Reverend Benjamin Cronyn, rector of the new frame church of St. Paul on North Street (Queens Avenue). There were four other churches in the village, again, according to Talbot, but they counted for little. The Church of England represented the Tory Establishment. All others, excepting the Roman Catholic, were "Dissenters" and therefore presumably Reform-minded.

The Anglican Establishment in London included such exotic figures as the Earl of Mount-Cashell, a land speculator; Captain Joseph Cowley, a relative of the Duke of Wellington; Henry Corry Rowley Becher, member of an old established Yorkshire family; Captain John Harris, Royal Navy (retired); Dr. John Salter, a former Navy surgeon, apothecary, and social reformer; Hamilton Hartley Killaly, an engineer, graduate of Trinity College, Dublin, and the Royal Academy of Science; and George Washington Busteed, former secretary to the governor of the West Indian island of St. Lucia.

The Episcopalians controlled to a large degree the economy and the society of the village. A similar but more powerful group presided over

1834
The Town of York incorporated as the City of Toronto, with William Lyon Mackenzie as first Mayor.

THE LONDON FOUNDRY ON FULLARTON STREET, 1838
Established by Elijah Leonard Jr., the London Foundry, later located on York Street, was one of the city's most enduring industrial ventures. In an age dominated by steam power, the foundry's chief lines of production — steam engines and boilers — enjoyed enviable reputations for quality and kept Leonard's blast furnaces in operation well into the twentieth century.

1835
London was granted the right to hold a public fair or market by letters patent of Lieutenant-Governor Sir John Colborne.

the life of the provincial capital, Toronto. Because of the many interrelationships among the Toronto proprietors, their enemies referred to them as the Family Compact. Although there was no such intimate bond among the members of the London Establishment, they came to be looked upon as a junior Family Compact.

It was easy to identify the members of the Establishment. They announced their affiliation every time they went to church. Their opponents were "chapel folk" — such as various Methodist sects, characterized by one writer as consisting of "The ignorant and uneducated; their adherents are principally the natives of the country, settlers from the United States, and emigrants from England." Worse still, they were staunch advocates of temperance, which brought down upon them the wrath of Colonel Thomas Talbot, who named them as members of "Damned Cold Water Drinking Societies."

In the hyperbole of the hustings, therefore, the equations were simple: Church of England = Tory; Methodism = Reformer. In reality, of course, the distinctions were much more subtle and complex.

Consider some instances.

Dr. Charles Duncombe of St. Thomas and Norwich, who was, next to William Lyon Mackenzie, the chief activist of the Reform movement, was a direct descendant of King James II of England through his mother Rhoda Tyrell.

The two Talbot brothers, Edward Allen and John, both prominent Anglicans, edited newspapers in London and St. Thomas respectively and were devoted to the Reform cause.

Charles Latimer, an English attorney barred from practice in Upper Canada because of rules inspired by the Family Compact, became a London merchant and ammunition-supplier to the Reform guerillas.

Elijah Leonard, an ironmonger from New York State, member of a family that had engaged in that trade since 1637, made no secret of his Reform sympathies, meanwhile buying surplus cannonballs from the British Army for eventual manufacture into stoves.

The Reverend William Proudfoot, minister of a schismatic Presbyterian church, was an intellectual radical whose congregation was, almost by definition, Reform.

The movement for political reform was gathering strength everywhere in North America and Europe in the 1830s and resulted, in 1834, in the election of a Reform majority in the lower house of the Legislature of Upper Canada. It is a coincidence worth noting that in that same year six farm labourers in the Devonshire village of Tolpuddle in England were sentenced to seven years' imprisonment in an Australian penal colony for organizing a farmers' union. Five of the six later settled in the London (Canada) area after their release.

In Devonshire and in Toronto the conservative Establishment was shocked, indignant, and frightened by these evidences of the spread of "revolutionary" sentiment. There had been rebellions in France and Poland in the 1830s; a slave revolt in Virginia and civil uprisings in Switzerland and Brazil in 1831, in Germany in 1832, and in Mexico in 1833. In such an atmosphere political rhetoric soon leaped the bounds of good taste and even reason, to become boldly inflammatory and irresponsible. A Conservative broadside printed at St. Thomas called for volunteers to attack a meeting of local Reformers:

NOTICE

The Ripstavers, Gallbursters, etc., with their friends, are requested to meet at St. Thomas, on the 17th of January, at 12 o'clock, as there will be more work for them to do on that day. The Doctors are requested to be in readiness to heal the sick and cure the broken headed. Let no rotten eggs be wanting. As the Unionists are all Yankees, a few pieces of pumpkin will not be amiss.

Whatever the Unions may be in England, it must be remembered that in this country with Republicans at their head, they are the next step to rebellion. ... Therefore, most notable Ripstavers, check the evil, in the beginning, that is, hoe them out — sugar them off — in short sew them up. The Dastards many think to screen themselves from the public fury by holding their meeting at a private house: but public or private put yourselves in the midst of them. You have a right to be there. It is a public meeting.

Whoever the "Gallbursters and Ripstavers" were, they turned out in force to do the Establishment's bidding, as Colonel Talbot, the local autocrat, gleefully reported a few days later:

My rebels endeavoured to hold a meeting at St. Thomas on the 17th, Dr. Franklin's birthday ... but in which they were frustrated by my royal guards, who routed the rascals at all points and drove them out of the village like sheep, members with broken heads leaving their hats behind them — the glorious work of old Colonel Hickory. In short, it was a most splendid victory.

The pot finally boiled over with the unfortunate appointment of a political incompetent, Sir Francis Bond Head, as lieutenant-governor of Upper Canada. Head called a new election in which he himself played a leading role, informing the voters that unless they returned a Tory government, Britain would disown the province.

London, with its population of 1,246, was now entitled to a seat in the Legislature. The Family Compact candidate was London's godfather, Colonel Mahlon Burwell. The Reformers put up John Scatcherd, a justice of the peace from Nissouri Township, a Reformer so radical in his views that he had termed King George IV a "Public Calumniator."

1836
Charles Dickens (1812-1870) publishes his Pickwick Papers, *inaugurating his career as Victorian England's most popular writer.*

The election campaign of the summer of 1836 was short, sharp and vicious. The London Establishment followed its parson into battle:

> The Rev. Mr. Cronyn is rendering himself as obnoxious to the farmers of this country as he was once to the people of Ireland. He is here as he was there, a busy meddler in the affairs of the State; and a violent stickler for the domination of his church, and the exclusive privileges of his order. He went along with the Tory candidates throughout the Township of London, soliciting votes.

SATURDAY, 2 JULY 1836

It's evening on the second and last day of balloting in London's first and most disgraceful election. By now nearly everyone entitled to vote has stepped up to the hustings and declared his choice, verbally. Only those who meet the stiff property qualifications may vote; the secret ballot is a generation in the future, and universal suffrage is a fragile dream in the minds of a few "radical" thinkers.

The town's in an uproar. Gangs of Tory bullies have been roaming the streets all day, hunting down known Reformers and Reform sympathizers announcing (on whose authority no one knows) an award of five pounds for every cracked Liberal skull.

All day Tory Orangemen from the back concessions of London Township have been streaming into town on horseback, by cart, wagon, and buggy. Now, with the polls about to close, comes the final attack on the democratic process.

It's a ragged, loud, torch-lit parade, led by a gigantic black man. It piles up in a disorderly rout on the courthouse square. A drunken Reformer is perched precariously on the roof of George Goodhue's general store, reciting the Liberal hymn, which is, fortunately for him, audible only to those nearest him:

> Up then, for Liberty, for Right,
> Strike home, the tyrants falter,
> Be firm, be brave, let all unite,
> And despots' schemes must alter.
>
> Our King, our government and laws,
> While just, we shall obey 'em,
> But Freedom's Heaven-born, holier cause
> We hold supreme above 'em!

Suddenly the mob, many of its members armed with clubs and stones, advances on the hustings where the candidates and their supporters are gathered. The main target is John Talbot, whose editorials in the St. Thomas *Liberal* have roused the wrath of the Family Compact supporters. As stones begin to rain on the wooden platform, Talbot finds himself in very real danger. He and his friends take shelter in the courthouse. The mob follows. Talbot goes to ground in the nearby home of his brother Edward Allen. This is a mistake; it's an obvious bolt-hole. As the first stone crashes through the front window, John dives out of a back window and claims a last-hope refuge in the home of the government's returning officer, the lawyer John Wilson, who escorts him out of the village to safety.

When the dust clears and the broken heads are bandaged, the results are announced. Colonel Talbot's right-hand man, Mahlon Burwell, has ten votes more than the Reform man, John Scatcherd.

The Tories celebrated their triumph; tomorrow morning St. Paul's Church will be packed with hangovers. The Reformers go off to lick their wounds and plot redress.

1836
The first of William H. McGuffey's Eclectic Readers *is published; by 1920 they had sold 125 million copies.*

ENTRANCE TO THE WEST END OF LONDON
Although painted by George R. Dartnell in 1841, this scene serves witness to pioneer life in 1830s London. An existence was literally seized from the grasp of the wilds.

By the fall of 1837 armed rebellion seemed inevitable, but its causes were only partly political. A poor harvest in 1836, followed by a late spring and a disordered growing season — rain when rain was not needed, drought when it was — early frosts, and a second scanty harvest brought severe suffering to a farm population largely dependent on a one-crop economy — wheat for export, mainly to the United States. In that country similar weather conditions had depressed farm incomes and wrought havoc on the nation's financial institutions. Hundreds of private banks were forced to suspend specie payments. On Wall Street the financial heart of North America suffered cardiac arrest:

> New York, April 27, 1837. ... Matters very bad. ... Confidence annihilated; the whole community, big and little, traveling to ruin in a body. Strong fears entertained for the banks, and if they go, God only knows what the consequences will be.

George Templeton Strong was a student at Columbia University in New York City. His diary records what was very nearly a complete collapse of the financial structure of the American republic:

> May 2 — Matters worse and worse in Wall Street. Workmen thrown out of employ by the hundreds daily. Business at a stand. ...
>
> May 4 - ... Fears entertained that tomorrow the attack will be general on all the banks; if so, they'll go down and then all the banks from Maine to Loui-

1836

Texas, the "Lone Star State," becomes an independent republic with Sam Houston as President.

barracks. This fortunate entrepreneur was Edward Matthews, an Englishman who had arrived in London in the early 1830s.

The military reserve on which the barracks were erected occupied roughly eight square blocks, extending from what is now Dufferin Avenue north to the right-of-way of the Canadian Pacific Railway and eastward from Clarence Street to Waterloo Street. Two sets of buildings enclosed the parade square. The first, built in 1838-1839, consisted of thirty-six buildings, constructed of hand-hewn logs. The second set, built of sawn lumber and generally referred to as the "Framed Barracks," was completed sometime before 1843. Altogether the complex cost the British Government about one hundred thousand pounds ($400,000) — a truly enormous sum for the time and place.

Inevitably the life of the village began to revolve around the huge reserve on its northern limits. Officers and enlisted men had needs, which the host community made haste to fill. The requirements of the men, being simpler, were probably the first to be met. Very soon, a row of grog shops and whorehouses sprang up along that portion of the present Richmond Street, then known as Sarnia Street, opposite the reserve.

The officers, many of them scions of old established English families, had physical needs too, but they exercised them in less overt ways, sublimating their sexual drive in sports. A section of the parade square became a cricket ground. Over the years cricket was gradually superseded by the North American game known as baseball (first introduced in the Oxford County community of Beachville in 1838). Other officers went in for the more exciting sports of horse-racing and the steeplechase.

Brawn was more easily satisfied than brain. For the intellectual, New London offered little. It was obvious that if the military required stimulation in this area, it would have to provide its own:

> The residence of the military in our midst, the contract for the barracks, and the start given to building generally, made life easier. ... As Dr. O'Flarity, of the 83rd Regiment, lived quite near us on the southeast corner of Richmond and Horton Streets, we saw a good deal of what was going on, and were once allowed to attend an amateur performance at a theatre on Wellington street, where the public library now stands. Standing trees supported the board roof and stumps, sawed off pretty evenly, supported the rough board seats. We went in a dark passageway by a door on North street. Dr. O'Flarity acted the part of a ghost; so I suppose the play was Hamlet, but that I don't remember.

The building recalled so vividly more than sixty years later by Mrs. Gilbert Porte was known as the Theatre Royal. It was a half-completed, abandoned Methodist chapel that stood in the southwest corner of Wellington Street and Queens Avenue. Ownership of the building had been casually and ruthlessly transferred by the local land baron, Colonel Thomas Talbot, by simply erasing from his land map the pencilled name of the church society and replacing it with the name of commandant of the London garrison.

The military theatricals were greeted with great enthusiasm by the townsfolk who until now had to content themselves with such entertainment as the occasional public hanging or the exhibition of an educated pig.

These early performances created a theatrical tradition in London that has been maintained up to the present. From time to time London amateur

GENTLEMEN AMATEURS PLAYBILL

As this 1844 playbill suggests, London's proud tradition in the performing arts is rooted in strong beginnings.

1840

Queen Victoria marries Prince Albert of Saxe-Coburg,-Gotha; Edward Prince of Wales (later King Edward VII) born 1841.

players have achieved notable success on the professional stage. The first to do so was Graves Simcoe Lee, a son of the innkeeper-physician Hiram Davis Lee. An early member of a civilian drama club, Lee turned professional and established his name as a Shakespearean actor in New York and elsewhere.

While some played cricket and others played Portia or Macbeth, still others painted. Many of the officers had received instructions in watercolours at the Royal Military Academy at Woolwich, England, under the great Paul Sandby or his son and successor Thomas Paul Sandby. Thanks to this group we have an excellent idea of how London looked in its village days.

It was an attractive village.

There is a pleasing symmetry to the view painted by a succession of artists from a favourite spot, a hill on Wortley Road, south and west of the Forks. From that distance the mud, dust, and the untidy ranks of the stumps, the ash pits, and the malodorous ditches were mercifully invisible. The scene, in fact, could be that of a prosperous English village.

Close to, the reality was quite different.

At the top of the social pyramid, life was very good, if occasionally boring. The round of parties, balls, teas, conversaziones, gaming, and visiting differed little from what one might find in an English garrison town of two thousand inhabitants. The daughters of John and Amelia Harris lived a life remarkably free of restrictions. If they danced until the small hours with a retinue of army officers and then slipped off for a moonlight sail across Lake Erie to Cleveland — what then?

An unknown writer of the period captured something of the essence of those carefree days — and nights:

Sing the delights of London society -
 Epaulette, sabretache, sword-knot and plume;
Always enchanting, yet knows no variety -
 Scarlet alone can embellish a room.
While spurs are clattering,
Flirting and chattering,
 Bend the proud heroes that fight for the crown;
Dancing cotillions,
Cutting civilians,
 These are the joys of a garrison town.

Little reck we of you black coated laity;
 Forty to one upon *rouge* against *noir*;
On soldiers we lavish our favours and gaiety,
 For the rest we leave them to feel *desepoir*.
Odious vulgarity,
Reckless barbarity,
 We have for such *canaille* as these but a frown;
While flirting with fusiliers,
Smiling on Grenadiers -
 These are the joys of a garrison town.

London's own social nucleus consisted of a very few families. Among these must be considered the Harris, Becher, Killaly, and Cronyn families. Some had money, all had position. Others had money, but no position. Money was acceptable, but only if a sufficient distance could be established

GRAVES SIMCOE LEE, c. 1870
Graves Simcoe Lee, whose name appears in the playbill on the opposite page, was a popular actor on London's early amateur stages. He later turned professional and gained fame in New York City as a Shakespearean performer.

1840
First Brock's Monument, built 1824, blown up 1840, in the first recorded "terrorist" attack in Canada.

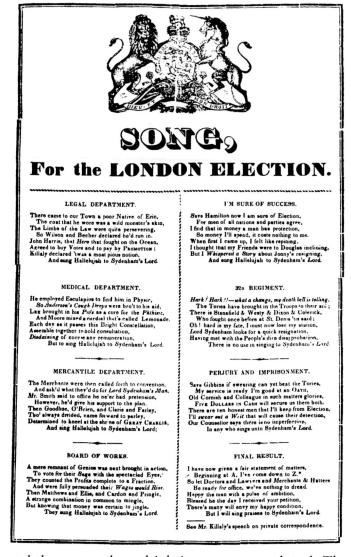

ELECTION
"SONG", 1841
Political satire was a common and often witty feature of early Canadian public life. This "Song" is a gentle ribbing of Hamilton Killaly, who won the election for the seat of London in the first Legislative Assembly of Canada, 1841-1844.

between it and the means by which it was accumulated. Thus, George J. Goodhue, who in 1840 was elected first president of the village board of police, was acceptable because his funds came from usury, which leaves the hands physically clean. Dealers in wood ashes (from which soap was manufactured) and similar products might bear on their persons embarrassing olfactory evidence of that abomination of nineteenth century — *trade*! For witness, the following anecdote:

> Society began to assert itself in 1841, when the line was drawn pretty tight to preserve intact a select few of the better class of business men as being the only ones qualified for admission to the drawing rooms, which were always open to military tinsel, from colonel to captain. Upon a certain occasion an assembly was invited which admitted none of the citizens proper, but such as had (or were supposed to have) a good bank account. All right so far, but when the cards of admission were collected and it was discovered that one of them smelled very strongly of soap or fish oil, it raised a tempest in a tea pot, which nearly upset the whole affair.

While there were members of the "codfish aristocracy" (as the social climbers were known) who would have done almost anything for a card of admission to one of these gatherings, there were other men who would have spurned an invitation. Men like Simeon Morrill, the tanner, and Elijah

1841
Great Britain proclaims sovereignty over Hong Kong, from which it must withdraw now by 1997.

Leonard, the foundry-owner, belonged to churches that opposed drinking, dancing, and gaming. While the Church of England did not encourage these practices, it carried out no active campaign against them. It is true, however, that on one occasion, after a particulary lavish affair given by George Goodhue at his home on Bathurst Street, Benjamin Cronyn preached a rather pointed sermon on the theme of Belshazzar's feast and its unfortunate consequences.

Not everyone, however, took to heart the preachings of the clerics. Mrs. Anna Jameson, author of *Winter Studies and Summer Rambles in Canada*, had this to say about leisure activity in London:

> The population consists principally of artisans — as blacksmiths, carpenters, builders, all flourishing. There is, I fear, a good deal of drunkenness and profligacy; for though the people have work and wealth, they have neither education nor amusement. Besides the seven taverns, there is a number of little grocery stores, which are, in fact, drinking houses. And though a law exists, which forbids the sale of spirituous liquors in small quantities by any but licensed publicans, they easily contrive to elude the law; as thus: - a customer enters the shop, and asks for two or three pennyworth of nuts, or cakes, and he receives a few nuts, and a large glass of whisky. The whisky, you observe, is given, not sold, and no one can swear to the contrary. While I was in London, a person who acted in this capacity [district magistrate] was carried from the pavement dead drunk.

Then, of course, there were the politicians. Some of those who apprenticed in the rough-and-tumble of local politics went on to compete in larger, if no less noisy, arenas. They were the professionals. Others engaged in the electoral battles more as a kind of sport. They were the amateurs. They had more fun.

London's first municipal elections were held on Monday, 2 March 1840. The four wards of the village were named for the patron saints of the United Kingdom: St. George's for England, St. Andrew's for Scotland, St. Patrick's for Ireland, and St. David's for Wales. Each ward elected one councillor to sit on the village board of police. A fifth councillor was chosen by the other four.

In this initial election the Yankee storekeeper George J. Goodhue became councillor for St. George's; Dennis O'Brien, his Irish business rival, was appropriately named to represent St. Patrick's; Simeon Morrill represented St. Andrew's; and John Balkwill, the brewer, was returned for St. David's. The fifth member was the lawyer James Givens, son of the Lieutenant James Givens who had accompanied Lieutenant-Governor Simcoe on his 1793 reconnaissance of the forks of the Thames.

At the first meeting of the village board, the members elected Goodhue as president — another step in his inexorable rise to political patronage and financial power. It was a time for the establishment of community reputations. Dennis O'Brien, London's leading Roman Catholic layman, came out of the experience with his prestige enhanced. He seems to have had few detractors, even fewer enemies.

The member for St. David's was of a different sort. He had founded, in 1828, the brewery that became Labatt's. He was apparently an enthusiastic consumer of his own product. In witness there are two surviving notations concerning a council meeting of Monday, 23 October 1843:

1841
Queens University, Kingston, Ontario, founded.

John Balkwill, Esq., having attended the Board in a state of intoxication: ordered that the constable do remove him; he having done everything in his power to impede the proceedings of the Board. Carried. ...

John Balkwill, Esq., one of the members of the Board, having broken the windows of the office, or instigated the same to be done: ordered that the Board adjourn until to-morrow morning.

It was further noted that Dr. William King Cornish, clerk of the board, submitted his intention to resign, "owing to Balkwill's conduct." It so happened that the building in which the board held its meeting was owned by Cornish, who then turfed out the board and demanded the arrears of rent, amounting to ten pounds ($40) for three years' use. The building, which was London's first "town hall," was described by the late Dr. Cl. T. Campbell:

The first "City Hall" was a small frame building plastered on the outside, situated on the corner of Fullarton and Talbot Streets. ... It remained there for many years. ... When I first knew it, Dr. Jas. Lee occupied it as his office. It was a little one-storey building, with a verandah — the platform of which was level with the street. It was a very unpretentious affair; but the municipal authorities found it sufficient for their purposes.

Dr. Cornish was an English lawyer who emigrated to Canada and, finding he could not practise law here, turned to the study of medicine under Dr. Charles Duncombe. He came to London in 1831, in which year his son Francis Evans Cornish was born. William King became successively (and sometimes concurrently) surgeon to the gaol, district coroner, justice of the peace, surveyor, road overseer, and land agent — a man for all seasons.

Deprived of their former meeting place, the village solons decided to build. A two-storey frame building was erected on what was to become London's Covent Garden Market. Later, it was moved across the street to the northwest corner of King and Talbot streets and bricked over. The only surviving relic of London's town hall is its silver-toned bell, now enshrined in a memorial in London Township's "ghost village," Carlisle. The town hall, along with the rest of the "Talbot Block" was demolished in 1991, in spite of eleventh-hour attempts to save the original frame building discovered under the layer of brick.

Before the bell was installed, village emergencies were signalled by means of a trumpet or bugle sounded by some designated individual. For less emergent occasions Londoners had three means of communication. Gossip was conveyed by word of mouth, commercial news by an officially-appointed town crier, and political intelligence by the weekly newspaper press.

London has always been a good town for gossip. Reputations by the hundreds have been made, broken, or enhanced over the tea pot or the coffee urn. The decade of the 1840s was a particulary juicy period:

Which young officer was currently courting which daughter of John and Amelia Harris?

What public official was said to be dipping into which public find?

Was it true that the lady wife of Casimir Gzowski, the Polish engineer-in-exile, was in the family way again?

PROSPECTUS of a weekly conservative newspaper, to be published in the town of London, and to be entitled "THE LONDON HERALD."

The present extensive and fast increasing population of the Town and District of London, connected with their great commercial and agricultural resources, affords ample encouragement for the establishment of another public journal, in addition to the existing one. And the fact that a large portion of the population who are favorable to the principles of British Conservatism, being destitute of a legitimate channel through which to give publicity to their sentiments and views on the various topics of Government, Legislation and general politics, is a sufficient reason of itself to justify the immediate establishment of a Journal of the kind contemplated.

Accordingly, it is the intention of the subscriber, who has published the *Western Herald* in Sandwich for upwards of four years, to remove his printing materials to London with as little delay as possible, and to commence forthwith the publication of the London Herald, which will be printed on an imperial sheet, (about the size of the late *London Gazette*) at Three Dollars per annum, including postage.

The limits of a Prospectus will not admit of the subscriber entering into an exposition of his political views and sentiments; but he trusts that his undeviating consistency in the conduct of the *Western Herald* on those principles of loyalty and fidelity which saved Canada from the thraldom of Yankee republicans and Canadian democrats, will be a sufficient guarantee of his future course.

The interests of that valuable class of men who are justly regarded as the main dependance of every country, the *Farmers*, shall always be considered of vital importance and will command the particular attention of the Editor.

As the proposed publication, though exclusive in its politics, is intended to benefit all classes of the community, it is expected that none who can command the subscription price will withhold his support. And in order to ensure the publisher from risk and loss it is necessary that a large accession to the subscription list be obtained without delay.

Post Masters and others to whom this Prospectus may be sent, are requested to act as Agents, and to forward their returns to Thomas Hodgkinson Esq., London, who has kindly consented to act as general agent in the subscriber's absence. No payments will be required until the appearance of the first number.

Advertisements will be inserted at the usual rates, and a liberal discount made to yearly and quarterly advertisers.

All kinds of Job Printing will be executed in the neatest and most expeditious manner at the office of the "London Herald."
HENRY C. GRANT,
Editor and Proprietor.
October 10, 1842.

LONDON HERALD PROSPECTUS, 1842
The London Herald, a decidely Tory journal, was established in 1842 by Henry C. Grant of Sandwich, Upper Canada. Grant promoted his brand of British conservatism in direct opposition to the editorial columns of the London Inquirer, a Reform newspaper.

Some bits of gossip found their way into the official records.

In November 1843, Father Patrick O'Dwyer, pastor of the Roman Catholic frame church at the southwest corner of Richmond and Maple streets, was arrested and fined for riding his horse on the downtown sidewalks. There was no way of keeping that quiet.

Then, of course, there was the scandalous case of Four-Eyed Stuart and the British officer.

In 1834 John Stuart, an attorney, married Miss Elizabeth Van Rensalaer Powell, daughter of Dr. Grant Powell and grand-daughter of the Honourable William Dummer Powell, chief justice of Upper Canada. Soon afterward, the couple moved from Toronto to London, where Stuart entered into the practice of law. Three daughters were born to the couple in the ensuing five years. All was apparently well with them until 1839.

In 1838, as we have seen, the 32nd Regiment of Foot was moved to London as a consequence of the Upper Canada rebellion. One of its officers was Lieutenant John Grogan. In the tight little society of "New London" it was inevitable that John Grogan and Elizabeth Stuart should meet. When they did, something happened. They soon became lovers. Then, in 1840, the regiment was moved to Toronto. Mrs. Stuart informed her husband that she was going to visit her mother, about whose health she was concerned. Once in Toronto, Elizabeth Stuart left mother, husband, and daughters to live with the handsome British lieutenant. As soon as he heard of this, Stuart hopped a stagecoach, called on Grogan, and demanded satisfaction, according to the ancient code of the duel.

The two men met, on a misty morning in June 1840, on Toronto

LONDON, c. 1845
Though the size of the buildings in this painting are somewhat exaggerated, the Village of London, as viewed from the banks of the Thames River, delivered a fascinating panorama. Designed with classic Greek lines, the building to the right is the London Mechanics' Institute, the forerunner of the city's public library.

1842
First Census of Province of Canada is taken; the census year later set in 1851 and every tenth year thereafter.

Island. Stuart fired first — and missed. Grogan then fired into the air. Satisfaction had been demanded and given.

Stuart, however, was not finished. He sued Grogan for "alienation of his wife's affections," won, and was awarded the astounding sum of £671 14s 3d Provincial Currency ($2,686.85 US) — a very large amount in those days.

Finally, Stuart took a step that made legal history. He petitioned the Parliament of Canada for a divorce from his erring spouse. The Act of Divorce (3d Victoria, Chapter 72), passed on 18 June 1841, was the first of its kind ever enacted by a Canadian parliament.

The Stuart-Grogan affair must have awakened unhappy memories in a second London household. On another June day, eight years earlier, John Wilson had shot and killed a fellow-law-student, Robert Lyon, in the last fatal duel ever fought in Canada. The meeting took place on the banks of the River Tay, at Perth, Ontario, on Thursday, 13 June 1833. In his subsequent trial on the mandatory charge of murder, Wilson defended himself and won acquittal. The following year he married Miss Elizabeth Hughes, the young lady whose honour he had defended in the field.

It would take an Edward Gorey to suitably illustrate these two early-Victorian dramas. In the American artist's inimitable style we would see the adulterous couple in the Stuart-Grogan affair merrily dancing their way from one mess dinner to another, living happily ever after while the cuckolded husband takes to drink and totters off down the road to ruin and obscurity.

In the Wilson matter we would see the virtuous John Wilson and the virtuous Miss Hughes plighting their virtuous troth and proceeding on their virtuous path, she to raise a brood in the fear of God, he to rise step by step to national prominence as lawyer, judge, and successful politician. Not exactly in the true Gorey tradition, one must admit, but in the final panels Gorey's Gothic magic could work its fey wonder, as we see John Wilson in his annual commemoration of the fatal duel, brooding, close closeted in his private chambers, seeing no one, speaking to no one, the albatross of memory peering bleakly down on him from the bookcase. ...

Say what you will, the Victorians knew how to live, how to drink from the cup of life, from the bubbles winking at the brim to the dregs lurking at the bottom!

In a society such as this, gossip became almost an art form, tea-pot fiction in many cases being overtaken by courtroom fact.

Information of a more serious nature was conveyed by the town crier. The initial two men named to this position were blacks, of whom the first and better-remembered was "General" George Washington Brown. Brown dressed in cast-off military uniforms, gleefully provided by young officers at the garrison. When Brown died in May 1845, his passing was marked by an eleven-stanza piece of doggerel verse in the London *Times*, of which the following is a sample:

> What man is there, who claims the rank
> Of "Londoner" who will not own
> How much he feels the common blank
> Made by the death of Gen'ral Brown!

1843
*The first successful
typewriter
patented
by Charles Thueber
of Norwich,
Connecticut.*

To Medical Students.

DOCTOR PHILLIPS will devote two evenings in the week, Mondays and Thursdays, to giving private instructions, and examinations, to Medical Students, in the following branches, Anatomy, Physiology and Pathology, Theory and Practice of Medicine and Surgery, Chemistry, Obstetrics, and diseases of women and children. Dr. Phillips has letters from Professors of the Universities of London, Dublin and Edinburgh, as to character and qualifications.

For further particulars, apply to Dr. Phillips, M. R. C. L.

King Street,
London, Jan. 9, 1843. 23m3

THE OLD ESTABLISHED
LONDON BREWERY.

THE Subscriber having succeeded Mr. Shepherd in the above Establishment, begs to acquaint his friends and the public, that he is prepared to supply any orders for ALE they may favor him with. He flatters himself he will be enabled to give his customers as good satisfaction as when carrying on the St. Thomas Brewery, and hopes by strict attention to business, and making a uniform good article, to obtain their support.

SAMUEL ECCLES
London, March 6, 1847. 19c.

MEDICAL ADVERTISEMENT, 1843
Dr. Phillips was one of several physicians who practised in London during the early 1840s. Like many of his professional contemporaries, he offered private lessons in the healing arts — foreshadowing the city's later role as an important teaching centre in the field of medicine.

LONDON BREWERY ADVERTISEMENT, 1847
The London Brewery was established in 1828 by John Balkwill. In early 1847, the brewery passed into the hands of Samuel Eccles, who, later that year, formed a partnership with a relatively unknown farmer named John Kinder Labatt. Under the Labatt name, the establishment would grow to be recognized as one of the country's largest nineteenth century breweries.

Brown was succeeded by "General" Don Kean. Within two years a white man, William Williams, was named to the position by the town council and served under a variety of administrations until the 1860s, when the city's daily newspapers made the job obsolete.

For many years the town crier and the weekly newspapers were competitors in the field of advertising. The crier had the obvious advantage of immediacy. A merchant-client could have him "cry" a sale as soon as he decided upon it, instead of waiting for the next publication day of the local weeklies, among which were the *Inquirer*, the *Herald*, the *Times*, the *Western Globe*, and the *Gazette*. The advertisements in these journals tended in consequence to be of an institutional nature. The first of the standard four pages was usually given over to "business cards," announcing services offered on a continuing basis by the advertisers. The third page usually contained such current advertisements as municipal announcements, coach and ship schedules, real-estate notices, and birth, marriage, and death announcements. A regular feature of the inside pages was a list, often a column in length, of letters being held at the post office awaiting their intended recipients. Sometimes the letters were prepaid, while others had to be paid for by those to whom they were addressed (Postage stamps were not introduced into the Canadas until 1851.)

Meanwhile, there was another side to the society of London in the 1840s that has seldom been touched upon, either in the contemporary records or in the selective memories of those who lived through the events.

There were poor people in London from the very beginning, and they had no protection against poverty and hunger except the sometimes chilly charity of the churches and church people. There was no official structure in place to answer the needs of those whom we today refer to in our oblique way as "the disadvantaged."

Only a few years earlier indigent widows were auctioned off to the highest bidder. Quite often the unfortunate females stepped from the auction block into that form of unpaid servitude called Christian marriage; but marriage was not a condition of sale. If the buyer didn't choose to formalize his relationship to his chattel — well, that was a matter between him and his conscience.

Nor was there any provision in the community's budget for the care

Like as the smoke vanisheth, so shalt thou drive them away and like as wax melteth at the fire, so let the ungodly perish at the presence of God.

Before the rector can continue with verse three, a hysterical cry from the street below is heard.

"Fire! Fire!"

There is immediate panic. People in wooden towns fear matches. The auditorium is on the second floor of the Institute. The stairs are narrow. A rush for safety can have tragic consequences. An unspoken message passes between the parson and the chief justice. The rector continues reading:

But let the righteous be glad and rejoice before God; let them also be merry and joyful.

With great equanimity the justice reads in a clear, loud voice:

O sing unto God, and sing praises unto his Name -

Other voices join in:

- magnify him that rideth upon the heavens, as it were upon an horse. ...

Quietly, but swiftly, the sidesmen lead the people down the steep stairs to safety while the parson and the chief justice continue their reading. Only when the last member of the congregation has reached the exit do the two men follow them. There's much to do. The Chief Justice is a guest at the Robinson Hall Hotel, at the corner of Ridout and Dundas streets, where the fire had started. His robes and other belongings are in his room. By this time the hotel is ablaze from front to back. At considerable risk to himself Judge Robinson rescues his belongings.

Marcus Gunn, a Scot from Pictou, Nova Scotia, is attentively listening to a "luminous Sermon", by Rev. A.G. Lawrie, at the Universalist Church when he hears the cry "Fire!". He too rushes to the Robinson Hall Hotel where, since arriving in London the previous November, he has left his heaviest trunk and a green box with the innkeeper. He is less fortunate than Robinson. The box, which contains most of his diaries, dating from 1822, is burnt or lost. To add insult to injury, the boarding house into which he, his new wife, and a son had moved but the previous day, also apparently falls victim to the flames. Fortunately, the family has several relatives in the countryside who will take them in.

The Reverend Benjamin Cronyn, always at his best in emergencies, is helping the occupants of nearby buildings to move their valuables to the street, where they are stacked up for later retrieval. The fire, fed by gale-force winds, northwest by north, is spreading rapidly. The Robinson Hall Hotel is now gone and so are the adjacent structures on Ridout Street.

A squad of artillerymen under Captain John Herbert Caddy has placed itself under Cronyn's direction. By dint of great effort they manage to evacuate residents' belongings ahead of the fire, but the men are tiring. Suddenly there's a cry from the rear. Sparks from the burning buildings have touched off one of the stacks of furniture carefully piled in the middle of the street.

It has become a losing battle, Soon every building on the block bounded by Dundas, King, Talbot, and Ridout streets is ablaze, and structures south of the river are in imminent danger.

1844

Samuel F.B. Morse (1791-1872) invents the Morse code by telegraph and transmits the first message from Washington to Baltimore.

Before nightfall more than two hundred buildings are in ashes. The smoke and flames can be seen as far away as St. Thomas and have attracted sightseers, scavengers, and looters from the surrounding countryside.

A further appeal to the garrison brings a number of men from the 2nd Royal Regiment of Foot to stand guard over the ruins with fixed bayonets to repel looters.

At the end of the day, Parson Cronyn, soot-stained and weary, retrieves the Preacher's Book of St. Paul's from the Mechanic's Hall. Later, in the rectory, he records a laconic note under the current date:

"No collection ... Great Fire."

Almost before the ashes of London's business district had cooled, money was being collected to aid the sufferers. Like the nasty business of the looters, there were ugly aspects to this effort, too. Some fraud artists, representing themselves as victims of the disaster, began collecting funds in Toronto. They had the effrontery to call upon the Anglican Bishop of Toronto, the Right Reverend John Strachan, who at once wrote to Benjamin Cronyn suggesting that the latter call a public meeting of "the best-known and respectable of your inhabitants" to organize a proper relief fund.

The proposal was swiftly acted upon, and soon donations were pouring into the stricken community from cities and towns all over Canada, from the United States and Great Britain, for the story of the fire had received widespread publicity.

Estimates of the damage caused by London's "Great Fire" ranges as high as £125,000. No final accounting of the relief fund has been found, but more than £460 is recorded as having been sent from outside London.

Not wishing a repeat of this disaster, many of those who erected build-

DUNDAS STREET, 1842, LOOKING WEST FROM NEAR WELLINGTON STREET

As the sharp division between urban concentration and freshly cleared land indicates, the Village of London abruptly greeted the weary traveller from the eastern reaches of Middlesex County.

1845

First failure of the potato crop in Ireland causes the Great Famine; hunger brings enormous migration to North America.

ings downtown following the fire chose to build with the much safer local white brick. It wasn't until June, 1850, however, that city council passed a by-law prohibiting the erection of frame buildings in the downtown area.

The busy parson of St. Paul's Church had much to occupy him that year. In addition to heading the campaign to raise relief money, he was deeply involved in a parallel effort to finance the building of the ambitious new St. Paul's. The architect was William Thomas of Toronto, who may have been a pupil of Sir Charles Barry, architect of the British Houses of Parliament. The inside dimensions of the new church were commodious — fifty-nine feet in width by eighty-five feet in length. The walls of the tower were six feet at the base. Crowned by four slender pinnacles, it rose to a height of 114 feet, making it the dominant feature of the London skyline.

Despite the rector's acknowledged skill as a financier and money-raiser, the congregation faced a formidable debt of £4,100 ($16,400 US) when the building was opened on Ash Wednesday, 25 February 1846, two years after the destruction of the first St. Paul's. According to the editor of the London (Canada West) *Times*, Dr. John Salter, 1,400 people crowded into the church, which had a seating capacity of one thousand, while several hundred more were unable to get in. Salter gave a knowledgeable account of the architecture, noting in passing that the style adopted "is that which prevailed throughout the greater part of the fourteenth century." The scholarly description descends into babbitry in the concluding paragraph:

> The erection of such a church in this part of the province is a marked step and feature in that curious but interesting ... process by which a Country passes from the savage wildness of nature to that state of population, health and intelligence, in which the finest comforts of civilization are enjoyed in companionship with the blessings of religious ordinances and instruction.

The reference to the former primitive nature of the site was an obligatory feature of any public address, ever since the days of Edward Allen Talbot, who wrote in his prospectus for the London *Sun*, back in 1831, that the site had formerly been only "the abode of the wolf and the haunt of the savage." Fourteen years after the opening of St. Paul's the then-mayor of London, James Moffat, drew to the attention of the then-Prince of Wales (later Edward VII) that "at most it is only 40 years since, in the locality where you now stand, none but the red Indian dozed under the shade of the primeval forest."

A good cliche is a joy forever ... and forever.

The financial institutions that by the 1840s were doing business on "Banker's Row" on Ridout Street north of Dundas were certainly not trading in wampum. These were solid, conservative branches of Toronto and Montreal banks. Their managers and directors were reluctant to loan money to such insubstantial organizations as the Church of England and the board of police of the village of London. Both were refused loans on the grounds of "insufficient security."

Despite the dyspeptic cynics of Bankers' Row, the new year seemed to promise nothing but good news for the thriving — and growing — community. At the beginning of 1847 the population was more than 4,000, and steps were being taken to grant it full town status. Additional num-

1845

John L. O'Sullivan coins the phrase "Manifest Destiny" to justify the relentless westward movement of the United States.

bers were expected with the opening of navigation in the spring. Immigration from the United Kingdom was on the rise again.

It was well known that the newcomers would be mostly Irish and dirt poor. Throughout the winter of 1846-1847 Canadian newspapers reported at great length on the famine that had followed two years of crop failure. In fact, Canadian journals and their readers showed more compassion for Ireland's suffering paupers than did the English press.

Even so, until the tattered legions actually arrived in Canada, no one had any real conception of the true horror of the Irish situation. As it was, the enfeebled skeletons who limped, crawled, or were carried off the ships at Grosse Isle were pictures of health compared to the human wreckage they left behind:

> At Castlebar people lay in the streets with green froth at their mouths from eating soft grass. Inquests brought in verdicts of "starvation," "Hunger and Cold," and "Died of famine." ... "As to holding more inquests," said the *Galway Vindicator* ... "it is mere nonsense. The number of deaths is beyond counting."
>
> In the parish of Kilgless, Roscommon, seven skeleton bodies were found in a hedge, half eaten by dogs. The police shot seven dogs. In the mouth of one of them was a heart and part of a liver.

Canadian generosity and compassion were very soon stretched to the breaking point, for the immigrants were not only sick, but their sickness was contagious. They called it "ship's fever;" we call it typhus.

Typhus is carried by body lice. The Irish paupers were generous hosts to the little horrors. Typhus is a disease of the blood vessels, the skin, and the brain. The symptoms are shivering, headache, congested face, bloodshot eyes, muscular twitching, and a stupid stare, as if the sufferers were drunk.

The disease made its appearance in Canada on 14 May. By the end of the month there were more than a thousand cases, and the medical superintendent on Grosse Isle had trouble finding enough people able to dig graves. He wrote to the chief immigrant agent at Quebec:

> I never saw people so indifferent to life; they would continue in the same berth with a dead person until the seamen or captain dragged out the corpse with boat-hooks. Good God! what evils will befall the cities wherever they alight. Hot weather will increase the evil. Now give the authorities at Quebec and Montreal fair warning from me. I have not time to write, or should feel it my duty to do so. Public safety requires it.

On 8 June the Canadian government ordered all municipalities to provide sheds to house healthy immigrants and hospitals for the sick. By that time the contagion had spread to Montreal, Kingston, and Toronto.

At this time London had two public markets — the present Covent Garden Market and the "New Survey Market," in the block bounded by York, Bathurst, Wellington, and Waterloo streets. The board of police commandeered the New Survey Market House for the reception of the healthy Irish and had constructed two hospitals, each twenty by forty feet, and a shed of the same dimensions for cooking and washing, the whole at a total cost of £200 ($800 US). Houses in the vicinity were rented for the accommodation of the chief physician, dispenser, stewards, and nurses.

1845
Richard Wagner (1813-1883), German operatic composer, publishes his Tannhauser.

The board of police named its president, Dr. Hiram Davis Lee, as physician and employed Daniel Brown, a veteran of the Battle of Lundy's Lane (25 July 1814), as steward and a woman named Ann Peel as nurse.

For a few weeks all was well and the elaborate precautions seemed unnecessary. Then, towards the end of July, the epidemic struck with a ferocity not seen since the Asiatic cholera outbreak of 1832. All the village's doctors were pressed into service in an attempt to check the disease, but to little purpose. Potter's Field, west of Waterloo Street and north of Dufferin Avenue, gaped wide to receive the bodies of the known and the unknown. The burial register of St. Paul's Church lost its desperate battle to remain current. There is now no way of knowing how many died between 15 July and 30 October 1847.

Throughout the epidemic Dr. Lee and his staff fought like lions to contain the disease. Lee visited all his patients twice a day, pacing the packed-dirt floor between the rows of pallets laid on the earth, breathing the fetid breath of fever. It was inevitable that the plague would win the uneven contest. Daniel Brown died on Monday, 30 August; Ann Peel died on Wednesday, 1 September. With the fever abating finally, Lee struggled through the rains of September, but by the middle of October it was apparent to his friends and helpers that he was sick and confused, exhausted past caring. On Friday, 29 October, he visited the hospital one last time. He had been fighting to save the life of one particular patient, for no special reason. Perhaps in his fever-addled brain he felt that this was a battle he must win, or perish. He did not win. According to a contemporary, he looked at his dying patient and was seen "to turn aside with irresistible loathing."

He died later that day.

Nowhere in London is there a memorial to mark the name, career, and selfless sacrifice of the only chief executive of the city to die a martyr's death in office.

While Lee was fighting his last, lonely battle at the south end of the village, an old dream was being fulfilled at the north end.

On 29 March 1845, the act incorporating the London and Gore Railroad Company (1834) was revived under a new name — the Great Western Railroad Company. A year later the British government enacted a similar piece of legislation enabling British investors to participate in the colonial venture.

The infusion of the English capital made it possible to proceed immediately with a survey of the proposed rail line, initially intended to link Hamilton and London, with later extensions planned to spots on the American border at Niagara Falls and Windsor.

The route chosen for the line through London was that later followed by the Canadian Pacific Railway. In 1847 the site proposed for the rail station was out in the country, by village standards. It was to be built on the west side of that part of the present Richmond Street then known as Sarnia Street, between Ann and Oxford Streets.

The property in question was still forested, although it was adjacent to the northern boundary of the military reserve, roughly marked by a meandering watercourse known as Carling's Creek. The waters of this stream supported three local industries — Carling's Brewery on Waterloo

1846
United States declares war on Mexico; after the treaty of peace in 1848 USA had annexed about one-third of Mexico.

Street, the Hamilton Brewery on Ann Street, and Water's Mill, west of Talbot Street where the creek empties into the north branch of the Thames River.

On Saturday, 23 October 1847, the site of the new station was the scene of the largest public gathering London had yet seen, as virtually the entire population of the village turned out to celebrate what George Brown, editor of the Toronto *Globe*, referred to as "the ceremony of breaking ground on this great national undertaking."

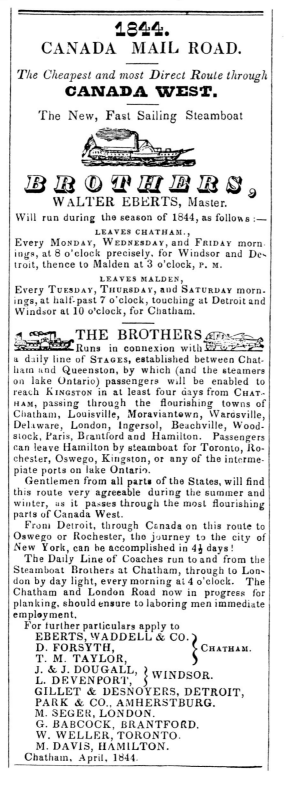

1844.
CANADA MAIL ROAD.

The Cheapest and most Direct Route through
CANADA WEST.

The New, Fast Sailing Steamboat

BROTHERS,
WALTER EBERTS, Master.

Will run during the season of 1844, as follows :—

LEAVES CHATHAM.,
Every MONDAY, WEDNESDAY, and FRIDAY mornings, at 8 o'clock precisely, for Windsor and Detroit, thence to Malden at 3 o'clock, P. M.

LEAVES MALDEN,
Every TUESDAY, THURSDAY, and SATURDAY mornings, at half-past 7 o'clock, touching at Detroit and Windsor at 10 o'clock, for Chatham.

THE BROTHERS Runs in connexion with a daily line of STAGES, established between Chatham and Queenston, by which (and the steamers on lake Ontario) passengers will be enabled to reach KINGSTON in at least four days from CHATHAM, passing through the flourishing towns of Chatham, Louisville, Moraviantown, Wardsville, Delaware, London, Ingersol, Beachville, Woodstock, Paris, Brantford and Hamilton. Passengers can leave Hamilton by steamboat for Toronto, Rochester, Oswego, Kingston, or any of the intermediate ports on lake Ontario.

Gentlemen from all parts of the States, will find this route very agreeable during the summer and winter, as it passes through the most flourishing parts of Canada West.

From Detroit, through Canada on this route to Oswego or Rochester, the journey to the city of New York, can be accomplished in 4½ days !

The Daily Line of Coaches run to and from the Steamboat Brothers at Chatham, through to London by day light, every morning at 4 o'clock. The Chatham and London Road now in progress for planking, should ensure to laboring men immediate employment.

For further particulars apply to
EBERTS, WADDELL & CO. }
D. FORSYTH, } CHATHAM.
T. M. TAYLOR, }
J. & J. DOUGALL, } WINDSOR.
L. DEVENPORT, }
GILLET & DESNOYERS, DETROIT,
PARK & CO., AMHERSTBURG.
M. SEGER, LONDON.
G. BABCOCK, BRANTFORD.
W. WELLER, TORONTO.
M. DAVIS, HAMILTON.
Chatham, April, 1844.

TRAVEL ADVERTISEMENT, 1844
Before the railway, a journey through Canada West was a demanding task. In the spring of 1844, Walter Eberts guaranteed the passage between Chatham and Kingston in at least four days! The run from Chatham to London departed at 4 a.m., and followed a course over the Chatham and London road.

1846
First formal rules for the game of baseball written by Alexander Joy Cartwright.

**B.A. MITCHELL,
c. 1870**
Establishing his drug store in 1846, Bossom A. Mitchell was one of London's most notable nineteenth century pharmacists. Mitchell not only developed a strong retail trade, he also trained numerous apprentices. After learning the art, many of Mitchell's students subsequently opened their own drug stores throughout Ontario.

1847
Britain's tragic Bronte sisters produce two works of "remarkable passion and imagination," Jane Eyre, and Wuthering Heights.

It was one of those crisp, sunny days October often confers on this part of North America, and the town was on holiday. All the stores closed at noon, and dignitaries from far and near began to assemble at the courthouse square. At one o'clock the procession set out, moving along Dundas Street to Richmond Street, and thence north.

The scene at the station site was described in colourful detail by the Toronto *Globe*:

> On the ground, preparation had been made for the ceremony which was now to ensue; a wide space had been cleared in the forest around, and stand erected for the accommodation of the guests and spectators. The logs gathered from the clearance were piled around the scene of the action, and ere the procession had reached the ground, these forest galleries were covered with people, and the ladies' stand was thronged with the beauty and fashion of the Metropolis of the Far West. The riflemen kept the ground clear in the centre, and as the procession arrived the several bodies took up their stations around the inside of the large circle, forming as it were a spacious amphitheatre. The number present has been estimated at from 3500 to 5000 persons, and we feel certain that the smaller number is below the fact.

George J. Goodhue, now a member of the Legislative Council of the Province of Canada (a post roughly equivalent to that of a senator in our present terms), was chairman and opened the proceedings with the obligatory remarks comparing the "then and now." He then called upon the guest of honour, Colonel Thomas Talbot, to turn the first sod. According to the florid wording employed by the Globe, the aging founder of the Talbot Settlement (he was seventy-seven) "took the spade and inflicted the first wound on Mother Earth."

A man of few words, Colonel Talbot said them and sat down to thunderous applause and a salute from a battery of the Royal Artillery.

Lesser men followed and said a great deal more. Either because of the accumulated weight of the dignitaries or because of the burden of their rhetoric, the main stand collapsed towards the end of the proceeding, throwing them all to the ground. No bones were broken, there was a good deal of laughter and applause, Mr. Goodhue said that that was all there was, the crowd gave "three times three" hearty cheers for the Queen, the procession re-formed for the march back to town — and that was the end of the public celebration.

At six o'clock that evening, 120 guests gathered in the dining room of the Western Hotel. This was Dennis O'Brien's original five-storey brick building on Dundas Street at Ridout. It was a large structure, one hundred feet by fifty-five feet, and contained sixty rooms; at this time it was operated by the firm of Paul and Bennett.

A copy of the menu for the evening, with a wine list on the reverse side has been preserved. For the benefit of oenophiles, it may be noted that a Medoc could be had for 6s. 3d. ($1.25 US) a bottle. There was "champaigne" (Reinhart or Sillery) at $2 a bottle, in addition to madeira, port, sherry, brandy, ale, porter, and stout. The most expensive item was Hunts' Very Old Port, at $2.50 a bottle. When it is realized that a skilled artisan (like a newspaper compositor) could not hope to take home more than $8 or $9 US a week, it will be seen that the Western Hotel was no workingman's pub.

The "bill of fare" was a weight-watcher's nightmare. The diners had a choice of meats, roast or boiled — beef, pork, veal, lamb, mutton, turkey, chicken, duck, goose, ham, corned beef, tongue, and calf's head (ugh!) Accompanying this Lucullan fare were the "vegetables of the season" — "kole-slau," tomatoes, cress, and celery. It may be noted that is was a rather early appearance of the tomato on a restaurant menu. Originally considered to be poisonous, tomatoes did not become a popular edible in the United States until the 1860s.

Within the ensuing few hours no less than sixteen toasts were proposed and responded to. George Brown, on behalf of his paper, was keeping careful notes of all the toasts and responses (especially his own); but as the evening wore on, his notes got skimpier. All he could write about Lawrence Lawrason's response to the toast to "Agriculture and Commerce," was that it was given "happily." Since that was the twelfth toast, the adverb was probably well chosen.

Halfway down the lengthy list came the toast to the guest of honour. George Goodhue's introduction of "the Hon. Thomas Talbot" was rather fulsome, and the cheers with which it was greeted were slightly sycophantic or perhaps only maudlin. The Colonel's response was terse and humorous; his humour, however, had its usual cutting edge:

> I thank you gentlemen most gratefully for the honour you have done me this day. I have witnessed a scene which I never hoped to behold in this settlement — it is an event never to be forgotten. I believe I am the oldest inhabitant. I slept on this spot 55 years ago, when my best friend was a porcupine. We were often excessively hungry in those days, but we all used to declare that we never were so hungry as the night we ate the porcupine. (Cheers and laughter.) What a change has occurred since then! Now I see different beings around me — no porcupine — no bristles; but in their place a company of half-civilized gentlemen.

This last sally was greeted with laughter and cheers.
They thought he was joking.

1847
Alexander Graham Bell, inventor of the telephone, born at Edinburgh, migrates to Brantford, Ontario, 1870.

**THE COURT
HOUSE, c. 1854**
*This, the earliest
known photographic
image of the struc-
ture, shows the Court
House as captured by
the camera of Graves
and Prudden. Though
based in New York
State at the time,
E.R. Graves and Henry
Prudden displayed
their talents at the
1854 Upper Canada
Provincial Exhibition
held in London. The
partners won first
prize for a collection
of their daguerreo-
types.*

The most illustrous of all the pioneers of southwestern Ontario, Colonel Thomas Talbot, died in London on Sunday, 6 February 1853, sixty years after he first saw the site of the city in the company of Lieutenant-Governor John Graves Simcoe. He was eighty-two.

The world in which Thomas Talbot died was vastly changed from the leisurely world into which he had been born. As he lay dying, not far from the forks of the Thames, the rails of the Great Western Railway Company were nearing the eastern outskirts of London. When the first train reached the city, later that same year, the journey from London to Hamilton had been reduced from a matter of days to a matter of hours.

When Talbot was born at Castle Malahide, near Dublin, Ireland, in 1771, the fastest speed attainable by a human being was astride a horse. Over a short distance a horse could run at perhaps thirty miles an hour. That had been the outside limit for many thousands of years.

In 1848 — months after London became a full-fledged town — a locomotive on England's Great Western Railway managed to reach a speed of *seventy-eight miles per hour!*

The ordinary people of London, Canada West, refused to believe these reports. Seventy-eight miles an hour? Madness! A sober Londoner with pretensions to scientific knowledge told the *Free Press* that if a passenger thrust his arm out the window of a carriage travelling at such a speed, he would have the member ripped right off!

When the wood-burning locomotive and its two coaches rolled into London early in the evening of Thursday, 15 December 1853, the gaggle of Very Important Persons who comprised the passenger list was intact as to limbs, but tired and grubby. The trip from Hamilton had taken six hours. William Bowman, mechanical superintendent of the GWR, recorded his memories of the occasion a half-century later:

> As I remember it, the weather was cold and raw, and the mud along the line was simply appalling.
>
> We left Hamilton, where I was living at the time, early in the afternoon and it was near dusk when we arrived at London. The time was very slow, slow even for those days, owing to the condition of the roadbed; and it was my opinion at the time that it was a foolhardy notion to attempt the trip on such a roadbed. The rocking of the coaches was frightful, and I thought at times we would go into the mud in the ditch.
>
> We stopped at all the stations along the line, but it was difficult to leave the coaches, as there was no platforms as yet erected, and the mud was too deep to wade into. Woodstock was the largest place between Hamilton and London in those days, and it was small enough to be ridiculous.
>
> We made the journey without incident, however, and upon our arrival in London we were met by a large crowd of people, who had awaited our coming. ...
>
> The station at the time was a little frame building, which was shortly afterwards replaced by the present structure.

The artist who recorded the scene for the *Illustrated London* (England) *News* took a considerable amount of artistic license. The clean, sharp lines of the woodcut give no hint of the dull skies, rain, and mud that the passengers actually experienced. The railway station shown is not the little shack that received them, but the later, permanent station.

1851
First Canadian postage stamps, the famous "Three-Penny beaver," "Six Pence Albert," and "Twelve-Penny Black."

THE ARRIVAL OF THE GREAT WESTERN RAILWAY
After a six hour trip from Hamilton, on December 15, 1853, the first Great Western Railway train puffed into London, ushering in a new era of prosperity. Of monumental importance, the arrival of the railroad guaranteed London's place as the wholesaling and manufacturing capital of the southwestern peninsula.

1852
Uncle Tom's Cabin, *by Harriet Beecher Stowe (1811-1896), an instant bestseller, galvanizes opinion against US slavery.*

The idealized picture conveys no suggestion as to the physical location of the event. It had nothing to do with the site where Thomas Talbot had wielded the ceremonial spade in 1847. This, the site chosen by the directors of the Great Western, was considered by the London merchant and financial community to be much too far away from the town centre. It was, after all, nearly a mile from the corner of Dundas and Richmond streets! The predecessors of today's Downtown London Business Association put pressure on the town council. The council put pressure on the Great Western. The company cited the additional cost a more central location would entail, and in effect said, "Put up or shut up." The town "put up" to the extent of investing £25,000 ($100,000 US) in the company — money, incidentally, which the municipality did not have and which the banks were unwilling to advance.

To compound this act of financial lunacy, the municipality proceeded to invest heavily in its very own railway line. The London and Port Stanley Railroad was incorporated by act of Parliament on Monday, 23 May 1853; capital stock, £150,000 ($600,000 US).

Among the incorporators of the new road was Freeman Talbot, youngest brother of Edward Allen Talbot, the dreamer who, nearly a quarter-century earlier, had captured the vision of a nation whose cities would be linked by iron rails and iron horses.

Although the London and Port Stanley Railroad never, in its century of operation, achieved financial success, a second project with which Talbot was associated made handsome profit for all its investors.

In 1849, Freeman Talbot was the chief architect of the Proof Line Road Company, a privately-owned toll road, the first such cooperative company in the history of the province. The Proof Line Road, which now forms parts of Highway 4, ran north from London to Ryan's Corners (Elginfield), on the townline between London and Biddulph townships.

By the time the Great Western's locomotive chuffed its way into London in 1853, the area already had the finest transportation network in the province, thanks largely to the efforts of Hamilton Hartley Killaly, an Irish civil engineer, who represented London in the Legislature of the United Provinces of Canada East (Quebec) and Canada West (Ontario) from 1841 to 1844. Killaly became chairman of the Canadian Board of Works and spent nearly the whole of his first appropriation of £100,000 ($400,000 US) on improving the roads in the western portion of the province, which included his own riding.

With the completion of the Proof Line Road and the entry of the Great Western Railway, London had truly become the hub of one of the richest farming areas on the continent, a pre-eminent position never seriously to be challenged.

Long before the rails of the Great Western reached London, the town was already in the grip of as wild a real-estate boom as has ever afflicted any area in North America. Property along the right-of-way suddenly assumed fantastic values. As in London so in the surrounding countryside. Property not on the railway but in areas where it might reasonably be expected feeder lines would later be constructed also rose sharply in value. It was a rich field for the speculator. Packages of land changed hands with dizzying speed and frequency. Fortunes were made overnight — on paper. In very few cases was the full amount of the purchase price paid on the line. An instance is recorded of a lot of land changing hands several times in the course of a single day — and no actual cash involved. It was margin buying on a scale equalled only once since in this area — in the hectic days preceding the stock market collapse of 1929.

The fever reached its most insane pitch in London. Real-estate promoters commissioned the survey of suburban building lots as far west of Komoka, north of Arva, east to Dorchester, and south to St. Thomas. All these areas are still well outside the perimeters of the modern city of London.

As an example of the inflated values placed on London real estate in the years between 1851 and 1857, it will suffice to cite the case of the businessman who bought a building lot on the eastern fringe on the downtown shopping district during the boom. Unlike most of his fellow speculators, he paid cash. For the ensuing fifty years he paid city taxes on the lot and the building he had erected on it. Finally, in 1905, he sold out for what was then considered a good price. It lacked a dollar of what he had paid for the land alone a half-century earlier.

As the land boom approached its giddy peak, events far removed from London thrust themselves forcibly on the attention of the townsfolk. The ancient political cauldron of the Middle East had boiled over again. Turkey declared war on Russia on 4 October 1853, launching attacks across the Black sea on Russian positions in the Crimean Peninsula. Before the end of the year England and France were allied with Turkey, and troops of both nations were on their way to the battle zone. Faced with a major war, Britain recalled its troops from their Canadian garrisons.

Five or six years earlier the loss of London's garrison would have had a catastrophic effect on the town's economy. By 1854, the drying up of this source of income was scarcely noticed. Indeed the war resulted in a greatly increased demand for Canadian wheat. At the same time a

FREEMAN TALBOT, c. 1880
A dynamic individual, who marked London's earlier years, Freeman Talbot was a man of seemingly limitless energy. At various times during the 1840s and 1850s, he was involved in enterprises that included newspaper printing and publishing, contracting, road building, as well as serving as county engineer. Talbot left London in the mid-1850s, and eventually he became a widely respected American state senator.

1853
Counties of Middlesex and Elgin separated municipally; court house built at St. Thomas.

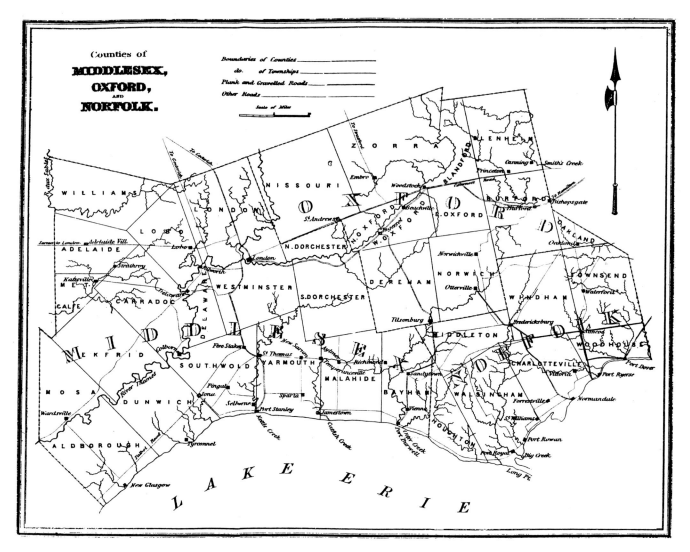

Counties of
MIDDLESEX,
OXFORD,
AND
NORFOLK.

Boundaries of Counties _____
do. of Townships _____
Plank and Gravelled Roads ___ _ ___
Other Roads _____

Scale of Miles

ROAD MAP, 1851

By the early 1850s, a rudimentary network of roads was evident in Middlesex, Oxford, and Norfolk counties. London benefitted from a web of plank, gravel, and dirt roads that linked it with outlying communities.

1853

Death of Colonel Thomas Talbot (b. 1771), soldier, settlement promoter; spent 50 years developing the Talbot settlement.

reciprocity treaty with the United States, arranged by Lord Elgin, opened the southern frontier to a duty-free flow of natural products.

In the result the economic heart of London moved from the army barracks to Covent Garden Market, where a handsome new market building had been erected.

Meanwhile the town council, led by the mayor, Marcus Holmes, a carriage-builder, was pressing the Canadian government to pass the necessary legislation for the incorporation of London as a city. A population of 10,000 was required, and London had passed that milestone in August 1854 when the official census was taken and the population was found to be 10,060 (not a large margin, considering this figure included those lodging, if only for the night, in the town's hotels!).

Not all newcomers to the city were wealthy or healthy. Many were neither. They didn't stay at the town's numerous hotels, inns, and taverns. Some sixty-eight newcomers, including a group of six Norwegian immigrants, went straight from the railway cars to the city's pest house, and thence to Potter's Field, off the Hamilton Road. London's latest encounter with Asiatic cholera was short, sharp, and nasty. The town council decreed once again that all victims of the epidemic should be buried by night. Then as now, municipal authorities strove to preserve the fiction

of a 100-per-cent-healthy citizenry. As an expression of the American South-land has it: "What the eye don't see, the heart don't grieve."

The poor immigrants whose remains were interred under cover of darkness were not the only exiles from the general paper prosperity. The inflationary spiral engineered by the rising values of land and wheat seriously inconvenienced middle-class Londoners and devastated the poor.

Over the years between 1848 and 1855, wages rose perhaps 20 per cent, while the cost of sheltering and feeding a family sky-rocketed by from 100 to 300 per cent.

As a consequence, those who could least withstand the economic turbulence suffered the most. So it was that a period of London's history superficially marked by financial progress and high expectations also saw the establishment of the municipality's first relief department, as some of the town's leading churches opened soup kitchens in an effort to meet some of the basic needs of the poor.

Meanwhile the flow of black refugees from the slave states continued. Harriet Beecher Stowe's phenomenally successful serialized novel *Uncle Tom's Cabin*, which appeared in book form in 1852, focused public attention on the humanitarian work of the Underground Railroad. As a highly visible, persecuted minority, the fugitive blacks won much sympathy from Londoners; more, in fact, than the indigent newcomers from Ireland.

The community that was about to achieve municipal maturity as Canada's newest city, was a far different place from the stump-strewn "New London" that had so amused the officers of the British garrison in the early 1840s. Its municipal limits were to remain unchanged, however, from 1841 until the annexation of London East in 1885.

THE TOWN OF LONDON, 1854
On the verge of city-hood, London beamed with pride. The arrival of the Great Western Railway, a healthy and expanding business community, the constant influx of new arrivals, the dynamic civic leadership all combined to help propel the town to its next municipal milestone. On January 1, 1855, London officially became a city. This engraving depicts a flourishing London as viewed from the northern edge of today's Thames Park.

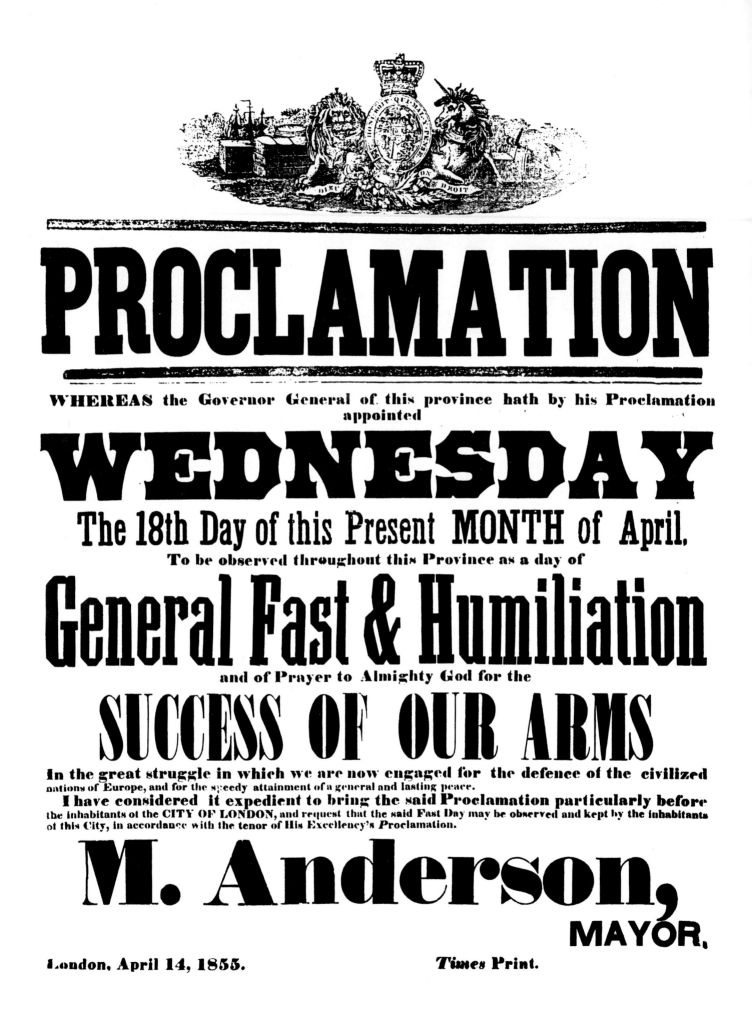

PROCLAMATION

WHEREAS the Governor General of this province hath by his Proclamation appointed

WEDNESDAY

The 18th Day of this Present MONTH of April,

To be observed throughout this Province as a day of

General Fast & Humiliation

and of Prayer to Almighty God for the

SUCCESS OF OUR ARMS

In the great struggle in which we are now engaged for the defence of the civilized nations of Europe, and for the speedy attainment of a general and lasting peace.

I have considered it expedient to bring the said Proclamation particularly before the inhabitants of the CITY OF LONDON, and request that the said Fast Day may be observed and kept by the inhabitants of this City, in accordance with the tenor of His Excellency's Proclamation.

M. Anderson,
MAYOR,

London, April 14, 1855.   *Times Print.*

CHAPTER FIVE

City

The City of London ... shall include all that part of the Province within the county of Middlesex, and lying within the following limits, that is to say: all the lands comprised within the old and new surveys of the Town of London, together with the lands adjoining thereto, lying between the said surveys and the River Thames producing the northern boundary of the new survey until it intersects the North Branch of the River Thames, and producing the eastern boundary line of the said new survey until it intersects the East Branch of the River Thames, and the eastern boundary line be known as Adelaide street. ...

— Proclamation signed by P.J.O Chauveau. Provincial Secretary, Quebec City, September 1854.

CITY OF LONDON COAT-OF-ARMS

The heraldic description, crest and motto and supporters are as follows: Per chevron gules and azure a chevron argent between in chief two garbs, or, and in base a beaver on a log of wood in sinister base and in dexter background a tree vert.

CREST: A locomotive and tender.
MOTTO: Labore et perseverantia.
SUPPORTERS: Dexter a deer and sinister a brown bear.
City of London Municipal Year Book 1981-1982.

A town is merely a large village. A city is another creature altogether, and no society has ever entirely succeeded in coping with the difference. Given a stable physical environment, a village may endure for thousands of years, as instance ancient Jericho. Cities, on the other hand, are subject to acute stresses that may eventually destroy them. The planet is littered with the bones of cities.

London's transition from village to city took only fifteen years, during which time the population soared from less than 2,000 to an estimated 12,000. The sleepy little market town of 1840 became, in a decade and a half, the bustling transportation hub of what the people of Toronto thought of as "The West." (Many still do.) For the construction industry, the building trades, the railways, and the land agents it was a bonanza time. Almost overnight, the corner of Dundas and Richmond streets became the heart of the community. Commercial and public buildings shot up like mushrooms, obliterating the former dominance of the courthouse's medi-

PROCLAMATION BROADSIDE
One of Murray Anderson's earliest political obligations as the first mayor of the City of London, was to declare April 18, 1855 as a day of hope in observation of the then occurring Crimean War. Though nearly half a world away, a British victory in the war against imperial Russia was close to many Londoners' hearts.

1854
Crimean War begins; England, France, Turkey against Russia; ends 1856. Over 800,000 soldiers die.

ALTERATION OF FIRM.

THE Firm hitherto trading under the title of WILLIS, DIXON & CO., has been altered, and will for the future be known as
WILLIS, BELTON & CO.,
Dundas Street.
London, Oct. 27, 1855.

WILLIS, BELTON & CO.,
GROCERS AND LUMBERMEN,

BEG respectfully to direct the attention of the Public to their large and superior stock of GROCERIES, which they are disposing of at their Store, situated on the corner of Dundas and Wellington streets.
THE LUMBER YARD
Contains a large assortment of Lumber, including Plain Flooring, Shingles, &c., which they are able to sell at low prices, and very cheap for cash.
An early inspection is invited.
London, Oct. 27, 1855   d150-kg-w350-kn

WILLIS, BELTON & CO. ADVERTISEMENT
This notice, which appeared in the London Free Press *of November 9, 1855, announced the newly formed partnership of William Willis, James H. Belton and William Sharp under the trade name of Willis, Belton & Co. Recognizing more lucrative opportunities in the lumber business, the firm soon discontinued its grocery line. By the early 1900s, under the Belton name, the company had grown to be one of London's largest.*

1854
Reciprocity Treaty with United States opens markets for Canadian products; along with railway building, the economy is buoyant.

aeval battlements. Now, only the tower of St. Paul's Church (114 feet high) could look down upon the architectural Johnnies-come-lately.

Committed now to the god of Progress, Londoners knew this was only the beginning. There were some optimists who predicted a population for the city by the turn of the twentieth century of one million, and none was prepared to say them nay. To launch this ship of destiny the citizens were asked to elect twenty-eight men to the first city council — nine more persons than form the corporation of the 1990s. There were seven wards, and each ward elected four incumbents — two aldermen and two councillors. The councillors were junior to the aldermen who, by virtue of their office, were also the magistrates and entitled to sit on the bench of the city police court, now for the first time served by a paid police force consisting of a chief and seven constables, one for each ward.

Since among the illustrious twenty-eight there were seven future mayors of London, two knights, and a senator, their names are worth noting here:

Ward One — aldermen, Peter Schram and James Moffat (mayor, 1860); councillors, John Blair and Barnabas Wheeler. Ward Two — aldermen, Murray Anderson (mayor, 1855) and Elijah Leonard (appointed a Canadian senator, 1867); councillors, William McBride (mayor, 1859) and George M. Gunn. Ward Three — aldermen, James Daniell and Joseph Gibbons; councillors, Arthur Wallace and John Clegg. Ward Four — aldermen, R. Abernathy and J.W. Kermott; councillors, Frank Smith (mayor, 1867; knighted, 1894) and David Glass (mayor, 1858, 1865-1866). Ward Five — aldermen, Daniel Lester and George C. Magee; councillors, Thomas Carter and Robert Smith. Ward Six — aldermen, John Carling (knighted, 1893) and Thomas Peel; councillors, William Glen and P. Phipps. Ward Seven — aldermen, William Barker (mayor, 1856) and William Darby; councillors, Robinson Orr and John Wells.

From this galaxy of business and professional men, the council itself named the senior alderman of Ward Two, Murray Anderson, as first mayor of London City. Anderson was a pioneer Londoner, having arrived in 1835. He was a manufacturer of tinware and a dealer in furs, a rather strange combination. In the fur markets he had an international reputation and often boasted of dining in New York with John Jacob Astor. Under his able guidance the city started off with a great verve on its first year of corporate existence.

One of the first pieces of business accomplished by the new council was a decision to publish the official proclamation of incorporation in the city's three weekly newspapers — the London *Times,* the *Prototype,* and the *Canadian Free Press.*

The last-named had been bought in 1852, by a young Englishman, Josiah Blackburn, who had done some professional writing in England and in Canada. The name of the paper was changed, in 1855, to the London *Free Press.* Under that name and its Gothic masthead, the journal has continued in the ownership of the Blackburn family to the present time.

The occasion for the change in name was the appearance, on 5 May 1855, of a daily edition. The previous owner, William Sutherland, had launched a daily version of his little weekly in January 1852, but it had

"He [Simcoe] judged it to be a situation eminently calculated for the metropolis of all Canada."

THOMAS TALBOT
A member of Simcoe's expeditionary force, Colonel Thomas Talbot permanently settled in Upper Canada in 1803. Although he resided in what became Elgin County, Talbot played an instrumental role in London's early affairs.

JOHN GRAVES SIMCOE
Arriving at "The Forks" on March 2, 1793, John Graves Simcoe envisioned great promise for the site. Though "The Forks" never became his provincial capital, Simcoe, nonetheless, would be pleased with London's position today.

BLACKFRIARS MILL

Another of London's early industries, Blackfriars Mill, located where Harris Park is today, was constructed in 1833. Using natural power supplied by the Thames, the grist mill continued in operation until a few years before the First World War.

Blackfriars Mill, London, Ont., Canada

JENNING'S DISTILLERY, c. 1837

Painted by James Hamilton, John Jenning's distillery, at the foot of Hitchcock Street (Dufferin Ave.), is an example of the industrial enterprise tied to London's early prosperity. This view looks south from Blackfriars Mill, and shows Eldon House on the ridge in the background.

". . . London was, in its village days, a reasonably attractive, reasonably happy, and prosperous community. . ."

RIVER THAMES, c. 1843
*Looking north from West-
minster Bridge, this view,
painted by George Russell
Dartnell, a military physician, captures the serenity
that a forgiving winter
could offer London.*

*". . . a young
Metropolis was
growing upon the
banks of the Upper
Canadian Thames."*

**FROM THE RIVER
THAMES, c. 1840**
*James Hamilton managed
to reveal a silken calm to
the Thames River when he
painted this marvellously
executed perspective.*

**FROM THE BANK OF
THE THAMES, 1842**
*An early example of
George Dartnell's work in
London, the eerie cast to
this moonlit scene seems to
radiate from the village's
largest structure, the Court
House.*

**OUR HOUSE: LONDON,
U.C., c. 1843**
*By rendering his own resi-
dence and grounds, George
Dartnell has successfully
conveyed that domestic
comfort could be found in
the frontier village of
London. The house may
still stand, much altered,
as part of 17-21 Stanley
Street.*

*"The British
Army became
the source of
all good things."*

BARRACKS AT LONDON, MAY 1842

When made a garrison town in 1838, London was elevated to a new level of respectability. The infantry barracks, as painted by Henry Ainslie looking south from near Oxford Street, were erected in 1839.

LONDON, 1842

After the garrison's arrival, John Herbert Caddy, from atop the Wortley Road hill, seized a thriving district town for his canvas. With the Westminster Bridge in the foreground, the Court House stands as the village's most prominent feature.

ENCAMPMENT OF THE ROYAL REGIMENT, JUNE, 1842

Under the "Union Jack" flown by the military, London assumed a decidedly British character. With loyal feelings of patriotism abounding, the soldiers' pay was a gladly accepted boost to the local economy. Displaying a stump-ridden field, Henry Ainslie painted this scene.

". . . officers went in for the more exciting sports of horse-racing and the steeplechase. . ."

GRAND MILITARY STEEPLECHASE
On May 9, 1843, London was witness to its first steeplechase. Held on the flats near the Thames, the chase "was a dashing one; there were some heavy falls, two right into the ditch; but great courage and skill were displayed by the gentlemen sportsmen.

One story connected with the royal visit has more basis in fact, although few of the details can now be confirmed. It depends on family tradition and a few scanty and discreet references in the papers of Marcus Gunn (1799-1878), diarist, newspaper editor, and land agent.

Gunn, a staunch anti-royalist and avowed republican, was also an inveterate writer of letters to the editors of various London newspapers. When the announcement of the prince's visit to London first appeared, Gunn launched a letter-writing campaign inveighing against the expense involved in entertaining the royal visitor, to whom he always referred as "the so-called Prince of Wales."

It appeared that his publicly-expressed sentiments met with approval of another visitor to the city, a member of the Fenian Brotherhood, the Irish terrorist secret society. The unnamed Fenian, in a state of aggressive insobriety, called on Gunn to congratulate him on his stand. In the course of the conversation the Fenian made an unguarded reference to a "reception" the Brotherhood planned for the prince when he visited New York City.

Over the next few days Gunn brooded over his classic dilemma. Since he was an anti-royalist, a conspiracy directed against the heir to the British throne should have given him no cause for concern. On the other hand, Gunn was not a man of violence. Coincidentally, the young prince was the same age as the diarist's favourite son, Donald Marcus, at his death in Boston.

Gunn's letterbook for the period in question contains a laconic reference to a letter he sent to the Duke of Newcastle, Prince Albert Edward's principal equerry and adviser. Later, there is a notation concerning a letter Gunn received from the duke. It conveyed the duke's thanks. There is no indication of the contents of either letter.

The certain facts are these. There was a plot by the Fenians to assassinate the prince in New York City. Acting "on information received" American authorities were able to thwart the attempt on the life of the "so-called Prince of Wales."

There the matter rests.

Another plot connected with His Royal Highness's visit to London was more successful. While the cream of the city's society was cavorting in the ballroom of the Tecumseh House, a clever gang of burglars was robbing their homes. The loot was calculated to be at least $1,200, a large amount for the times.

Among the civic dignitaries who surrounded Mayor James Moffat as he read his stilted address to the Prince of Wales was the senior alderman for Ward Seven, Francis Evans Cornish. The alderman was destined to become an even more towering figure in local legend than the future king of England.

Cornish was the son of "Old Dr. Cornish," the protean doctor-lawyer-surveyor-land-agent whose career was touched on briefly earlier in this history. Born in London Township, baptized in St. Paul's Church, London, he was named queen's counsel in 1857, becoming, at age twenty-six, one of the youngest men to be granted that honour in the history of the province.

1860
Birth of "Grandma Moses" (Anna May Roberts 1860-1961), primitive painter of American life.

This was the man, who, in January 1861, was elected seventh mayor of the city of London. The elegant James Moffat had served his turn nicely; now, in the year the American states went to war against themselves, perhaps it was the time for a brawler. The electorate got one.

Before he launched his career as the four-term "uncrowned king of London," Cornish was already well known to the gossip-mongers. For once, gossip was outdone by the facts. What fiction, for instance, could improve on the veritable facts of the story of Frank Cornish and the city hall arcade?

Answer comes there none.

The arcade was a pedestrian walkway linking Richmond Street with the Market Square. It was not intended for vehicular traffic.

On a certain day, in a state of non-sobriety, the mayor drove his horse and carriage through the arcade. He was arrested by a constable. The following morning police-court spectators, including the press, were treated to a unique spectacle.

Mayor Cornish, in his official capacity as chief magistrate, called out his own name. He responded to it. He read himself the charge, delivered himself a lecture on the evils of drink, and fined himself four dollars, an amount carefully removed from his right-hand trouser pocket and placed on the magistrate's desk.

Now it so happened that city magistrates received no salary, being entitled instead to collect all fines. Mayor Cornish accordingly transferred the four-dollar fine from the desk to his left-hand trouser pocket. Finally, after communing with himself, the chief magistrate decided to remit half of the fine on the grounds of the defendant's previous good conduct and subsequently transferred two dollars from the left-hand pocket to the right-hand pocket.

The mayor's lenient treatment of himself was not extended to other drunks. During his term of office there was said to have been a marked decline in the number of charges of "drunk and disorderly." On the bench, the mayor was an unrelenting foe of public inebriety. He had a simple remedy for intemperance. Regardless of the social position of the offender, the penalty was the same. Clad in distinctive prison garb and toting a ball and chain, he was set to work grading, gravelling, raking, and otherwise improving the streets of the city. One such appearance in public was often sufficient to cure the most hardened toper. It was the principle of the old-fashioned pillory, somewhat modernized.

It would be prolix (but highly diverting) to list all the juicy incidents that speckled the career of Francis Evans Cornish. They included public assaults on the persons of the city's chief of police and an officer of the British Army, numerous charges of public drunkenness, one charge of bigamy, and a noisy suit for a divorce.

The man suited the times that, like himself, were flamboyant and dramatic. Cornish entered into office the same year as did the sixteenth president of the United States, Abraham Lincoln. The London newspapers, like most of the Canadian press, tended to look on the new Republican head of state with disfavour; the *Free Press* considered him a dangerous demagogue.

1861
US Civil War begins with attack upon Fort Sumter, S.C.; 11 states form the Confederate States of America.

When the seceding Southern states formed themselves into the Confederate States of America, they elected as their first and only president Jefferson Davis, a senator from Mississippi who had been secretary of war under President Franklin Pierce. There is a persistent local legend that says Davis had friends in London and that he drafted some of the clauses of the constitution of the Confederacy while a guest at the Tecumseh House Hotel. It is barely possible. Certainly the Confederacy had many supporters in this city, mainly among the members of the Establishment.

Nevertheless public opinion generally began to swing towards Lincoln and the North in February 1861, when a plot to assassinate the president was thwarted by the swift action of Allan Pinkerton, a private detective. This attitude hardened into active support when the Confederacy fired on Fort Sumter, South Carolina, on Friday, 12 April. Three days later Lincoln issued a call for 75,000 volunteers and one of the bloodiest civil wars in history had begun. Some of those who presented themselves at the recruiting offices were Canadians. Among them were some young Londoners. A few left their bodies on the battlefields.

The American Civil War had a deep and lasting effect on the history of Canada, and nowhere was it felt more strongly than in London. The issues were more clearly understood by the common people than they seem to have been by the politicians. The North stood for *paid* labour, the South for *slave* labour. The North represented the working man, the South, the Establishment. However many words the politicians wrapped around these issues, this was how London's artisan population — what an earlier generation had known as the "mechanics" — saw the matter.

That London's citizens did have some disagreements about the issue of slavery can be found in one particular incident that took place at the Great Western train station in 1859. This story, involving the kidnapping of a black child into slavery was told by two rather different people: Elijah Leonard, the foundry owner who was an immigrant from New York, and Mrs. Amelia Harris, matriarch of one of London's leading "Establishment" families. Said Leonard:

> I was at the Great Western Station ... when I first noticed a dandy sort of fellow pacing up and down the platform with a bright negro boy at his heels, acting as his body servant, and sending the little innocent to buy his papers and cigars. He was rather communicative, and told in my hearing how much the boy was worth when he got him south. I had heard stories of this illegal traffic going on in the North but had never come face to face with it. I knew in a moment this creature had been east and had enticed this boy, perhaps from his home. In turning around I saw on the station Anderson Diddrick, the colored man who carried the Union Jack in front of our firemen when in procession. I told him I was afraid that boy was going into slavery and it was too bad to see him dragged off free British soil to work all his life for someone else, and perhaps be badly treated. The train started, the man whistled to the boy, and off they started for Detroit. This brought tears to Diddrick's eyes. I asked him if he knew anyone in Chatham. "Yes, several." "Would they take this boy away from this man?" "Yes, they would," but he added he had no money to telegraph. I gave him some, and he immediately wired the state of affairs ... When the train stopped at Chatham, sure enough there were nearly a hundred colored men and women with clubs and staves who surrounded and boarded the train and demanded the boy. He was hand-

FRANCIS EVANS CORNISH, c. 1864
Perhaps no other politician brought more colour to London's public arena than did Francis E. Cornish. Serving as the city's mayor from 1861 to 1864, Cornish was known more for his antics than his actions of office. He influenced the electorate with bribes in the form of free beer, fist-fought a British military officer to defend the honour of his wife, and, in his capacity as mayor, fined himself for public drunkeness.

1861
Louis Pasteur proves that micro-organisms cause fermentation and disease.

ed over by his greatly surprised master without much ceremony and taken up town.

Leonard noted that although the railway company was angry and attempted to prosecute, the charges were eventually thrown out of court. As for the boy, he was taken into the Shadd household in the Chatham area, where he lived for some years.

Now, Amelia Harris also talked about the incident in her diary, but she, unlike Leonard, was indignant that the man be robbed of his "property":

> "Sept. 30, 1859: A great outrage has been committed on the Great Western at Chatham. A southern gentleman was passing through with a slave boy ten years old. Some negroes made the discovery here and telegraphed to the coloured people at Chatham who assembled in a mob of 300 and when the train stopped at the station they took the boy forcibly from his master although the child cried and did not wish to go. Mr. Brydges, the manager of the railroad is much annoyed and intends to prosecute and punish with the utmost rigours of the law. It will turn the American travel from Canada. Actually the message from London had been sent by Elijah Leonard, a strong abolitionist.

Clearly, her concern for business ("It will turn the American travel from Canada") over freedom for the child, shows where she stood on the issue. The politicians — American, British and Canadian — however, tried to muddy the waters. William Henry Seward, Lincoln's secretary of state, tried to patch up the quarrel between the North and the South by proposing that the two join together to invade and annex Canada. Some of the Northern newspapers waxed enthusiastic about the suggestion, but Lincoln refused to adopt it, fearful of expanding the conflict by bringing in England, allied politically with its colonies and economically (cotton) with the Confederacy. Faced with these confusing developments, the politicians of British North America adopted the traditional national policy of speaking very softly and carrying a twig.

Meanwhile there was plenty of local news to engage the attention of Londoners. The economic picture had changed rapidly. The farmers of the western part of the province had greeted the outbreak of the Civil War with some enthusiasm, expecting an increased demand for their wheat. They were disappointed. The newly-developed Kansas fields now provided the needed wheat. The armies of the North wanted beef. Canadian farmers responded. The changeover to beef production came just in time. The fragile soils of the peninsula were quickly wearing out under the merciless drain of a one-crop farm economy. Before the war was over scores of handsome new farm homes testified to the financial success of their region's beef barons.

The sand-and-clay soils of the peninsula, harrowed by the grinding teeth of the retreating glaciers ten millennia earlier, now revealed new hidden riches. The first commercial oil well in North America started production at Oil Springs, in Lambton County, in 1858. By 1861 the oil boom had replaced the real-estate boom. One account published in 1878 tells a graphic story of the feverish activity associated with the opening of the fields:

1861

The hymn "Abide with me," composed by Henry Francis Lyte and William Henry Monk.

The success achieved by a few of the first operators fired the whole community with a desire to become millionaires and everybody got the "oil fever" and for a time the staple of conversation in the street, the store, hotel or office was oil mad; nearly every man became an oil speculator and nearly every acre of land in probable or improbable localities which could be leased, was leased for oil purposes, and lands worth intrinsically next to nothing were held at fabulous prices. ... Speculators rushed to the scene from all parts of the country and joint stock companies were formed by the dozen; test wells were sunk in every likely and unlikely locality and in every direction until the ubiquitous derrick disfigured the whole landscape. Staid and sober business men, yielding to the allurements of the day, became sanguine and visionary speculators in oil lands and spouting wells and immense fortunes were made in a day and lost in a night. London was the centre of this speculation and was the market where the oil land in several counties were bought and sold.

While some Londoners were making money in oil, others were making whoopee at the City Hospital. The nature of this institution was quite different from that of today's hospital. In the 1860s it was a refuge and treatment centre for the very poor. In the frequent outbreaks of epidemic disease of those days, it served as a pest house. Dr. Robert Hobbs was for a time the official physician. His duties were to "attend to and render medical aid to all sick persons at the City Hospital and to all poor persons within the limits of the city ... to provide and furnish all Medicines, Medicinal and External applications for the restoration of health (Bandages excepted) ...to vaccinate all poor persons who may attend for that purpose, the fee to be charged not in any case to exceed fifty cents."

The city's relief committee, headed by Councilman David Hughes, was responsible for the operation of the hospital. Mr. and Mrs. John Helstone were steward and matron. For some time rumours had been circulating about the rather hedonistic behaviour of the staff. Finally, in early 1861, as the result of a complaint laid by Dr. Hobbs, an investigation was carried out. The report "charged a few of the aldermen with being too intimate with the matron and other female attendants at the hospital." Councilman Hughes admitted "that the Matron would throw her arms around his neck and kiss him as would the other servant girls in the establishment and he would kiss them in return."

It is difficult to tell from the report whether favours other than kisses were exchanged. It is clear, however, that Councilman Hughes was most assiduous in his duties, being seen at the hospital "four or five times a week."

OIL REFINERY ADVERTISEMENT, 1863
This advertisement represents a long since disappeared era in the city's industrial past. In the early 1860s, London entrepreneurs found ripe opportunities presented by the oil fields of Lambton County. Rather than refine the crude at the site of the wells, many saw economic advantage in building refineries in the London area. While the majority of the refineries were located in what became East London, the Petersville Rock Oil Refinery distilled crude just west of the city limits.

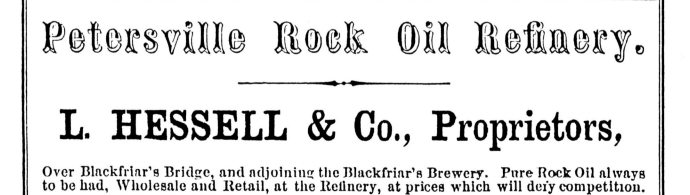

Petersville Rock Oil Refinery.

L. HESSELL & Co., Proprietors,

Over Blackfriar's Bridge, and adjoining the Blackfriar's Brewery. Pure Rock Oil always to be had, Wholesale and Retail, at the Refinery, at prices which will defy competition.

In the result the Helstones were dismissed and the husband-and-wife team of Thomas and Helen Warren appointed in their stead. The new steward and matron had barely time to get settled in when the peripatetic City Hospital had to move its operations again. On Monday, 18 November, the city council received word that the Crown authorities would again require the use of the hospital and the other buildings on the barracks grounds for military purposes. Before the end of the year the city had taken on the appearance of an armed camp, with an estimated 2,000 British troops overflowing the facilities of the military reserve. A number of downtown buildings were rented for officers' quarters and administration offices. The premises formerly occupied by Hope, Birrell and Company, general merchants, at the southeast corner of Carling and Ridout streets, became a military prison.

The unexpected return of the Imperials was owing to what came to be called the *Trent* Affair. A British ship bearing that name was stopped on the high seas and boarded by a Union vessel, the *San Jacinto*, and two Confederate diplomats bound for England were forcibly removed. When the news reached Britain, the government reacted angrily. An army of 10,000 troops boarded transports bound for Canada. The Prime Minister, Lord Palmerston, sent an ultimatum to Washington: apologize and return the Confederate commissioners, or prepare for war.

Palmerston's precipitate action was taken during the temporary absence from London of the Queen. The royal consort, Prince Albert, although gravely ill, insisted on taking a hand in the affair. The belligerency of the British demand was toned down. The troops, already on their way to Canada were ordered distributed among the existing garrisons rather than being sent to the frontiers prepared for a state of war.

By the time London's quota of nearly a fifth of the expeditionary force had reached the city, the worst of the crisis had passed. The North was not in a position to fight a war on two fronts. The mutual threats were reduced to the normal mutterings and mumblings of diplomatic communication. It had been a near thing, and Londoners continued to have bad dreams about the possibility of a Yankee invasion.

While the crisis was still very much current, nervous Londoners were treated to a charming diversion. On Friday, 15 November, General Tom Thumb (Charles Sherwood Stratton) visited the city under the auspices of Phineas Taylor Barnum. The midget was then in his twenty-fourth year, nudging three feet in height, and was at the peak of his fame. To the delight of the cheering crowds, he rode in his miniature carriage from Strong's Hotel on the north side of Dundas Street, between Richmond and Clarence streets, to the city hall where he was received by Mayor Cornish and other members of the city council.

1862

Victoria, incorporated as a city and becomes the capital of British Columbia.

Happy memories of this pleasant evening were still being savoured when the sad news was received of the death on Saturday, 14 December, of Queen Victoria's beloved Prince Albert. The news cast gloom over the Christmas celebrations of citizens and soldiers alike, as the flags of the garrison and the city hall stood at half-mast.

Frank Cornish was returned to office in 1862. A new generation of municipal politicians was emerging as death and boredom removed some

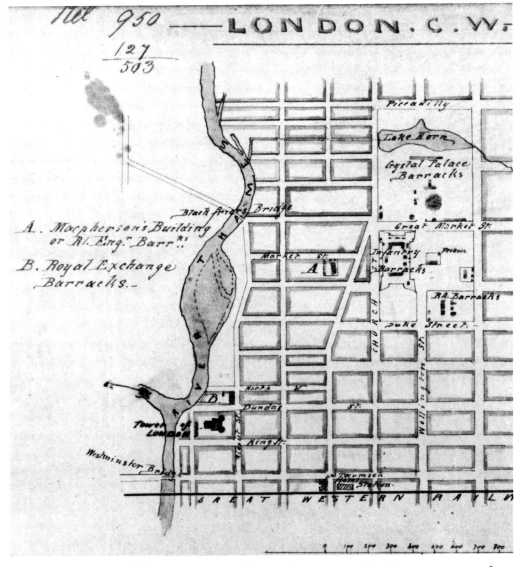

MAP OF LONDON, CANADA WEST, 1865
Although larger than the defined scope of this map, in 1865, London's urban concentration was still chiefly confined to the east of the River Thames. Note that the city's most familiar landmark at the time, the court house, is designated as the "Tower of London."

of the older men. The new council members were businessmen, professional men, and artisans; few belonged to the old London Establishment. One who shared some of the characteristics of the old clique was Simpson H. Graydon, a native of Ireland and, like Bishop Cronyn, a graduate of Trinity College, Dublin. Graydon first visited the area in 1840 as a member of a group of young adventurers who came to Canada "for the hunting." Still looking for thrills, the young men drifted on to the Australian gold fields. Graydon, when he finally decided to settle down, chose London for his home and entered into the study, and subsequently the practice, of law.

Meanwhile, relations between the citizens and the British garrison were not as friendly as they had been formerly. There were many more soldiers than there had been back in the forties. They had overflowed the military reserve into the downtown areas of the city. Soon there was friction.

In the eight years since the redcoats had marched off to the Crimean War, civilians had virtually taken over the barracks property. To the north, Lake Horn had become a community playground. South of it, on the northeast corner of Central Avenue and Wellington Street, a large octagonal building known as the Crystal Palace was built to house the annual Provincial

1862
The Gatling gun (rapid fire machine gun) patented by R.J. Gatling of Indianapolis.

CIRCULAR SHOWING LONDON'S EXHIBITION BUILDING

Built for the 1861 Provincial Exhibition, the Crystal Palace, as it came to be known, was a grand structure indeed. Its octagonal features made for a pleasing design, while the 28,000 square feet of display space offered by its main floor and upper galleries gave the building the utility required for annual fall fairs. Located just north of today's Victoria Park, the Crystal Palace was designed by London architect William Robinson.

1863

International Red Cross founded; Geneva Convention follows 1864; first appears in Canada 1885.

Exhibition of September 1861. As has already been noted, the city was using one of the two hospitals on the reserve. Many of the other buildings had been taken over by poor squatters. Part of the parade square, which the Imperials had used as a cricket pitch, had been pressed into use by London sportsmen for the more plebian game of baseball, which had been steadily increasing in popularity.

As invasion fears receded, local tensions increased. Succeeding barracks commanders faced a difficult double task of pacifying the civilian population while at the same time finding peacetime occupations for the troops. They were, after all, fighting men who chafed at inaction. There was a fine old war going on just a few hundred miles away. Furthermore the Union's pay-scale was better than the Queen's. The recruiting officers at Windsor and Port Huron asked few questions. The rate of desertions increased dramatically.

Frank Cornish was re-elected Mayor in 1863, but this time around victory didn't come quite so easily. His perennial opponent David Glass, a former mayor (1858), was steadily building a powerful challenge to the incumbent. Cornish's ace-in-the-hole was his use of the British troops. The story is that he bribed a considerable number of soldiers to take up temporary residence in tents pitched on Tipperary Flats, in the city's north end, for a time sufficient to entitle them to a vote in the municipal elections. Factually true or not, this story has become a part of the Cornish legend.

The next incident in the Cornish saga is solidly factual. It happened during a ball at the Tecumseh House Hotel sponsored by the garrison in honour of the marriage of the Prince of Wales to the Princess Alexandra of Denmark, which took place that very day (10 March 1863) in St. George's Chapel, Windsor.

A Major Bowles, of the 63rd Regiment, second-in-command of the garrison, was the official host of the event. Rumours had been circulating linking Bowles' name with that of the Mayor's wife, the former Victorine Leon Clench. Cornish set out to confront the Major.

The confrontation took place in the hotel in the early morning hours of 11 March. It was short, sharp, and farcical. A brief bout of fisticuffs ended with the victorious mayor landing a magisterial boot on the major's posterior. Despite the attempts of two other officers to prevent further assaults on the honour of the regiment, Cornish succeeded in ripping off the Major's decorations and hurling them in his face.

At the city police-court hearing that followed, Cornish was found guilty of unprovoked assault and fined six dollars. In defence the Mayor said only that he had been denied admission to the ballroom and had been aggravated by the Major's abrupt manner. This restraint on the part of Cornish stimulated the gossip concerning the alleged relations between the Major and Mrs. Cornish.

The Major, for his part, created a bad impression when he explained with some *hauteur* that he had been stopped at the entrance to the ballroom "by a civilian whom I at first took for a cabman, but afterwards recognized as the Mayor of the City of London."

Such an unfortunate remark insulted not only the Mayor but the coun-

THE FIRE OF DECEMBER, 1862
Ravaging fires plagued Victorian London, especially its downtown. On Sunday evening, December 28, 1862, fire was discovered in Mr. Baxter's dry goods store. The flames quickly spread to two adjacent shops. When the last glowing spark fizzled out, the conflagration had consumed the grocery of T. Forbes & Co., Shaw and Vennor's hardware, and Mr. Baxter's establishment. Resulting in damages of about $73,000, the flames left in ruins the mid-point of the north side of Dundas Street between Richmond and Talbot.

1863
Emancipation Proclamation frees about 3 million slaves in 10 southern states.

these rather petty considerations. Dr. Hellmuth, as dean of Huron and later as the second bishop of the Diocese, introduced the kind of academic secondary schools known as collegiate institutes and was instrumental in founding and funding the University of Western Ontario in 1878. His stature as the greatest educator in the history of the peninsula cannot seriously be challenged.

Meanwhile, with the aid of his coterie of bully-boys and his British Army pals, Francis Evans Cornish was elected to his fourth and final term as mayor in January 1864.

It was to be a vintage year.

The Canada Trust Company under its birthing name — the Huron and Erie Mortgage Corporation — got its start in life. So did the James Cowan Hardware Company.

It was the tercentenary of the birth of William Shakespeare. The Perth County town of Stratford, after a slow start, staged a modest little celebration. London had a much bigger, three-day "monster" festival capped by a performance in the city hall auditorium of *The Merchant of Venice*. In keeping with Elizabethan stage tradition, all the female roles were played by young, clean-shaven men. (Portia was Edmund Meredith, a leading lawyer.) Graves Simcoe Lee returned to the city to take part in the festival. A former member of the Gentlemen Amateurs, he had gone on to become what was called "a luminary" of the American professional theatre.

Another cultural event of consequence was the laying of the cornerstone of Dr. Hellmuth's London Collegiate Institute (not to be confused with the later secondary school bearing the same name). Citizens came to know it better as "Hellmuth College."

The year was marked by some less pleasant events, of which the worst was an outbreak of incendiarism. It would appear that arson is the oldest signature activity of the urban guerilla. London's tiny police force, consisting of a chief and seven constables, was unable to cope with the firebug. The city council appointed forty citizens to serve as special constables and offered a reward of $200 for the apprehension of the arsonist. (It should be noted, parenthetically, that decimal currency had been adopted by Canada in 1858.) The money was never claimed.

The police had no "fraud squad" in 1864, and so when William Oakley, a municipal collector of taxes, was found to have a notable shortage in his accounts, the matter was settled by the parties themselves. All of Oakley's real estate, goods, and chattels were seized, and his two sureties paid the city's claim. No one yet knew that the city treasurer, John Brown, had already embarked on his unparalleled thirty-year-career of embezzlement of the city's funds.

These local affairs were minor irritants compared with the major anxiety Londoners were subjected to in that critical year. In 1864 the American Civil War impinged directly on the lives of the people of London. Driven to desperation by the growing certainty of its defeat by the Union, the Confederacy tried a mad scheme involving the use of Canadian territory as the base for an attack on the cities of the North. The so-called Northwest Conspiracy was led by Jacob Thompson, a member of Jefferson Davis's cabinet. From his headquarters in Toronto Thompson presided

1864

The Charlottetown Conference of Canadian politicians the first step towards Confederation.

JONES'
COMMERCIAL
COLLEGE,
c. 1864
*J.W. Jones, the
proprietor and prin-
cipal of the business
school bearing his
name, billed himself
as a "Professor in
Theory, Banking and
Mathematical Depart-
ments; Instructor in
Commercial Law
&c." In 1864, under
the careful tutelage of
Jones and his team of
instructors, one could
receive a thorough
schooling in a variety
of commercial
studies, telegraphing,
drawing, and mono-
chromatic painting.
Twenty-four lessons
in penmanship were
a bargain at five
dollars.*

over a network of Confederate spies, guerilla fighters, refugee Southern soldiers (said to number 2,000 in Canada West), Canadian sympathizers, and dissident Northern Democrats. Chief among this last-named group was Senator Clement Laird Vallandigham, of Ohio. Banished by Lincoln for his treasonous activities as leader of the anti-war Copperhead movement, Vallandigham spent at least part of 1864 in London.

In London, conveniently situated with respect to the cities of Toronto, Detroit, and Buffalo, Vallandigham met and parleyed with Thompson's agents, among whom were an unidentified young woman from Maryland and a dashing young officer from Kentucky. The officer, Captain Thomas Henry Hines, was a physical double of the actor and Confederate sympathizer John Wilkes Booth. Hines was the military commander of the Northwest Conspiracy.

Hines's plan, in broad outline, was reported to his secretary of war in June 1864:

> Two regiments [of guerrilla fighters] now in the process of formation in Chicago will be placed under my command to move upon Camp Douglas and free the prisoners.

*1864
George Mortimer
Pullman begins the
construction of his
railroad sleeping
cars.*

Simultaneously with this movement, the Democrats in every county of Illinois and portions of Indiana and Ohio will rally to arms. A force of 3,000 Democrats under a competent leader will march upon Rock Island &Illinoisé for the release of the 7.000 prisoners at that place.

The remainder will concentrate upon Chicago and Springfield. State governments of Indiana, Ohio and Illinois will be seized and their executives disposed of. By this means we hope to have, within ten days after the movement has begun, a force of 50,000 men.

In the crunch, thanks to excellent intelligence work in Ottawa, Washington, and London, England, the conspiracy fizzled out, with nothing to show beyond an abortive naval excursion on Lake Erie, fire-bomb attacks on twelve buildings in New York City, and a border raid on the community of St. Albans, Vermont. It was a pitifully meagre return for an investment of several million dollars.

None of this, of course, was known to the Londoners of Canada West in the summer of 1864. They only knew the worry of it all. The streets of the city swarmed with Confederate and Union spies, counter-spies, double agents, and moles, along with the sprinkling of Allan Pinkerton's men, Canadian secret agents, and a clutch of eager newspaper reporters. The situation in London was similar to that experienced in Toronto by the head of the Confederate mission. Jacob Thompson complained of "the bane and curse of carrying out anything in this country due to the surveillance under which we act. Detectives, or those ready to give information, stand on every street corner. Two or three cannot interchange ideas without a reporter."

Londoners did have some idea of what was going on. So did the Northern press, which grew more and more belligerent in its demands for the final elimination of British power in North America. In these circumstances London's Imperials began to look more like saviours and less like nuisances. The late unpleasantness with Mayor Cornish was glossed over. But then the 63rd Regiment was replaced by the 47th. The men of the 47th were a tough, hard-bitten crew. They cared nothing at all for the feelings of the "colonials." Little frictions became big tensions, resulting finally in the "Battle of the Gore."

The "Gore," as noted before, was a triangular piece of land bounded by Central Avenue and Richmond and Clarence streets. The Clarence Street allowance was within the boundary of the military reserve, which was marked in part by the big stump fence. During the eight-year absence of the troops from the city, local people had breached the fence and used the street allowance as a short-cut to downtown London. The 47th replaced the fence. Citizens tore it down. The soldiers replaced it again and, with loaded guns, prepared to confront and repel the invaders. Undaunted, the citizens again began dismantling the fence. On command, the Imperials fired a volley over the heads of the activists, who paid no attention whatever to it. Three or four subsequent volleys likewise had no effect. A blank charge fired from one of the barracks cannons succeeded only in setting one of the stumps on fire. While the troops laboured to extinguish the blaze, the London loyalists triumphantly drove farm wagons down the reactivated street allowance, which experienced no further blockage.

1864
Canada Temperance Act (the "Dunkin Act") passed.

In September and October, the Charlottetown and Quebec conferences launched the British North American provinces on the road to national unity. London's member of parliament, John Carling, played a special role behind the scenes in smoothing the way for cooperation between the two great political enemies, George Brown and John Alexander Macdonald.

The first of the municipal elections of January 1865 followed the pattern of the four previous years. The candidates were, as usual, Frank Cornish and David Glass.

There were many signs that the London electorate was becoming a little bored by the Cornish antics. Glass shrewdly took advantage of the mood.

The first day's vote went to Cornish.

That evening David Glass met with some members of the 1864 council. He claimed that the voting had been marked by so much violence that a fair contest had been impossible. He asked that balloting be continued for a second day in order that all who wished might vote, and that the militia be called out to guarantee the security of the polling stations.

The next morning Frank Cornish's supporters found a ring of armed militiamen surrounding every polling place in the city. The news spread rapidly. Assured of a fair opportunity to voice their choice, the Glass men turned out in great numbers. When the count was complete, London had a new mayor.

One of the first problems Mayor Glass faced was the bill for the militia-

COVENT GARDEN MARKET, c. 1865
Established in 1845, and taking the name of the fruit and vegetable market in London, England, the Covent Garden Market is one of London's most enduring traditions. The market building to the right was constructed in 1853 and served vendors of fruits, vegetables, and meats. A fish market building, located at the left-centre of the photograph, was constructed as a separate, relatively isolated structure for reasons that only became apparent in the heat of summer.

ANDRUS BROTHERS ADVERTISEMENT, 1867

An expensive item given the time, the melodeon was a small organ equipped with reeds activated by the suction of an accordion box. Since melodeons, organs, and the like were a required fixture of the mid-Victorian parlour, the Andrus Brothers enjoyed a steady trade during the 1860s.

1865

Salvation Army founded by General William Booth; first appearance in Canada at London, 1882.

men — $282.60. There was much opposition to the discharge of the debt. Those councillors who were faithful to Cornish claimed there had been no necessity for the show of military strength and, furthermore, there was some question whether the council's action had been decided by a legal quorum of that august body.

The account was finally paid, under protest.

April brought an end to the savage war across the border. General Lee surrendered at Appomattox courthouse on Sunday, 9 April. Five days later Abraham Lincoln was assassinated by the actor John Wilkes Booth. On the following evening, Saturday, 15 April, the Confederate officer Captain Thomas Hines fled from a mob in Detroit, Michigan, who mistook him for Booth. At the point of pistol he commandeered the Detroit-Windsor ferry and joined friends in London and, eventually, Toronto.

In common with other communities throughout North America, London mourned the death of the man whom less than five years earlier the London *Free Press* had dismissed as a ranting demagogue. Josiah Blackburn, in company with a number of other Canadian newspaper editors, visited the White House toward the end of the war and came away with a totally different impression. The power of the president's personality affected the Canadians deeply.

The North Street Methodist Church, on the southwest corner of Queens Avenue and Clarence Street, which on its completion in 1854 was said to be "the finest church west of Great St. James Street, Montreal," was chosen as the site of a memorial service. The huge church was packed to hear a funeral address delivered by W.G. Moncrieff, a former Presbyterian minister, newspaper editor, historian, school-teacher, and acknowledged dean of London letters.

The death of the martyred president was not viewed with compassion by everyone. At Lucan, north of London, a village already notorious because of an imported Irish feud, the community's flag had been lowered to half-staff in tribute to Lincoln. A Southern refugee named White fired a shot at the flag.

The end of the war did not mean the end of danger to Canada. Northern newspapers were still trumpeting their demands for the annexation of Canada. By their posturings they actually hastened the advent of the Confederation of the British North American colonies. As George Etienne Cartier declared, "When we are united, the enemy will know that if he attacks any province he will have to deal with the combined forces of the Empire."

An anxiety closer to home was the epidemic of burglaries that broke out in 1865. The police force was unable to cope with it. Eventually the situation became so bad a citizens' vigilance committee was formed to patrol the streets at night. A reward of $200 was offered for the capture of the burglars. Like the earlier reward for nabbing the mysterious arsonist of 1864, this one, too, was never claimed.

In the folklore of the United States the citizens' committee of vigilance is usually represented as a spontaneous expression of the community's need to establish law and order where no official legal machinery exists. In these cases the community takes the law into its own hands, with often tragic results.

This was not the intent of the ancient English *posse comitatus* (power of the county). The "posse," as it is more generally known, does not exist *outside* the law. It is called into being by representatives of the law, to assist them in carrying out their legal functions.

The London area has had examples of both kinds of committee — the vigilance committee and the posse. The notorious vigilance committee of Biddulph Township, which was responsible for the mass-murder of five members of the Donnelly family in 1880, was organized outside the law. It later arranged for some of its members to be appointed as justices of the peace and constables, to give its murderous work the colour of legality.

On the other hand, the citizen committees of London of the 1860s were true examples of *posse comitatus*. They were called into being by legally constituted authority (the city council) to assist the official police force in carrying out its legal tasks of protecting life and property.

Before 1865 was out, there was even more serious work for the city's volunteer peace-keepers. This time the threat came from outside the city; indeed from outside the provincial border. The Fenian Brotherhood had enlisted thousands of disbanded and jobless veterans of the American Civil War in a mad adventure — to invade and conquer Canada in order to use it as a base to drive the English out of Ireland.

By early fall, thanks to superb intelligence gathered by Canadian and British operatives (including one working within the Fenians' executive circle), it was known that one of the principal centres of Fenian activity was Chicago, and that a major attack was to be launched from there on the Canadian border at Sarnia. Sarnia was chosen because of its excellent rail connections with such Canadian nerve-centres as Stratford, London, and Toronto. Sufficient credence was given these reports that on Wednesday, 15 November, Lieutenant-Colonel James Shanly was ordered to hold the London militia in readiness to defend the frontier.

(It was Shanly who, earlier in the year, had defended the city against its late mayor, Frank Cornish.)

Time passed. There was no invasion. A reaction set in. Mocking editorials and news stories belittling the "Finnigans" began to appear. John A. Macdonald, however, had access to secret information that led him to consider the Fenian threat a very real one. Accordingly, in March 1866 a call went out for 10,000 volunteers for the Canadian militia. More than 14,000 presented themselves for duty.

Nothing happened. As the weeks dragged by, London's factory-owners and businessmen became restive at the continued inconvenience and expense caused by the volunteer call-up. On 30 May the *Free Press* editorialized:

> The prolongation of the Fenian sensation is a sad bill of expense to Canada, and the people are anxious to see a period put to the Volunteers' term of service. ...

Two days later the balloon went up. The *Free Press* was on the streets by five o'clock on the morning of Friday, 1 June, with disturbing news:

> We had hoped we had got to the bottom of these Fenian scares, but it seems

1865
"Alice's adventures in wonderland" *published by Lewis Carroll (pseud of Rev. C.L. Dodgson, 1832-1898).*

**CITY HOTEL,
c. 1866 (above);
c. 1887 (below)**

As early as 1856, the City Hotel was located at the southwest corner of Dundas and Talbot Streets. A devastating fire completely destroyed the original building in 1865, but within a year, a larger, more commodious replacement had been constructed (pictured above). Involved renovations were undertaken in the mid-1880s, resulting in a large addition to the west and a mansard roof capped with slate shingles (below). As the only survivor of the razed Talbot Streetscape, Londoners are more familiar with this building as the Talbot Inn.

1865
Ku Klux Klan established at Pulaski, Tennessee.

we were mistaken. ... the redoubtable Sweeney is assembling his Fenian loafers at Buffalo for a raid on Canada. ...

Within an hour anxiety had replaced irritation. An "extra" issued free at 7:30 am reported that a large force of Fenians had landed at Fort Erie on the Niagara frontier. At 1:30 pm the city council held a special meeting to consider the question of the formation of a home guard for the protection of the city.

By the afternoon both the *Free Press* and the *Advertiser* had published extras reporting much in the way of sensation but little hard news. All that was certain was that the Fenians were in Canada in undisclosed numbers.

Some idea of the size of the invading force was spelled out in a story from Port Stanley, on Lake Erie:

> All day yesterday, a fleet of between thirty and forty schooners were cruising off Plum Point and Port Stanley. It is expected they carry supplies for the Fenians. During the afternoon, about five, they all tacked off in the direction of Port Colborne.

By nightfall the *Free Press* had its own war correspondent in the field. He was Malcolm G. Bremner. Another Londoner, Donald Cameron, who later became sheriff of Middlesex County, represented the Toronto *Globe*.

A telegram from the front, routed via Paris, Canada West, was received some time before midnight:

> News has just been received that the Fenians are entrenched about four miles from Fort Erie, and our troops are closing in at Chippewa, Port Colborne and Dunnville.

There was little sleep for anyone in London that night. The telegraph offices and the newspapers were fully staffed, but no trustworthy information was received. The first news was not available until late afternoon, Saturday, 2 June, and it was bad:

> A skirmish took place about eight this morning between 600 Fenians, under Col. O'Neill, and about an equal number of our Volunteers. Troops firing was heard for about three-quarters of an hour in the neighbourhood of Frenchman's Corners. Three of our dead lie in the road. No other dead reported. It is said our men were repulsed, and retreated in good order. ... The march has been exceedingly fatiguing, and Corporal Wm. Corrington, of the 4th, is now lying at the point of death from sunstroke. ... A number of Fenian rifles have been captured. A hard battle is expected tomorrow.
> M.G. Bremner,
> *Free Press* Correspondent.

The decisive battle — "skirmish" would be a better word — was fought near the village of Ridgeway the following day, Saturday. It resulted in the rout of the Fenians and their retreat back across the border.

News of the victory did not reach London until late on Sunday. It was the strangest Sunday London had ever known. The city had become a war zone. Rumour had a field day. The *Free Press* reported:

> The most excited state of feeling prevailed in London all day Sunday. Crowds gathered at every corner in the most intense state of excitement after news. ...
> At 12:30 Sunday morning the bugle sounded an alarm in London, and the fire bells rang, causing an intense excitement. People turned out of the churches in crowds in a state of the utmost alarm. The occasion was a report

1866
Fenian Raids by disaffected Irishmen based in USA begin, end early 1870's.

that the Fenians had landed at Sarnia and Windsor. It turned out to be false, however.

Many years afterwards William Hayman, a soldier in the British 53rd Regiment, recalled the tensions of that day:

> Many a Sunday I have gone to St. Paul's Church with my rifle on my shoulder and forty rounds of ball ammunition in my cartridge pouch, expecting to have to fight my way back home from the church to the barracks ... Col. Harence was our commanding officer then, and a fine fellow he was too. Many a night I have seen him on the streets until morning, ready at a moment's warning to turn his men out.

By Monday morning, 4 June, the "war" on the Niagara frontier was over. That evening 4,000 Londoners gathered at the Great Western Railway depot to greet the returning volunteers. Later, at a banquet honouring them, Mayor David Glass proposed a toast: "To the health of our guests, Her Majesty's troops, and the noble volunteers who have gone to the front in the hour of danger."

That's where most popular accounts of the Fenian raids end. It wasn't over for London and the western peninsula. The threat of invasion via the St. Clair River border was very real. On at least three separate occasions British troops and Canadian militiamen were ordered to Sarnia to repel threatened attacks by Chicago-based Fenians. The threats proved false alarms. The fears remained and finally proved the glue, however, to bind together the eastern provinces of British North America in a defensive union.

As the curtain came down on the seriocomic drama of the Irish adventure, London buried its saint on Wednesday, 3 October 1866.

He was Ensign The Honourable Henry Edward Dormer, late of the 60th King's Royal Rifles. He was the youngest son of Joseph Thaddeus Dormer, eleventh Lord Dormer, and his wife Elizabeth Anne Tichborne. Both families had long histories of deep attachment to the Roman Catholic faith; in the case of the Tichbornes the record extended back to the twelfth century. The Dormer family motto expresses well the fervour of that connection: "Cio che Dio vuole io voglio" (What God wills, I will).

From his arrival in London in February 1866 until his death some seven short months later, the young Englishman was an exemplar of the life in Christ. Attaching himself to a preaching mission being conducted at St. Peter's Church by the Dominican Order, he made of himself an honour-guard for the priests taking the Eucharist to the poor and ill. There were many sick in London at this time, owing to the twin outbreaks of Asiatic cholera and typhoid fever.

It was while attending an old lady suffering from the latter disease that Dormer contracted the fever himself. It swiftly proved fatal. He left a personal estate of $13.95 and a reputation for piety and charity that has endured. His closest London friend, Father Stephen Byrne, a Dominican friar, wrote to Dormer's parents:

> In all sincerity of my soul I believe, my dear Lord and Lady, that you have brought into this world and reared to manhood a great saint.

Posterity has not seen fit to challenge the good friar's judgment. It

1867
USA buys Alaska from Russia for $7,200,000, equal to two cents per acre.

survivors, hauling up bodies, and getting in one another's way.

The first light of morning revealed a slime-coated, tangled mass of wreckage in what had been the path of the runaway river from the Oxford Street bridge to the main branch of the Thames. Smaller buildings, of which there were a great number, for this was a modest, workingman's suburb, had been reduced to matchwood. Larger structures were twisted, gouged, and scarred as though they had been the toys of a demented giant.

William Thompson and the *Advertiser* had grabbed the newspaper "scoop." It was Lambert Payne and the *Free Press*, however, which obtained the "colour story." Payne, covering his third disaster in four years, was appalled by what he saw. At one place a mother, standing at an upper window, had passed down her baby to willing hands below, only to see it snatched out of the rescuer's hand by a runaway barn and ground to death against the sidewall of its parents' home. There, against the wall near the window, was the crimson imprint of the child's body.

Lambert Payne turned away, sick at heart.

The scene was chaotic. Wreckage and bodies were strewn over a large area. One thing was certain. The residents of London West had been fortunate. In spite of the fact that the flash flood had struck at an hour when most people were in bed, the death toll had been remarkably low. The best estimate was seventeen or eighteen.

It took some time for the lesson of the July flood to register with the people of London and the Thames River basin — something over sixty years, in fact. Floods on the Thames have occurred at every season of the year — spring, summer, fall and winter. Since the first really damaging flood in 1851, the cause has been constant. The removal of the forest cover throughout its 163-mile (262 kilometre) length has left the stream susceptible to uncontrolled run-off. That was precisely what happened in 1883 when the denuded soil of the watershed had nothing on it to hold back the immense amount of water suddenly dumped upon it.

In August 1883, the volcano Krakatoa, in Java, blew up, sending shock waves around the world, and thousands of tons of dust into the stratosphere to change the world's weather patterns for several months and to leave a legacy of green suns, blue moons, and spectacular sunsets.

The year also marked the eclipse of one of the brightest careers in Canadian education. The Right Reverend Dr. Isaac Hellmuth submitted his resignation as bishop of the diocese of Huron in the summer of 1883. He cited as the principal cause of his surprise decision the grave illness of his wife. (She died on Wednesday, 21 May 1884.) This was not, however, the only reason. The two colleges named after him were in financial difficulties. The Hellmuth Boys' College (later named Dufferin College) had ceased operation in 1882. The mother-church of the diocese, St. Paul's, was heavily in debt. The clergy and laity of the diocese were sharply divided on the matter of the bishop's grand plans for his new cathedral and the new university. In addition there were many who resented his autocratic administration.

The reluctance of Dr. Egerton Ryerson, director of the Ontario school system, to acknowledge his debt to Hellmuth is unfortunately typical of

**C.S. HYMAN,
c. 1903**
Charles Smith Hyman, mayor in 1884, was one of London's more colourful public personalities. Nicknamed "Champagne Charley" for gallivanting about in private train cars, Hyman found politics greatly to his liking. Elected as a Liberal member of parliament in 1900, he was Sir Wilfrid Laurier's minister of public works until 1907.

1883
Greatest explosion in modern times: volcano Krakatoa, Indonesia; 36,000 died.

his contemporaries' reactions to Hellmuth and Hellmuth's ideas. It is true that the bishop drove others as he drove himself; it is true that in the pursuit of his own goals he could be stubborn to the point of intransigence; it is true that he often rode roughshod over the feelings of others and could not bring himself, even in Christian charity, to suffer fools gladly; but the great tragedy of this brilliant man's life lies in something much more basic and intellectually shocking than these human faults of character.

Isaac Hellmuth was a *converso*, to use the Spanish term — a converted Jew. Furthermore he had that intellectual arrogance that so often characterizes the scholar of the Diaspora. It is barely possible that his provincial Canadian fellow-citizens could have accepted a properly humble *converso*, but never one of such obviously superior intelligence.

The very silence of his contemporaries and his later biographers in respect of these facts is in itself eloquent evidence of the ambivalent character of the community's reaction to the son of a Warsaw rabbi. Today, approaching a century from his death (1901), there is still a tendency among Londoners in speaking of Hellmuth to emphasize rather the fact that he was a former Jew than that he was the founder of the University of Western Ontario.

In fact he was, and still is, regarded as something of an anomaly, grafted to the family tree of the Church of England in Canada. It is for this reason,

PLAN OF KENSINGTON HEIGHTS, 1884
Kensington Heights, an early suburb of London, was surveyed on land owned and developed by William and Samuel Glass, respectively the sheriff and deputy sheriff of Middlesex County. Located in the neighbourhood of present-day Woodward Avenue and Riverside Drive, this area was annexed by the city in 1897.

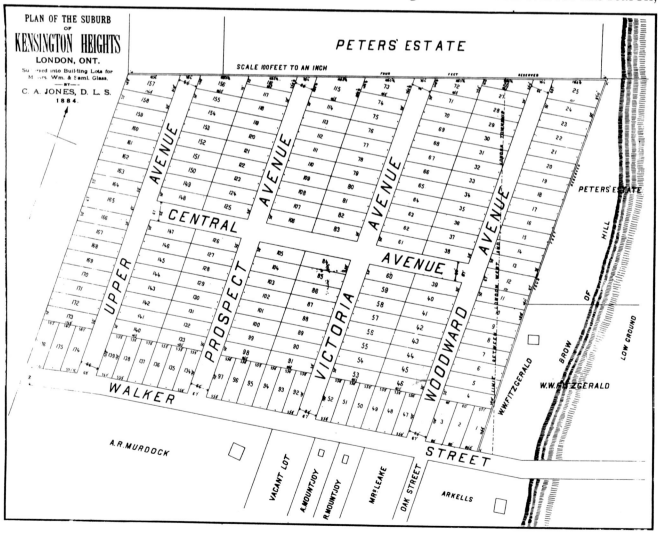

disturbing as it may be to the good conscience of the "Anglo-Saxon" founders of London, that the failure of Hellmuth's Canadian career must be attributed. His lonely, unequal battle ended, as it had to, in his defeat. The man who had a foot in each of two camps had a home in neither. Of him it could be said, as of the Master he followed so faithfully, "Foxes have holes, and birds of the air have nests; but the Son of Man hath not where to lay his head."

Of quite a different nature was the ebullient young man whom Londoners elected as their mayor in 1884. Charles Smith Hyman, aged thirty, was head of the tannery founded by his late father Ellis Walton Hyman. The younger Hyman had launched his political career just as the province of Ontario marked the centennial of its first settlement by the United Empire Loyalists.

The success of the UEL celebrations in Ontario and New Brunswick sparked an enthusiastic interest in local and regional history. This in turn led to the establishment of historical societies, libraries, and archives in both provinces.

A distinctive London institution also made its first appearance in that landmark year. The Baconian Club is still pursuing its aberrant course more than a century later. The club is variously described as a literary society devoted to the proposition that Sir Francis Bacon wrote the plays and sonnets attributed to William Shakespeare; as an association of professional eccentrics; and as a debating society conducted somewhat along the lines of a "roast." It is all of these things and none of them. It is, quite simply, the Baconian Club.

There is no such ambiguity about the club to which the mayor belonged — the London Club. After an abortive beginning in 1875, the club was incorporated by an act of Parliament in 1880, and by 1884 it was settling into its present quarters on Queen's Avenue, in the heart of the city. Both this club and its sister-organization, the London Hunt and Country Club, were socially exclusive and until recent years denied membership to both Jews and women.

The long financial recession that gripped Canada for the last quarter of the nineteenth century claimed two London banks as victims. Fawcett's Bank collapsed in 1884, and the Bank of London three years later. The Fawcett disaster involved a shortage of $47,000 and a number of lost or destroyed bank records, and resulted in severe hardship for many depositors. It was a very unfortunate period for the private banks in the London area. Ten of them went belly-up between 1879 and 1887.

Many of the banks had invested heavily in land and timber in northern Ontario and Manitoba. Political developments were coming to a head, with the second insurrection of the Metis under their leader Louis Riel.

On Thursday, 26 March 1885, the Metis fought an engagement with a force of the North West Mounted Police at Duck Lake, Saskatchewan. The Mounties were defeated, suffering a loss of nine men. One of the dead was Skeffington Connor Elliott, son of the Middlesex County judge, William Elliott.

Within a few days orders were received for the mobilization and dispatch of the 7th Fusiliers, City of London Regiment, to the scene of the

THE LONDON CLUB, c. 1890
Erected in 1881 to house the London Club, an exclusive association of the city's leading businessmen, this stately building still stands at 177 Queens Avenue.

1884
Great celebrations of Ontario's first century of Loyalist settlement.

RETURN OF THE 7th BATTALION, 1885

Fought over 1,500 miles away, for many Londoners, the Northwest Rebellion of 1885 was more tangible than mere, contemporary news reports. Dispatched to help put down the Louis Riel led uprising, London's own 7th Battalion returned home to an uproarious and hearty welcome.

1884
Standard Time proposed by Canadian Sir Sandford Fleming.

rebellion. The "call to arms" was sounded by a bugler mounted on one of the popular "penny-farthing" bicycles, tootling on his instrument while guiding his unwieldy vehicle over London's gravel, dirt, and cobbled streets. It was a courageous feat, but received little notice from the members of the regiment. One by one they woke up, remembered the date, snorted, and went back to sleep. It was the morning of Wednesday, 1 April — April Fool's Day.

Eventually assembled, the regiment, under the command of Lieutenant-Colonel W. DeRay Williams, travelled west on the nearly completed line of the Canadian Pacific Railway. They returned in July without having fired a shot in anger. The heroes received a great civic welcome. One Fusilier, an employee of Hyman's Tannery, was greeted by a banner stretched across Richmond Street that read:

"ARE YOU THERE MORIARITY?"

Moriarity was.

Like the other members of the regiment Moriarity received a big dinner and a cigar later that day. One of the city's cigars, encased in a glass tube, survived into the fifth decade of the twentieth century, one of the less-treasured objects in the short-lived museum of the London and Middlesex Historical Society.

In fact, the manufacture of cigars had become a booming local industry. By the late 1880s there were at least ten firms producing many different brands, some with exotic names. An allied trade was the manufacture of cigar boxes. One of the most successful of these was the Beck Brothers Cigar Box Manufactory, which moved to London from Toronto in 1884. One of the two Beck brothers was Adam (later Sir Adam), who became one of the city's most famous adopted sons, and the founder of Ontario's publicly-owned hydro-electric power system.

London had already been introduced to the joys of electricity. In a

THE RIDOUT STREET BRIDGE, c. 1885
The third bridge to span the Thames River at this point, the Ridout Street Bridge, like its counterpart at the foot of Blackfriars Street, was erected by the Wrought Iron Bridge Company of Canton, Ohio. Thirteen years later, the London Street railway extended its line over this crossing into South London.

public demonstration of Ball's Electric Light Machine in July 1882, 7,000 citizens came to see the lights turned on in Victoria Park. Thereafter, progress was swift. Within four years many of the principal streets were lit by electricity.

Electricity was but one symbol of the changes taking place in the lives of Londoners. The other was trade unionism. In earlier times, manufacturing of goods took place in small workshops, and the artisan-workers often toiled sidy-by-side with the owners. As mechanization of industry increased in the nineteenth century, so too did the problems encountered by the men and women who worked in these factories. Working conditions were difficult and sometimes dangerous. Pay was low, hours were long — ten to sixteen-hour-days — and a six-day workweek was common. Young children, employed as apprentices, ran around the shop floors amid the grinding machinery. In a time when governments offered little protection against workplace hazards and unfair wage cutting, forming trade unions was the only defence working people had.

London was a part of this continent-wide movement, although there were few unions here prior to 1880 (Typographical Union — 1856, Iron Moulders — 1859, Cigar Makers — 1864). The first united working class movement to make inroads in London was the Noble and Holy Order of the Knights of Labor. The Knights of Labor was a Philadelphia-based movement that seemed to combine the traditions of the secret fraternal organization (e.g. the Masons and the Foresters) and the worker education society with the newer ideas of trade unionism. London was a major centre for the Canadian branch of the Knights in the 1880s, with over 1,000 members adhering to seven "Local Assemblies". Although most of the London members were men, a few women joined the ranks of the Knights of Labor. In late-nineteenth century London, women workers were a sizable part of the workforce of several industries, mainly cigar and biscuit-making.

1885
Donald Smith drives last spike in CPR at Craigellachie, B.C.

FREDERICK A. FITZGERALD, c. 1885
An East London oil refiner blessed with imaginative vision, F.A. Fitzgerald was the industrialist who orchestrated the formation of the Imperial Oil Company. When incorporated on September 8, 1880, Imperial Oil was the nation's largest refining concern. Although born in London, the company left the city for Petrolia in the mid-1880s.

1886
Dominion Experimental Farm estab. at Ottawa by Ag. Minister Sir John Carling; fellow Londoner William Saunders is director.

While the movement itself declined in the late 1880s, the Knights in London did help working people get started on their journey to gaining more control over their everyday lives.

The founding of London's Trades and Labour Council (forerunner of the London and District Labour Council) in 1884 was one such step the Knights of Labor helped working people to make. The LTLC was an umbrella organization of labour groups in the city affiliated with the national Canadian Trades and Labour Council. It aimed to help workers improve their working lives by organizing unions in London industries, pushing for better working conditions, campaigning for equal pay for equal work for women, and better wages for all. The London TLC also helped working people in a more general way by organizing Labour Day parades, setting up educational programs, and supporting working class candidates in municipal and federal elections. One of their biggest projects was their campaign to encourage the public to support workers by buying only products with "union made" labels on them.

In just a few short years, the trade union movement had begun to gain some respectability in the eyes of the public. R.H. Hessel, one of London's early labour leaders, claimed things weren't easy for the men who started a union in the Burridge & Co. shoe factory in the early 1870s: "... at first their meetings were held in secret, sometimes in the cellar of one of their homes, for fear of prosecution if they were found out." By July 1886, however, city officials had rolled out the red carpet to welcome the thousands of labour delegates who poured into the city for London's first labour convention, the meeting of the International Iron Moulders Union, sponsored by the Knights of Labour and the London local of the Iron Moulders Union. The delegates took time out to play on Friday, 9 July, and invited the public to a parade and picnic. London Mayor Hodgens declared the day a half-holiday and he even led the parade. The parade had 4,000 marchers, including "seven carriages ... containing the lady members of the mixed assemblies of the Knights of Labor — Harmony and Confidence, and the ladies were greeted with hearty applause as they passed along." Afterwards, nearly 10,000 people gathered at the Western Fairgrounds eating, listening to the bands playing beneath the trees, racing for ribbons in the sports events, and watching the baseball game. No labour picnic is complete without speeches, and several of the international union representatives took the opportunity to address the lemonade-sipping crowd. Both the London *Advertiser* and the London *Free Press* heaped praises on the event and its organizers, the union members, the working people, and the weather. Said the *Free Press*:

> ...never before has such an influential representation of practical workers been seen in this section. The intelligence, respectability, and sobriety of the delegates is apparent at a glance and serves more forcibly to prove in a most conclusive manner that the representatives do not assemble for the purposes of pleasure but meet to transact the business of the most vital importance to their interests. ... The success of the movement should bring about more cordial relations between capital and labor, while giving the men more confidence and a firmer footing in their demand for an honest day's pay for an honest day's work.

THE MASONIC TEMPLE, c. 1885
Built in 1880-81, and dripping with the decorative intricacies so typical of Victorian architecture, the Masonic Temple boastfully offered its splendour to the northwest corner of King and Richmond Streets. Designed by renowned London architect George F. Durand, the grand structure barely survived a fire in 1900, and was demolished in 1967.

By this report, the London labour movement had come a long way from the days of hiding in basements. Yet, the most trying days for London labour were still to come.

Despite the long-dragged-out, continent-wide recession, London was beginning to earn its reputation as a solid, conservative money centre. Opulent family homes began to grace such thoroughfares — properly called avenues — as Queen's and Dufferin in central London, and Grand Avenue in the south.

Some of the mansions, like Charles "Champagne Charlie" Smith Hyman's home "Idlewyld," boasted ballrooms of elegant dimensions — and cramped, cell-like rooms for the domestic staff. An American writer, Joanna Barnes, in her recent novel *Silverwood* (New York: 1985), provides an evocative picture of the domestic arrangements in a large home in New York City:

> One day, though it was forbidden, I had surreptitiously made my way to the fourth floor of the Madison Avenue house, where the servants' quarters were. What I found there were not rooms at all but tiny cubicles, most of them windowless, separated from each other by thin, wooden partitions which denied all but an illusion of privacy. In each a single gas jet provided all the light and heat there was. The rooms were identically outfitted with a cot and a chamber pot, a washstand, pitcher and basin, a narrow chest of drawers and four clothes pegs. These were the dreariest, meanest surroundings I had ever seen, and I found it nearly impossible to believe that our mother, who was the soul of kindness and forever reminding us that charity began at home, could possibly be aware of the conditions in which our help lived.

Even the smaller, middle class homes usually had two staircases leading to the upper floors, the "front stairs" carpeted, with shallow risers; the "back stairs" uncarpeted and steep, leading to the "helps' quarters" under the eaves.

1886
Robert Louis Stevenson writes Dr. Jekyll and Mr. Hyde.

MOUNT HOPE ORPHANAGE, c. 1880

Founded in the 1870s by the Sisters of St. Joseph, the Mount Hope Orphanage, situated on the west side of Richmond Street between College Avenue and Grosvenor Street, served an important charitable function in Victorian London.

1888

"Jack the Ripper" murders six women in London, England; the case still an open mystery.

to the London Civic Employees Credit Union Limited.

London's churches were also active in philanthropical activities, especially those associated with the Roman Catholic Diocese of London. The Sisters of St. Joseph were the pioneers. They had already established a House of Providence and the Mount Hope Refuge, and in 1888 they opened their own hospital.

It must be pointed out that these institutions bore little resemblance to those with which we are today familiar. The late Victorians continued to tend towards the view that the poor and distressed were the authors of their own misfortune. There is an unmistakably censorious tone to many of the regulations guiding the administration of these places. This is especially true of the institutions operated by the municipalities. The rules laid down for the poor house of the County of Norfolk in 1871 are typical:

Rule IV   Every inmate, unless sick, shall rise at 7 1/2 o'clock, and retire at 8 o'clock, in winter; and rise at 5 1/2 o'clock and retire at 9 o'clock in summer. And all that are able to work must be kept employed.

Rule V   No inmate is allowed to leave the premises without a pass from the Inspector. If any one wishes to visit friends, or go away on business he, or she, must apply to the Inspector, at his usual visits, for a written pass, which must be presented to the Keeper before he or she will be allowed to leave the premises. ...

Rule VIII Any one infringing any of the above rules will be placed in solitary confinement, with bread and water diet, for such a period as the Inspector shall direct, subject to the approval of the Medical Superintendent.

Many of the occupants of these poor houses were local people who, for one reason or another, had fallen on evil times. The harsh rules represented a pretty general public attitude toward the distress of other people. The feeling about needy newcomers was even harsher.

The Guthrie Home for English orphans was established in the 1880s in an old building on the Commissioners Road east of London that dated back to the 1820s. In 1887 John T. Middlemore, founder of the Orphan Children's Emigration Charity, brought out a party of fifty girls and one hundred boys from Birmingham, England, to this facility. On that occasion a local newspaper had this to say about the philanthropic effort:

> This work Mr. Middlemore has made a study. During the 15 years of his career in ridding England of an unprofitable class of persons, he has bestowed upon Canada at least 2,000 members of that class, a few of whom are said to have made useful residents.

Before we condemn the Londoners of a century ago for their lack of compassion, however, it would be advisable for us to consider the difficulties experienced by the social agencies of the 1990s in locating group-homes in residential areas.

No Dust! No Rust! No Labor! Try it! The Best in the World.

We warn the public to beware of Imitations of our Nonsuch Stove Polish.

Use our MIRROR STOVE PIPE VARNISH Largest Bottle. Best Gloss.

STUART & PANTON LONDON, ONT.

INTERNATIONAL NONSUCH STOVE POLISH, —FOR— Stoves, Stove Pipes, and Sheet Iron.

No Rust! No Dust!

Easiest, Best & Most Durable Polish in the Market.

Every Bottle Warranted to give the best Polish in the World.

FOR SALE EVERYWHERE.

For Sale by all the Leading Wholesale and Retail Hardware and Grocery Firms.

STOVE POLISH ADVERTISEMENT
In 1889, Stuart and Panton proudly declared that their "International Nonsuch Stove Polish" was the best in the entire world. Apparently though, consumers thought otherwise and by 1892 the firm was no longer in business.

THE GUTHRIE HOME, 1889
Constructed as a tavern in the 1820s, this building, located at what today would be 871 Commissioners Road East, served as the Guthrie Home for English orphans. Vacant by 1974, the structure was burned during a training exercise carried out by the London Fire Department shortly after.

CHAPTER NINE

Horse-and-Buggy Days

The horse and buggy made the reporting of fall fairs an enviable assignment because on such occasions it was possible to take along the Little Lady, and while the reporter ... was engaged in copying the prize list, the L.L. could always be depended on to make a few notes about the women's fancy work, the cookery, and the preserves so dear to the housewives' hearts.

And then there was always the drive homeward — mostly by moonlight, as it seems in retrospect. And how surely those livery stables' nags could make their way, unguided and untended, until the lights of London appeared over the hill and it became necessary once more to come from out the clouds and pick up the reigns to restrain a now impatient horse from foundering on the last long mile that led to stable and to feed box. Steady Bess, old girl; whoa Dan!
— George W. Yates, Ottawa, in the London *Free Press*, 21 June, 1939.

The fact is, as the extract above illustrates, London liked the nineteenth century and was reluctant to give it up. It required two world wars finally to convince the die-hards that Queen Victoria really was dead and that the "good times" were no more.

Of course, the good times were never that good, in spite of the rosy memories of George Yates and thousands of others. The best that could be said of them was that those times were slower and less noisy than our present environment.

These memories are summer memories. In the spring and autumn the roads that Dobbin travelled that halcyon evening would have been deep in mud. What prevailed in the rural areas also held true in the city. London's streets were a hodgepodge of materials. Some streets were dirt on one side of the street, gravel on the other. Some of them were brick, covered with asphalt; others, in the downtown area, were paved with cedar blocks. All types froze in the winter, heaved and potholed in the spring — just like the ones we travel today.

The statistical relationship between rural and urban areas was changing rapidly. The farm population of Middlesex County began a slow decline,

"NIP" TUNE AND HIS BICYCLE, c. 1890
The bicycling craze that swept Canada in 1890s found ready participants in London. Here we see J.A. "Nip" Tune of the Forest City Bicycle Club posed with his favourite "high-wheeler".

1890
Norman Bethune, Canadian medical hero, born, Gravenhurst, Ont., d. 1939 in China.

SIR JOHN CARLING, 1896
Sir John Carling of Canadian brewing fame was also a well respected politician and statesman. Launching his public career as a school trustee in 1845, Carling found later success at the provincial and federal levels. In 1896, he was made a senator, a position he held until his death in 1911.

1890
Bismarck, the "Iron Chancellor," dismissed by Emperor William II of Germany.

while that of London began to rise. From a figure of 19,941 in 1880, London's population rose to 30,705 in 1890. A good part of the increase came from the annexation of the suburbs. London East "amalgamated" with London in 1885. Soon afterwards the factory suburb's smelly petroleum industry was relocated to Lambton County, where it had originated. In 1890 the city took over the unincorporated areas of what is commonly called London South. London West was added in 1897.

The atmosphere of the age served to enhance London's social insularity. Its citizens were intelligently aware that there was a world outside London and felt sympathetic towards its shortcomings. This attitude often infuriated or amused the city's critics. When a London newspaper once commented, smugly, that London was "better laid out" than its traditional rival Hamilton, an editor in the latter city wrote acidly that when Hamilton had been as long dead as London, it too would be "well laid out."

London modestly acknowledged its reputation as one of the wealthier Canadian cities. At the same time, its citizens were well aware of the social and economic gulf fixed between its richest residents and its poorest. They were proud of the first group and tolerant of the second.

London was, and is, a tolerant community. This is not to say that Londoners are incapable of racism. They have resented Jewish business success and erected subtle social barriers against blackness; but while these attitudes have been persistent, they have never been terribly popular. The people of London have always felt somewhat embarrassed by the *existence* of differences between individuals.

The city had few minority groups. The largest at this time was the Italian newcomers. They had begun to arrive, in numbers, in the 1870s. They were not penniless immigrants. They came with some capital prepared to establish businesses and to become full-fledged citizens of the new land. Many settled in the downtown area west of Richmond Street and north of Carling Street, a district later referred to by many as the "Latin Quarter." Almost inevitably, music was a common interest. Such family names as Cortese, Maiorana, Briglia, Vita, and later Lombardo and Niosi, became well known throughout the continent.

There had been Jewish families in London from almost the beginning of settlement, but they seem not to have established any formal religious institutions until the 1860s. Many of the founders of the oil companies were men with Jewish backgrounds. This was especially true of the Imperial Oil Company.

Of what we have come to call the "visible minorities" the blacks were, of course, the first. It was not until the 1870s that Asiatic immigrants became a feature of Canadian life. One local record, Goodspeed's *History of Middlesex*, states that "Wahelee Angnee was the first Chinese laundryman in London". He began business here in 1878. The census of 1881 reports 4,383 registered Chinese in the country, most of whom had been brought to Canada to undertake the back-breaking work of building the Canadian Pacific Railway through the Rocky Mountains.

As London society grew more complex, the nature of the charitable impulses of its citizens changed. Charity became more specialized, and specialized agencies arose to meet those needs. By 1896 there were no

CAMPBELL CARRIAGE FACTORY, c. 1890
The John Campbell Carriage Works at 75-85 King Street was one of London's more enduring industries. Established in the mid-1850s, the enterprise was still manufacturing carriages in the 1920s, though by then it had diversified into auto repairs. Here we see a selection of Campbell's finest models of trade in stock.

THE PARLOUR OF "WAVERLEY", c. 1890
Erected in 1883, "Waverley" served for many years as the residence of Thomas H. Smallman. The rooms of the stately mansion reflected the opulence of the Victorian age.

**THE MORKIN
HOUSE BAR,
c. 1905**
*The thoroughly
stocked "sampling
room" of the Morkin
House, a hotel situat-
ed at 89 King Street,
warmly greeted pa-
trons. The advertis-
ing etched into the
taproom's mirror
was chiefly for the
benefit of out-of-
town travellers who
were likely to
appreciate such
acquaintance with
the city.*

1894

*Labour Day
holiday celebrated
first time in
Canada by an act
of parliament.*

Canada's female head of state, the "Widow of Windsor" celebrated her diamond jubilee in 1897. It was even grander than the golden jubilee extravaganza of ten years earlier. Most Londoners had known no other queen but Victoria. The very name of the community spoke of its strong attachment to the capital of the Empire and to its Empress. During the jubilee year a visitor from the older London found great amusement in the duplicated street names — Pall Mall, Piccadilly, Grosvenor, Cheapside, and Regent. He was Harry Furniss, noted Punch cartoonist and illustrator of the novels of Charles Dickens, William Makepeace Thackery, and Lewis Carroll. Through him, London, Canada, made the scene in London, England, by way of a satirical cartoon.

The city made the international scene again in January, 1898, but this time it wasn't amusing. On municipal election night, Monday, 3 January, a crowd gathered in the second-floor auditorium of the city hall on Richmond Street. They were celebrating the mayoral victory of Dr. John D. Wilson. Suddenly, without a warning, a section of the floor gave way, pitching 250 people onto the ground floor. Seconds later, a 500-pound safe slid into the hole, crushing many of the victims. A total of twenty-three people died; 150 were injured.

Less noted nationally, a single death in April 1898 provided a local sensation. It was a murder case. Since it was a truly theatrical murder, it is necessary to set the stage for the telling.

The Mechanics' Institute building, 229-231 Dundas Street, erected in 1877, had been vacated in 1895 when the London Public Library opened its new building at the southwest corner of Wellington Street and Queens Avenue. The municipal library took over the function and the collections of the Institute.

The Dundas Street building, then, became the home of the Music Hall (later Bennett's Theatre, and later still, the Majestic Theatre). The box office was on the ground floor, the theatre auditorium on the second level.

On the night of Friday, 1 April 1898, the touring Wesley Stock Company, under its manager James Tuttle, was performing a play called *The Candidate*, which was billed as "a satire on Canadian politics." The male lead was played by an American actor, William D. Emerson, whose wife was also a member of the cast.

That evening, just before curtain time, there had been a dispute between Tuttle and Emerson on a matter of overdue wages. There was a confrontation on stage, in the course of which Emerson shot Tuttle in the face at point-blank range with a .32- calibre revolver, a stage property that unaccountably was loaded with live ammunition.

In the ensuing confusion someone told the crew to raise the curtain. As the bleeding corpse lay stage-centre, a member of the cast stepped forward to the footlights and cried out, "Is there a doctor in the house?"

This hoary stage line drew howls of laughter from the three hundred members of the audience as they recalled the date. Someone put a name to it:

"April fool!"

Eventually the audience was apprised of the true state of affairs, but unfortunately

— there *was* no doctor in the house.

After a long delay a doctor was found, some two blocks distant. Dr. Frederick P. Drake drove his finger into the facial wound of the obviously deceased manager and solemnly announced to the house, now eagerly assembled on stage:

"This man is dead."

This, the second theatrical cliché of the evening, was followed by a third when a member of the London police force stepped up to William Emerson, and declaimed:

"You, sir, are under arrest."

The second act of this real-life drama lived up to the promise of the first. From the beginning of the case the London public was on the side of the actor. When the grand jury brought in a true bill on a charge of first-degree murder, there was widespread indignation. The late manager, James Tuttle, weighing in at 250 pounds, had been unpopular with everyone. He had struck the first blow in the altercation with the slender actor. Emerson was a member of the United States Naval Reserve and was expecting to be called up for service in the Spanish-American War. That, in itself, made good newspaper copy. The female lead in the drama of the trial was Emerson's wan and weeping little blond wife Laura, who at every critical moment was to be seen "clasping her flaxen-haired little daughter to her breast."

In these circumstances the prosecution didn't have a chance, despite the unexplained loaded revolver in the hands of the defendant. The jury stayed out just long enough to appear to have considered the manner, then brought in the expected verdict:

"Not guilty."

The crowd inside and outside the courtroom was ecstatic. When Emerson, his wife, and daughter emerged, some men loosed the horses from the shafts of the carriage that was waiting for their hero, and themselves

STEAM ENGINE ADVERTISEMENT, 1897
A securely established industrial concern, George White and Sons, Limited was one of the leading producers of traction engines in Ontario. At the turn of the century, the company did a booming trade supplying the Canadian west with heavy farm machinery.

BICYCLE ADVERTISEMENT, 1898
The 1890s bicycling rage stimulated the development of a lucrative manufacturing industry. Responding to a voracious demand for "wheels", small bicycle factories sprang up across the country. To help satisfy the London market, the Alaska Cycle Company offered these three models at relatively cheap prices for the day.

DOMINION DAY PARADE, c. 1899
As these school children paraded along Dundas Street, the crowds proudly cheered for Canada!

1895
Babe Ruth, baseball great, and Jack Dempsey, boxing champion, born.

pulled the vehicle to Emerson's boarding house, preceded by an improvised band.

The story is worth retelling. It epitomizes the romantic sentimentalism of the period. A less lovely aspect of this attachment to the romantic ideal was the outburst of patriotic fervour for the cause of Britain in the South African War. Less lovely because the war cost Britain a great deal of credibility in world circles. The spectre of a powerful empire pitting half a million troops (including 7,300 Canadians) against a mere 88,000 independence-loving Boers was not a pretty one. Toward the end of the conflict, which began in 1899 and lasted until 1901, England's use of a scorched-earth policy and the establishment of concentration camps in which 20,000 men, women and children died, offended Britain's friends and enraged her enemies.

Nevertheless Londoners and English-speaking Canadians generally supported Britain. Citizens played tinny-sounding recordings of "Soldiers of the Queen," on their hand-cranked Edison phonographs and prayed for the success of the Empire's arms.

For a time in 1899 residents of the Forest City had plenty of excitement on their own turf.

Four years earlier, in 1895, the London Street Railway sold its horses and converted its trams to another kind of horsepower — electricity. This conversion did not come without a price, however, and the London interests of the LSR sold out to a Cleveland company, Everett and Grace. As far as service goes, this was an enormous leap forward, although the public was less than enthusiastic about the jump in fares. As for labour relations, things were not so rosy. In earlier times almost anyone could handle a horse-drawn vehicle. Now it required an engineer to operate the electric cars. The "motorman" came into his own. He joined a union, Branch 97 of the Amalgamated Association of Street Railway Employees

STREET RAILWAY SHELTER, c. 1905
The extention of street railway service to Springbank Park in 1896 endorsed the position of the park as London's most popular. On May 25, the day the branch line was opened, over 10,000 excursionists made the trip.

THE LONDON STREET RAILWAY, c. 1905
Incorporated in 1873, and electrified twenty-two years later, the London Street Railway answered growing transportation needs. Here we see the busy stop in front of the "Crystal Palace" at Queen's Park (now the Western Fairgrounds).

THE TUNE SODA WATER WORKS, c. 1900

Established in 1883, the James Tune and Son Soda Water Works, located at 132 York Street, catered to many of London's grocery stores, restaurants, and hotels.

TROOPS PATROLLING DUNDAS STREET

The streetcar strike of 1899 was a time of great friction in London's labour history. To maintain peace and order, the city called upon the military for assistance.

of America. On Thursday, 27 October 1898, the AASREA called its members out on strike. Their grievances: the company's practice of importing workers from the U.S., the difference in pay between the regular workers and the relief workers, and harsh discipline from the managers. It lasted less than a week. Besides an agreement regarding the above grievances, the employees won an extra one-third of a cent an hour on their former wage of fifteen cents an hour.

The labour peace lasted only a few months. The managers of the London Street Railway Company refused to honour the agreement made with the workers at the conclusion of the first strike. In fact, they tried to break up the union, and they regularly gave the unionized relief workers fewer hours than the non-unionized workers. On Monday, 22 May 1899, seventy-nine motormen and conductors walked off the job, without notice.

This second strike proved to be the most vicious of the city's history. It dragged on for more than a year and was accompanied by the worst civic violence London had ever seen. The striking workers, however, received a lot of support from the public, particularly the working people. A boycott of the LSR was observed by many, and several fraternal orders such as the Orange Lodge and the Masons promoted the strike slogan ''We Walk to Protect Labour.'' Men wore ''We Walk'' signs on their hats, and the young women who worked in the factories walked long distances to get to work rather than take the LSR. At one point, the striking workers actually borrowed buses and ran them along the LSR routes, so people would have an alternative way to work.

Much of the violence that took place during this strike was owing to the company's use of replacement workers, or ''scabs.'' So much damage was done to the rolling stock that the police were called out. Londoners were then treated to the astonishing spectacle of the trams and their strike-breaking crews being guarded by constables carrying loaded revolvers.

The violence reached a peak on Saturday, 8 July. Many businesses were now operating only a half-day on Saturdays. This meant that many employees were at liberty to join the crowd that was beginning to assemble in the downtown area. By 2:30 in the afternoon several thousand rioters had taken over control of the city's core. The authorities hoped against hope that the rioters would run out of steam as the supper hour approached. Hunger apparently only made the mob meaner.

At midnight, Dr. John Wilson, in his second year as mayor, called out the militia units to restore order. He then read the Riot Act to the noisy, unruly mob. It was the first and only time in the history of London that this legal instrument has been employed.

Taking a keen interest in the plight of the striking LSR workers was London's only labour newspaper, the *Industrial Banner*, the official organ of the Trades and Labour Council. Founded in 1892, the *Industrial Banner* was one of the oldest labour newspapers in the country, and was regularly shipped to Hamilton and Toronto. Edited for 28 years by London labour leader Joseph T. Marks, the paper offered a decidedly different view of the LSR strike than the *Free Press*. For example, in regards to the business community's reaction to the bus boycott, the writer notes:

NURSES, c. 1905
Mollie McConnell (left) and Mamie Robbins, both nurses at the London Asylum, were just two of the rapidly growing number of health care attendants who flocked to London's hospitals at the turn of the century.

1896
George Burns (Nathan Birnbaum), comedian, world's oldest active entertainer at time of writing, born.

DR. R.M. BUCKE, c. 1900
A visionary blessed with a kind heart, Dr. Richard Maurice Bucke, the superintendent of the London Asylum from 1877 to 1902, revolutionized the care and treatment of those suffering from mental illness. With his distinguished beard and rumpled old hat, the doctor and his family posed for the camera on the steps of their home.

...and the result is that a few misnamed public spirited citizens of professional capabilities, who never raised a blister on their fingers in their life by hard work, and who never laid a brick, or dug a drain, or set a row of type, or performed even the simplest act to help to build up the city, now raise their hands in holy horror and cry out that the city is being ruined and protest against the boycott.

In the end, however, the union lost. After more than a year, the strikers finally called off the strike. Most of the unionized workers lost their jobs to the replacement workers hired by the LSR during the strike.

A prettier tale, one that has long been held dear to the hearts of romantic Londoners, unfolded its fairy-tale climax in the Gay Nineties.

Cy Warman, an American journalist and poet, fell in love with a girl from Kansas, Myrtle Marie Jones, who was attending the Roman Catholic Academy of the Sacred Heart in London. After seeing her home one evening in mid-July, 1891, Cy sat down on a bench in Victoria Park and composed a poem to her, which he looked on as a proposal of marriage.

So did she. She accepted.

In 1893, Raymon Moore set the poem to music. The song was called "Sweet Marie." It made Cy Warman's fame and fortune.

In 1899, the Warmans returned to London, built the house at 100 Cheapside Street that still stands, and lived there happily ever after — at least until he died.

An important date was coming up and the "battle of the century" began on Monday, 1 January 1900. Thousands — perhaps millions — of people celebrated that New Year's Day as the beginning of the twentieth century. A fewer number of brave souls declared that the first day of the new century would not come until Tuesday, 1 January 1901. Although much outnumbered, the second group was right. The reader may work it out for himself, or herself. The next occasion for debate will come on Saturday, 1 January 2000.

The first year of the new century started out on a sad note. Queen

1897
First Women's Institute in the world founded at Stoney Creek by Adelaide Hunter Hoodless.

THE LONDON RUGBY-FOOTBALL CLUB, 1900
Bristling with confidence, these husky lads brought home London's first national football championship in 1900. Led by half-backs Jack Gilmour and Frank Taylor that season, on November 24, the "red, white and black" buried the McGill University squad by 14 to 5 for the Canadian intermediate title.

Victoria died on the Isle of Wight on Tuesday, 22 January 1901, to be succeeded by London's favourite prince, as King Edward VII. As a footnote to history, it may be noted that a remarkable number of boy babies born that year were christened Albert Edward in honour of the new king, just as another crop of local children forty-one years earlier had been given the same two names in honour of the same royal personage when he visited as the Prince of Wales.

The new king's son, Prince George (later George V), visited London later that year with his wife, Princess Mary. The city's greeting was a warm one, but somewhat marred by an unaccountable oversight on the part of the committee in charge. There was no official welcome at the railway station.

September 1901 marked the opening of the palatial new Grand Opera House on Richmond Street, between Fullarton and Maple (Dufferin) streets. The new theatre succeeded the former Grand Opera House, which had occupied premises in the Masonic Temple building on the northwest corner of Richmond and King streets. The building had been gutted by fire on Friday, 23 February 1900.

The new theatre was the queen of a massive chain of some ninety houses controlled by Ambrose Joseph Small, of Toronto, one of the best known and most cordially hated theatrical figures in Canada. The importance of the new theatre lay in its large seating capacity (1,850), its modern equipment, and the extraordinary dimensions of its playing area, which may be judged from the following description from Julius Cahn's Official Theatrical Guide for 1905-1906:

> LONDON — Pop., 50,000. Grand Opera House. A.J. Small, proprietor. J.E. Turton, bus. mgr. Communications regarding time at this theatre should be

1898
Imperial penny postage (2¢) established in the British Empire; Canada prints famed "Map Stamp."

After the aviator had taken his seat in the machine and the engine was started, several of the spectators held the big bird until the momentum was reached. Then with a rush along the field the machine lifted from the ground within 100 yards from the starting point and gradually climbed to an altitude of nearly 600 feet. In the downtown section of the city, Mr. Havens manoeuvred over the National Bowling Alley building, swaying at times, but keeping well on his course. He looked like a gigantic bird, traveling along at a terrific speed, a cloud of white smoke trailing behind him. The landing operation at the aviation camp was simplified. Making an abrupt circle over the C.P.R. tracks, Havens turned his machine toward the meadow from which he had made his ascent, drooped his planes and took a long, graceful glide to earth. When about 20 feet from the ground, he silenced his engines and brought the machine lightly to the field. ...

A 60-horsepower engine, developing a speed of over 70 miles per hour, faster than almost any ordinary railroad train, was the power behind the air voyage.

That was a big year for London. In May the governor-general visited the city, and unveiled the "Soldier Monument" in Victoria Park to those who lost their lives in the Boer War. In July, Dora, the daughter of brewer John Labatt, went for a ride in an aeroplane, the first London woman to do so.

The governor-general was His Royal Highness The Duke of Connaught. Elderly Londoners must have found it difficult to recognize, in the distinguished seventy-two-year-old soldier, the gay young officer who had officiated at the opening of Hellmuth Ladies' College back in 1869.

Few governors-general have had a closer association with Canada than the first Duke of Connaught and Strathearn. During his original posting to this country he was a member of the Red River expedition that was sent west in 1870 to deal with the first Riel Rebellion. Port Arthur, now submerged along with Fort William in the modern city of Thunder Bay, was named for him. In the European war that was a little over two years away at the time of his visit to London, the Duke organized the Canadian Patriotic Fund to help the dependents of the servicemen, and his daughter assisted in raising a regiment named for her, the Princess Patricia's Canadian Light Infantry. The "Princess Pats" served with distinction in both world wars. The Duke himself lived to see Great Britain go to war for the second time against the German state. He died on Friday, 16 January 1942.

Among the crowds that greeted the Duke in the spring of 1912 were many newcomers from the British Isles. The Liberal prime minister, Sir Wilfrid Laurier, and his minister of the interior Sir Clifford Sifton were responsible for attracting more than three million immigrants from the United Kingdom, the United States, and Europe in the years between 1897 and 1914. Like the earliest arrivals to the London area back in the 1830s, these new people brought little with them except a desire to "get ahead."

The effects in London were marked. Hundreds of "workmen's cottages" sprang up, with a concentration along the Hamilton Road in East London. Strange new languages were being heard on the city's streets. One of these languages was German. Suddenly, beginning in 1913, this was not a popular sound. Rumours began to circulate around one man, Otto Becker, an employee of the Public Utilities Commission. It was said he was a member of the German Reserve Army. It was said he was a spy.

LONDON NORMAL SCHOOL, c. 1910
As a training facility for elementary teachers, the Normal School on Elmwood Avenue graduated over 12,000 pedagogues during its 60 years of service. Later students attended U.W.O. The old building, now restored, houses the Mgr. Feeney Centre for Catholic Education.

CITY HALL, c. 1912
London's city hall on Richmond Streeet was an austere, conservatively crafted structure when held in comparison to its contemporaries throughout the province.

And then it was August 1914. A hot month.

Since the assassination of Archduke Ferdinand of Austria at Sarejevo, on Sunday, 28 June, things had been heating up in Europe. It was all too complicated for the average person to understand. It all came down, however, to the fact that Great Britain had served an ultimatum on Germany. The Kaiser had until 11 pm Tuesday, 4 August 1914, to withdraw his troops from the territory of the neutral state of Belgium.

Crowds began gathering in front of the newspaper offices in the early evening hours of that day. From time to time copy boys emerged to put up fresh bulletins on the boards in front of the offices, printed by hand with grease pencils on newsprint. The crowds were quiet until the last bulletin of the night was put up:

"GREAT BRITAIN DECLARES WAR: GOD SAVE THE KING!"

The following day the *Free Press* reported on the city's reactions to the news:

> Scenes of the wildest enthusiasm, with every display of patriotic regard for the motherland in the present European situation followed the official announcement of the declaration of war by Great Britain on Germany last night. ...
>
> Within a few minutes after the announcement was made on the *Free Press* bulletin and in extra edition a hundred patriots gathered in front of the *Free Press* and calling upon a group of bandsmen organized a procession and demonstration that grew as it proceeded through the business section.
>
> At midnight the throng was even greater. ... Wild cheers went up when the declaration of war was announced and gathering at Richmond and Carling streets the crowd lustily sang "God Save the King," "Britannia Rules the Waves," "The Maple Leaf Forever," "O Canada," and other national and patriotic airs.
>
> There was no thought save of victory, and while London has in the past at times born the reputation of strong and anti-military leanings, sentiment was unanimously to the contrary.

On the afternoon of 4 August, the Public Utilities Commission fired Otto Becker.

He left town immediately.

SENDING THE TROOPS OFF, 1915
For many, sending the troops off to the battlefields of Europe was a tearful, yet patriotic event. Unbeknownst to some, this scene at the Grand Trunk station would be the final farewell to sons, brothers, husbands, and friends. World War One abruptly ended the blissful age of innocence so familiar to the entire country.

1915
John McCrae publishes "In Flanders Fields," in Punch *magazine.*

CHAPTER TEN

Cry Havoc

Cry, "Havoc!" and let slip the dogs of war.
— William Shakespeare, *Julius Caesar.*

The high contracting parties solemnly declare in the names of their respective peoples they condemn recourse to war for the solution of international controversies, and renounce it as an instrument of national policy in their relations with one another.
— Frank Billings Kellogg, Peace Pact, signed at Paris, 27 Aug. 1928.

The history of London now enters a period of which many present residents have personal knowledge. Human memory being the selective faculty that it is, it will prove impossible to offer a truly balanced picture of the years under review. One must try to avoid too narrow a focus. Events within one's special frame of knowledge will inevitably overshadow those within other parameters. The only approach that would seem to promise an impartial overview is that based on the importance given to various events by the public media.

In what our generation called "The Great War" the first concern of Londoners was with our own. The news of the great Canadian victory at Ypres, for instance, was of less interest than the answer to the urgent question "Is my boy all right?" Casualty lists were scanned with agonizing intensity. Only after the absence of the name of a dear one from the lists could the reader show an intelligent interest in the progress of the war.

It's difficult to recapture the mood of Canadians in the first year of the war. Patriotism was a fever that affected nearly everyone. A contagious enthusiasm infused every act. There was a supreme confidence in the outcome. The Germans would be taught a lesson. The fighting would be over by Christmas. The question came to be: *What* Christmas?

The war bogged down in the trenches in France and the general enthusiasm waned. The casualty lists grew longer. Life on the home front became more difficult. Coal, among other commodities, was rationed. People living along the main lines of the Grand Trunk Railway (the former Great Western) and the CPR sent their children out to scavenge the soft coal that fell from the engine tenders. Sometimes a friendly fireman would toss a shovelful on the right of way. Ashes from domestic coal furnaces were raked over for bits of unburned fuel.

Rationing was a new experience for Londoners. On the whole they

DUNDAS STREET LOOKING WEST FROM RICHMOND, c. 1925
With the staid Victorian century, the innocence of the Edwardian age, and the harsh realities of one world war all firmly behind it, London approached the 1920s with great hope and confidence.

1915
Ontario implements Workman's Compensation Act.

McCORMICK'S BISCUIT FACTORY, c. 1915
Women have always been a vital part of London's twentieth century industrial workforce. Pictured here is the predominantly female staff of the packing department in McCormick's soda biscuit division.

MACHINE SHOP, SPRAMOTOR COMPANY, c. 1916
Throughout World War I, London's industry devoted its collective energies to the war effort. The Spramotor Company, at 68-74 King Street, through valuable munitions contracts, produced thousands of artillery shells. A propaganda piece designed to boost morale, the banner on the back wall reads: "TO KAISER BILL [the German leader], WITH COMPLIMENTS FROM THE SPRAMOTOR COMPANY."

1916
During the Battle of the Somme, British first use tanks.

coped with it quite well. It was the troops stationed in the encampment on Carling Heights that caused the greatest disruption in the community's life-style. At one time (1916) more than 16,000 troops were receiving training at Wolseley Barracks. It was inevitable that there should be clashes between soldiers and citizens. In many ways it was a return to the uneasy relationships of the 1860s. The "dirty 33rd" were the worst. This was the 33rd Battalion of the Canadian Expeditionary Force. On one occasion they created a riot in downtown London.

Not all Londoners supported the war, either. Some, particularly among the labour movement, saw things rather differently. Arthur Mould, one of the city's foremost labour leaders of the early 20th century, had this to say:

> ...I saw the Boer War all over again with a greater intensity and destruction than ever known. Moreover, I was older, with more experience and greater knowledge of world affairs than I had as a youth, the Imperialist Jingoism of saving the world for democracy, fighting for hearth and home, saving our Christian Civilization — when nearly all who were fighting were so-called Christians, all these things were nauseating when one knew — unless he were blind — that it was purely a war between powerful forces, for the retaining and gaining of more of the world's resources — particularly in oil.
>
> Germany's line to Baghdad was no different than the thin red line from the Cape to Cairo, and never was justifiable for the rivers of bloodshed and agonizing cries of mothers.

They were dreary days; grey days as the dreadful fighting went on. The Edwardian generation had no previous experience in these matters to draw upon. Napoleon was a century gone; the Kaiser was a nightmare figure of daunting ferocity. Anything German became abhorrent to all right-thinking Canadians. By order of George V the royal house of Saxe-Coburg-Gotha became the House of Windsor, and Berlin, Ontario, changed its name to Kitchener. The patriotic fervour that had hurled Canada into the European conflict within hours of the British declaration was beginning to ebb as the interminable battles resulted not in victory, but in longer and longer casualty lists. The cost to Canada in human lives was high: of 628,462 Canadians who served, 60,661 died.

New weapons appeared — the submarine, the tank, the aeroplane. Canadians made a name for themselves in all branches of the armed services, and by the end of the war it was apparent to the world that Canada was a country to be reckoned with. It has been said with much reason that Canada entered the conflict as a colony and emerged as an independent nation, a fact that was acknowledged when the British Parliament later passed the Statute of Westminster in 1931.

None of this was then apparent to the 20,000 war-weary Londoners who jammed Victoria Park on Monday, 11 November 1918, to celebrate the signing of the Armistice. The mood of the crowd verged on hysteria. A dummy representing Kaiser Wilhelm was strung up and burned. The celebration went on, in a lower key, for several days. Many of those who attended the spontaneous outburst of thanksgiving at the eleventh hour of the eleventh day of the eleventh month carried within their own bodies a new and even more savage enemy.

Spanish influenza, so called because it was first identified in Spain, wrought havoc among the troops in the trenches in France, and from there spread around the world. Like all the earlier epidemics and pandemics it appeared in Canada first in Quebec City and from there spread westward. By the end of the year it was everywhere. The final global toll was more than twenty-two million dead, 30,000 of them in Canada.

The disease reached London in October, and for three weeks raged with great severity. Schools, theatres, and all public places of assembly were closed for a time, and the streets of the city became deserted. One

GORDON C. McINTOSH
Gunner Gordon Cowan McIntosh, the son of the Rev. W.R. and Jennie McIntosh of 826 King Street, lost his life on the scarred battlefields of France. At age nineteen, a promising future was suddenly taken from him on July 14, 1917. That "He gladly died for the Freedom and the Glory of the world", as his memorial card patriotically stated, was of little comfort to his grieving family.

1917
Federal income tax introduced as a temporary wartime measure.

VICTORY BOND HEADQUARTERS, NOVEMBER 6, 1918
Taken five days before the Armistice of November 11, this photograph depicts the Victory Bond Headquarters at 361 Richmond Street. Victory bonds were vital to war financing. The London office staff collected more than one-fourth of the county objective and well over half the city objective mid-way through its October/November 1918 campaign.

1918
Roy Brown shoots down the "Red Baron," Von Richthofen, in aerial battle over France.

in every six persons contracted the plague, and those who hadn't walked in fear. Then, just as residents relaxed, feeling that the worst was past, the disease returned at the beginning of January 1919 in an even more severe form. Although fewer people were affected, the mortality rate was higher in the second outbreak.

At last it was over and London began to pick up the pace of normal city life again. In October 1919, Victoria Park again became the scene of a huge gathering of citizens as more than 20,000 Londoners turned out to greet the darling of the Empire, His Royal Highness Edward Albert Christian George Andrew Patrick David, the Prince of Wales. Men, women, and children lined up in orderly queues to shake the hand of the heir to the throne as Mayor Charles Ross Somerville looked on proudly. Those who were lucky enough to grasp the Imperial hand found themselves facing a slim young man of average height with a crooked, rather shy smile.

Such popularity as the Prince of Wales enjoyed has a price. That evening a former mayor of London, a physician, was called to the Tecumseh House Hotel by an equerry of the prince to treat an injured hand, grossly swollen by the overly-enthusiastic grip of hundreds of patriotic citizens.

The prince was well enough by the following morning to play a round of golf at the London Hunt and Country Club, where he was ambushed by a reporter from the London *Free Press*, Edmund J. Penny, and a pho-

tographer, Seward Lancaster. Penny got an exclusive interview. The prince met the Mayor's son, Charles Ross (Sandy) Somerville, Junior, who was that year launching a career in tournament golf that would take him to the top rank of North American amateurs.

The year the Prince of Wales visited was significant in another way — women voted for the first time in municipal elections. The Local Council of Women wasted no time in exercising their newly-gained right, and set out to get three women elected to the Board of Education. Their campaigning paid off, for Mrs. Lorna Harris, Mrs. Alberta E. Williams, and Mrs. A.T. Edwards became the first women elected to public office in London.

Ed Penny's newspaper, the London *Free Press*, suffered a grievous loss New Year's Day, Thursday, 1 January 1920, with the death of its publisher, Walter J. Blackburn, eldest son of Josiah Blackburn. Seven months later the paper lost its managing editor, Alfred E. Miller.

These two deaths resulted in the arrival of a trio of interesting and important men in leading roles in the London drama. W.J. Blackburn's brother Arthur stepped into the management of the newspaper. The founding member of the Blackburn dynasty had been primarily a writer and politician; the second was an astute businessman; the third was an amateur scientist. Arthur Blackburn had a keen interest in the fields of photography and wireless. Combined with a well-developed sporting instinct, his interest in photography led him to take the first action photograph ever published in the family's journal, a shot of the finish of the King's Plate race at Toronto in 1906. It was also he who introduced Linotype machines into the composing room of the *Free Press*.

Alf Miller died in August 1920. The search for a replacement resulted in the appointment of Arthur Rutherford Ford, a native of Point Edward,

1919
"Group of Seven" painters formed in Toronto.

LONDON AND PORT STANLEY RAILWAY REPAIR SHOP, 1916
Chartered in 1853, opened in 1856, and fully electrified in 1915, the London and Port Stanley Railway gave London essential access to a lake port. Here we see a solitary machinist tending to the maintenance of motor car no. 8 at the car barns built in 1916.

STREET SWEEPER, 1918
Long since replaced by motorized vehicles, this horse-drawn street sweeper, seen here at the northeast corner of Ridout and King Streets, was maintained and operated by the city's Roads Department.

ELMWOOD AVENUE, c. 1920
Looking west from between Wortley Road and Cathcart Street, Elmwood Avenue was typical of the tree-lined thoroughfares found in the quiet neighbourhoods of postwar London.

HUNT BROTHERS LIMITED DELIVERY TRUCK, c. 1920
Motorized delivery trucks first made their presence felt in London in the very early 1910s. Used extensively by both manufacturers and wholesalers, by the 1920s, they were a common sight throughout city streets.

DUNDAS STREET, c. 1920
Looking east from near Richmond Street, the Dundas Street of the 1920s was a greatly changed roadway from that of twenty years earlier. Electric signs protruded over curbed sidewalks, and pedestrians were learning to be wary of the discourteous automobile.

LONDON'S FIRST GASOLINE-POWERED BUS, 1923
In 1923, the London Street Railway introduced its first gasoline-powered vehicle. Owing to their greater reliability and increased safety, the buses gradually replaced the city's aging fleet of streetcars. The last operating electric trolley disappeared from London's streets in 1940.

THE "TALBOT STREETSCAPE"
With hay wagons on the southwest corner of the Market Square, this photograph, taken on December 12, 1922, shows the Victorian buildings on the west side of Talbot Street between Dundas and King. More familiar to Londoners as the "Talbot Streetscape", this grand stretch of mixed nineteenth century architecture, save the northern-most building, fell victim to the wrecker's ball in September, 1991.

1920
Ghandi (1869-1948) emerges as India's leader in the struggle for independence.

Ontario. Ford had been a member of the press gallery at the Parliament Buildings in Ottawa. He had covered the disastrous fire that destroyed the centre block on Thursday, 3 February 1916. During his Ottawa career Ford had met the *Free Press* correspondent Fred Landon there. Landon left the field of journalism in 1916 to become city librarian. In the summer of 1920 Ford, while on his vacation, stopped off in London to see his old friend Landon. One thing led to another, and by October Arthur Ford was settled at the ancient walnut desk that had served his three predecessors as managing editor.

No one could call London a "hot" news town. During the 1920s it lived up to its reputation as "the biggest small town in Canada" — and one of the wealthiest. It's an exaggeration to say that everyone knew everyone else, unless one inserts the adverb "nearly" in both places. The population growth was almost infinitesimal. In 1920 there were 181 more people in the city than in 1919. In 1921, the gain was 503. The year 1922 saw a big jump of 1,585, but the following year there was an increase of only 498 persons, to a total of 61,867.

Socially, also, the community lagged behind the times. True, there was sin in London, but it was generally discreet and well concealed. At the top and bottom of the social scale, there were "fast" girls and boys, and a rather startling number of hidden pregnancies and abortions. The great bulk of the population, the middle class, however, observed a Victorian rather than Edwardian code of morals. The majority of the girl children of this class were not rouged, short-skirted flappers, and the boy children wore short pants and long stockings until the magical age of sixteen, when these symbols of childhood were discarded for long trousers with the fashion-ordained twenty-two-inch cuffs that flapped around the feet like the skirts London ladies wore in the 1880s.

In 1923 the citizens elected another of London's unusual, even eccentric mayors. He was George A. Wenige, proprietor of Bicycle and Motor Sales Company, 425-427 Wellington Street, "phone 3182." George Wenige served in the mayor's chair for a total of nine terms, the most ever served by a chief magistrate in the city's history.

In spite of its slow growth the city had a town-planning commission as early as 1922. Its jurisdiction and that of the city stopped at Huron Street which had been the city's northern boundary since 1840. The expected extension of the city's mercantile life in that direction had never happened.

On Monday, 18 June 1923, the Honourable Ernest Charles Drury, premier of Ontario, laid the cornerstones of the arts building and the natural science building of the University of Western Ontario. The site was the former "Bellevue Farm," owned by the Kingsmill family, north of the city on the west bank of the north branch of the Thames River.

There was much criticism of the university's choice. The site was considered to be a long way from the city centre and, furthermore, inaccessible. A great deal of ribald comments were directed against "the college in Kingsmill's cowpasture," which, it was said scathingly, was "half way to Lucan."

With the financial support of the city and the province, a bridge across the Thames at the approach to the campus from Richmond Street was completed, however, in November 1923, and the two new buildings were officially opened on Wednesday, 24 September, 1924.

In a corner of the arts building, Fred Landon, former Great Lakes sailor, newspaperman, and city librarian, took on a new job as librarian of the university. As late as 1908 the library of the Western University (as it was then called) contained no more than two hundred books. Ten years later Landon, himself a Western graduate (1906), secured for the university the private library of John Davis Barnett of Stratford, consisting of more than 40,000 volumes. The agreement was signed Saturday, 10 August 1918, the financial consideration being one dollar. Dr. Barnett never got the dollar.

At the time of the acquisition the university was sharing the facilities of Huron College on St. George Street. From its founding by Bishop Hellmuth in 1878 the university had led an extremely precarious existence. The medical school is the only faculty to have maintained an uninterrupted history, from 1881 to the present. A reorganization in 1908 withdrew the university from the control of the Church of England.

Now, at last, in 1924, the renamed University of Western Ontario had its own 225-acre campus, two handsome new Collegiate Gothic buildings, and more than 40,000 books. The cataloguing of the Barnett collection went on for years under Fred Landon and his immediate successor Dr. James J. Talman.

For a season Londoners showed great pride in the addition to the city's educational mosaic, but they soon lost the first flush of hymeneal bliss. Despite the truly amazing growth of the university in the years since the opening of the new campus, London has never become a "university town" in the English sense. Town and gown have not always made sweet music together. Sometime in the 1960s, however, UWO became the city's largest employer and perhaps the largest annual contributor of outside money to the local economy.

THE HOLEPROOF HOSIERY PLANT, c. 1922
Arriving in London in the early 1910s, the Holeproof Hosiery Company of Milwaukee, Wisconsin erected this factory at 203-213 Bathurst Street in 1920. A thoroughly modern plant when built, it provided nearly 200 with work producing over 500 pairs of hose per day. Serving as a clothing factory until the late 1980s, the building is presently a storage facility.

1921
Insulin discovered by Canadian doctors Banting, Best, Macleod and Collip.

THE COURT HOUSE, c. 1925
Upon the eve of the 100th anniversary of its construction, the Court House served as a magnificent symbol of London's early history. An enlargement completed in 1878, and several subsequent renovations, accorded the structure an appearance which has, for the most part, survived until today.

1923

Centres of Tokyo and Yokohama destroyed by earthquake, 120,000 dead.

Much more exciting to the average person than these fusty academic doings was the erection of the city's first traffic tower at the corner of Richmond and Dundas streets in 1925. There used to be a piece of motion-picture film comparing, in speeded-up motion, the haphazard movement of pedestrians and motor traffic before the installation and the orderly, almost military precision of cars and people afterwards.

All traffic on Richmond Street North came to a halt in mid-August 1925 as the funeral cortege of the "Hydro Knight," Sir Adam Beck, moved south from his palatial residence, "Headley," through the heart of the city. It was probably the last such funeral to be seen in London. The procession consisted of dignitaries from near and far, top-hatted and frock-coated in the best nineteenth-century tradition. The men all wore black armbands.

Conspicuous among the formally-attired mourners was the mayor of London, dressed in a business suit and wearing a straw hat! Chided later for his lack of respect George Wenige denied the charge. It was his best suit, he declared, and the straw boater happened to be the only hat he owned.

Spectators by the thousands lined the route. Their reactions to the passing of the hearse were wildly mixed. There was no middle course where Adam Beck was concerned; in life he was either loved or hated. His coffin was greeted by both tears and snarls. Some men refused to remove their hats in tribute to the dead; women sobbed.

The city that Sir Adam Beck had helped to drag into the twentieth century marked the centennial of its founding in 1926. An Old Boys Reunion highlighted the celebration. Hundreds of old boys returned to the arena of their youth. "New Boys" were scarce. Between January 1925 and January 1926 the population of London increased by only nineteen persons! The biggest little town in Canada" was living up to its name.

The world (which included London) woke up with a start on Friday, 20 May 1927, to learn over the London *Free Press* radio station CJGC that a young man from St. Louis, Missouri, Charles Augustus Lindbergh, was somewhere out over the stormy Atlantic in a single-engine monoplane, trying to win a $25,000 prize for the first non-stop flight from New York to Paris. All that day and into the next Londoners neglected work and study to strain after what little news was available. When the remarkable young man put his craft down at Paris after thirty-three hours and twenty-nine minutes aloft, France — and the world — went mad.

The tremendous surge of interest in the flight led to many imitative ventures, one of which originated in London. The Carling Brewery and Malting Company seized on the opportunity to publicize its product. After a decade of Prohibition, Ontario had repealed the restrictive legislation passed during the Great War and the three major Canadian breweries — Molson's, Carling's, and Labatt's — were scrambling to get back into their pre-war markets.

Charles A. Burns, president of Carling's, came up with a natural. The company offered $25,000 for the first non-stop flight from London, Canada, to London, England. A call went out for flyers to undertake the hazardous adventure. Two veteran pilots took up the challenge. They were Captain Terrence Tully and Lieutenant James Medcalf. They and their families needed the money.

Carling's bought a Stinson monoplane in Detroit and had it flown into the local airport, a dirt field on Highway 4, between London and Lambeth. Hundreds of Londoners made the journey out to see the silver bird come in, the late afternoon sun flashing on her wings.

After several delays, the departure of the plane, the *Sir John Carling*, was set for the beginning of September 1927. It was a bad time of the year for an aerial crossing of the Atlantic. Tully and Medcalf knew it. Any Londoner who saw the two young men in the lobby of the new Hotel London prior to the take-off on Thursday, 1 September, will not soon forget the ashen faces and trembling fingers of the flyers.

The *Sir John Carling* took off from a field at Crumlin, east of the city, now the site of the Argyle Mall, and almost at once flew into bad weather. After a forced landing in Maine, they got as far as Harbour Grace, Newfoundland, before the flight was stalled again by weather conditions. The plane sat there for several days waiting for a break in the storms. Meanwhile the London public revealed some of its more unpleasant attitudes.

"They're just stalling" was a common comment, as was "They don't intend to go at all."

"It's just a promotion stunt" was another.

In the result, the two aviators took off from Newfoundland on Wednesday, 7 September, in spite of continued inclement conditions, and promptly disappeared forever somewhere in the sullen grey swells of the Atlantic.

The episode of the *Sir John Carling* was soon over-shadowed by the train of new sensations that marked the "Roaring Twenties." Of special interest to local people was the investigation into fraud charges against Aimee Semple McPherson, the Oxford County native whose "Four-Square

THE UNIVERSITY OF WESTERN ONTARIO, MARCH 28, 1924
Recognized today as University College, this facility, built in 1924, originally served as the arts building at the University of Western Ontario. At the time of construction, many saw little soundness in the choice to move the school's main campus to "Bellevue Farm" in what was then London Township. In hindsight, the space afforded by the location has greatly enhanced the university.

1924
The Red Ensign becomes Canada's official flag.

RICHMOND STREET LOOKING NORTH FROM DUNDAS, c. 1926
Blinding sleet and vengeful snow storms have marked every year in London's existence. Centred in an unforgiving snowbelt, the city has always played as an unwilling target for Jack Frost's delight.

THE CARLING FLIGHT, 1927
Amid mixed speculation, on September 1, 1927, Terry Tully and James Medcalf, aboard the "Sir John Carling" and bound for London, England, daringly flew out of London. The chase for the $25,000 prize offered by the Carling Brewery tragically ended six days later, when the plane was swallowed by the open seas of the Atlantic.

POST OFFICE, 1927
For the occasion of Canada's 60th anniversary in 1927, the post office building at the southwest corner of Richmond Street and Queens Avenue was patriotically bedecked with the "Union Jack". Another 38 years would pass before the country would fly its own distinctive flag.

McCLARY'S ADELAIDE STREET PLANT, c. 1925
Tracing its origins to Oliver McClary's 1847 tin shop, the McClary Manufacturing Company was London's largest industrial concern before World War II. The company's kitchen utensils, cooking ranges, and furnaces enjoyed international reputations in the mid-1920s.

MUNICIPAL BUILDING, c. 1930
Constructed at a cost of about $190,000 in 1928-29, this building served as London's City Hall until the present one was opened in 1971. Somewhat austere in design, the building still overlooks the northeast intersection of Dundas and Wellington Streets.

THE LONDON PUBLIC LIBRARY, c. 1920
Inheriting its initial volumes from the defunct Mechanics' Institute, the London Public Library was opened in a new building (pictured) constructed at the corner of Queens Avenue and Wellington Street in 1895.

Evangelism" had profited her mightily in Los Angeles.

Many Londoners in search of profit "without benefit of clergy" were playing the stock market. "Margin buying" was the name of the game. An investor borrows money to buy stocks and then puts up the stock as collateral for the loan. If the stocks rise, the investor may collect gains quickly. If they go down, he has to raise more cash to cover his investment. It's a socially-acceptable form of gambling, very popular with the middle class.

The castles in Spain proved to be built on quicksand. The disastrous slide in stock prices, which started on Thursday, 5 September 1929, hit bottom on "Black Tuesday," 29 October, when sixteen million shares were traded on Wall Street and losses reached billions of dollars.

The collapse was complete. The American economy went into a sharp decline, dragging most of the economies of the western world along with it. The depression that followed — the Great Depression — was the longest and the most severe in North American history.

There were still a few Londoners around who remembered the savage depression of the 1850s. The parents of 1859 passed on well the lesson of those wicked times to their children and their children's children. It was lodged deep in London's community consciousness. As a result, the city emerged from the suffering of the Dirty Thirties in better financial condition than any other Canadian municipality.

The above statement must be examined more carefully. It applies to the overall picture, but not to specifics. The members of the financial establishment came out of the trauma of those years relatively unscathed. The middle classes endured much hardship; all were forced to retreat to a lower standard of living, some were wiped out. The poor, the single unemployed, and the unemployables suffered with great intensity.

London's city council, like most municipal governments in Canada, was ill-prepared for the relief efforts required of them in the Depression. A Welfare Committee and several special committees were set up to control relief efforts. The members of the committees were mainly city councillors and representatives from London businesses — an arrangement that attracted heavy criticism from provincial welfare minister David Croll who said the London Welfare Committee was too tightly tied to city council. Along with the Welfare Committee, the city hired a number of full time relief workers to investigate the cases and administer the relief. They started small with a staff of only three, but as the Depression increased in intensity, so too did the demands on the city welfare office. By 1935 there were 38 full-time workers.

Record-keeping not being what it is today, it is difficult to determine exactly how many Londoners received relief. The numbers which follow should be looked at as rough guides. They do not include the countless people who applied for, but were refused relief for whatever reason, people being supported by relatives, and people living off their savings. In 1930, 1,620 were on relief, or 2.3% of the population. In 1931, the number had jumped to 2,730. By January, 1932, the number of people on relief had nearly doubled to 5,108. March, 1932 saw the number doubled again to 11,455. From 1933 through 1936, the number hovered between 8,500 and 11,000.

1928
The first Walt Disney "Mickey Mouse" film produced.

1932 HIGH SCHOOL HOCKEY CHAMPS
On February 5, 1932, this scrappy bunch from London Technical and Commercial High School soundly defeated cross-town rivals South Collegiate by a 5 to 0 spread to capture the city title. Left to right: Bud Ray, goal; Norm Putherbough, defense; James H. Brown, coach; Bordy Armstrong, wing; Burn Chalmers, defense; Clare Hodgins, wing; Mr. Riddel, Les Thomas, substitute; Bill Westhead, centre.

The city had to scramble to feed, clothe, and house this new burden. As a result, the relief payments were paltry, and when possible the welfare office gave out vouchers for food, rather than money. The city followed the provincial guidelines for food payments per week, which, even by the standards of the 1930s was meagre fare:

    1 person — $1.50
    2 people — $2.45
    3 people — $3.35
    10 people — $8.25

Food was, by far, the city's greatest expenditure. Yet, the welfare office also gave out coal for fuel, clothing, and at times helped families make their rent payments.

In those days before the large-scale welfare systems were in place, qualifying for relief was quite an ordeal. The city put many restrictions on who could receive assistance and who could not. The Welfare Committee's attitude was that people should not be getting welfare unless they were the poorest of the poor, and everything of even minimal value had been pawned off. So, welfare recipients in London were not permitted to own a telephone, or a car, or even own a driver's license. Single mothers had a particularly rough time applying for help. The London city welfare workers had a policy of telling women who had been deserted by their husbands that they had to sue their husbands for non-support before they could get help from the city. This practice ended, however, in 1936, after the Civil Liberties Association of London lodged a complaint against the Welfare Committee, saying it was humiliating for the woman and caused problems within families.

Besides the regular relief payments, the city was involved in a number of special employment projects, partly financed by the province. The Farm Placement Scheme sent single men onto farms to work for $5-10.00

1929
St. Valentine's Day massacre: 6 gangsters die in Chicago.

a month, plus room and board. This, however, was not particularly popular, especially among the industrial workers. Similarly, the Y.W.C.A. Domestic Training Program was mostly passed over by unemployed women, mainly because of the long hours and low pay. Many of the men opted to work at the Department of National Defence labour camps located outside the city.

For families who wished to stay together, there were few options aside from direct relief. There was one program for the adventurous, however, the Relief Land Settlement Scheme. Over two dozen London families were sent to Hearst, in rocky northern Ontario, to start farms. These settlers were essentially "homesteading," for they usually had to clear their own land and build log cabins. Not surprisingly, this was not a successful enterprise. The seeds they were given wouldn't grow, and they had little more than garden tools with which to work the land. The Welfare Committee received a number of letters of complaint from frustrated, hungry Londoners stuck in Hearst with no way to get back. Wrote Mrs. Corbin, one of the unlucky settlers:

> When I wrote to you a few months ago I gave you a good account but I was a bit too hasty, things are not so good now. To start with I do not see how we are going to make a living. There is absolutely no market in Hearst or any farmers in their own district, even the bank in Hearst is closing up, as are two grocery stores. That will leave only one so we cannot trade with them. We came here to try and make ourselves independent, but we will be worse off than before, and we are not satisfied at the way we are treated. Our supplies are bought from Eaton's at the cheapest rate they can get, which is all right, but Eaton's sends mostly old stock. There are several people here complaining about the food. Some of it could not be used at all, and our children cannot get any milk which they need, and we cannot get medical attention. I would like to know if there is anything you can do to help us get our children back and we will get back the best way we can. If not, we are going to take the children and start out to walk back. There are several people here who want to get back as there is no use staying here. Hoping you will answer this letter and thank you very much.

Most of these measures the city Welfare Committee took seem draconian to us, even in this day and age when complaints about "welfare bums" are frequent. Yet, it must be remembered that the Depression of the 1930s was before the era of the "welfare state" and the city simply didn't have enough money to help everyone who got caught by the ravages of the economic cycle.

For thousands, staying with their families and attempting to collect relief from the strapped city coffers was no longer an option. As a result, living tides of gaunt-faced men swept westward in summer, clinging by the thousands to wherever a handhold or a foothold offered on the freight trains, bound for harvest work in the wheatfields of the prairies — then ebbed again eastward as drought and despair reduced the western farmers to an equivalent state of indigent hopelessness.

By the mid-1930s the Canadian "dry bowl" was as bleak as the "dust bowl" of the United States, and the prevailing westerly winds were carrying tens of thousands of acres of prairie topsoil east to the sea. On a day in May 1934, night came to London at noon as the sun was blotted out

1931
Toronto's Maple Leaf Gardens is built.

by a mammoth cloud of dust on its way to fertilize the Atlantic Ocean. God alone knew how many Western Canadian farms went to sea that day.

Attempts to recapture the impossible dream of economic stability came from two main sources, both political. Governments on the municipal, provincial, and federal levels strove to ameliorate the sufferings of the middle and lower classes by legislative measures. These measures were more designed to avoid future suffering than to treat present injury. The legislation passed into law at that time — family allowances, old age pensions, unemployment insurance, and the like — proved of inestimable value to generations to come, but did little to assuage the deep wounds of the Depression years.

The second impetus to reform came from political parties not then in power. The politics of the left wing came into prominence at this time. The membership of the Communist Party reached its twentieth-century peak in the Depression period, attracting to its ranks many idealists of all ages and social backgrounds. The Canadian party was affiliated with the Third Communist International — the Comintern — founded in Moscow in 1919. For a time a member of the Comintern had his home in London, where he and his family lived under the constant surveillance of the RCMP.

The Communist Party, like all dissident groups, thrived on martyrdom and was aided greatly by the jailing of its leader Timothy (Tim) Buck, in 1931. This ill-judged action by the Conservative government of Prime Minister Richard Bedford Bennett played into the hands of the Canadian left wing. Small "l" liberals of all ages and classes reacted with anger to the government's use of the infamous Section 98 of the Criminal Code, which prohibited certain forms of public assembly.

Of the dissident political organizations that flourished in the dark thirties, only one made any lasting impact on the electorate. The Co-operative Commonwealth Federation, founded on Monday, 1 August 1932, under the leadership of the Reverend James Shaver Woodsworth, met with an immediate and favourable response across the nation. The party's Regina Manifesto of 1933 made a clear statement of socialist intent. The party attracted to itself interest from all groups striving for political and economic reform, from the old style Fabian socialists to the communists. In 1943, the CCF, as it came to be called, found it necessary to purge itself of its far-left supporters, if it were ever to achieve widespread public acceptance as a reform, and not a revolutionary, party. Early that year a meeting of the members of the Woodsworth CCF Club of London continued halfway through the night before a majority succeeded in ejecting from the Club four of its members, including the secretary-treasurer, for espousing, or appearing to espouse, communist principles.

The average Londoner cared little for these political efforts, some of which in time came to benefit him through the introduction of social and economic reforms. The really big news of 1934, so far as this hypothetical human statistic was concerned, consisted of two blockbuster stories — the birth of the Dionne quintuplets on Monday, 28 May, and the kidnapping of John Sackville Labatt, president of the Labatt brewery, on Tuesday, 14 August.

DOMINION PUBLIC BUILDING DECORATED FOR THE 1939 ROYAL TOUR
Intended as a public works project to help relieve unemployment figures during the Great Depression, the Dominion Public Building was erected in 1935-36 and replaced the city's inadequate post office built in 1858-60. Still standing at 457 Richmond Street, the imposing edifice is a striking example of the Art Deco influence.

1932
The Lindberg baby is kidnapped, later murdered.

The Labatt kidnapping and its confusing aftermath partially revealed the unsavoury underside of the Prohibition era. The kidnapping itself was bungled. Labatt was taken by his captors to a cottage in the Muskoka area. A note demanding a ransom of $150,000 was directed to the brewer's brother Hugh Labatt. The note was signed "Three-Fingered Abe." After three days the kidnappers apparently panicked and released John Labatt in Toronto.

The subsequent arrests and trials of five persons did little to clarify the issues. While public opinion has never been completely satisfied with the explanations given at that time, it is possible to draw some conclusions from the affair.

The two local breweries, Labatt's and Carling's, as well as the Hiram Walker Distillery at Windsor, were involved in a "rum-running" operation across the Detroit River. This is not to say that the three companies were themselves actively engaging in illegal activities, but their products certainly were being shipped in quantity over the international border by persons who may or may not have been employed by those companies.

The border traffic was controlled by an organized-crime syndicate in Detroit. The group had decreed a levy on each bottle or case transported across the river from Canada. This "tax" was to be paid, directly or indirectly, by the producing companies. Both Labatt's and Carling's had refused to pay or to allow it to be paid. The Labatt kidnapping was apparently a means to enforce compliance.

Overlooked by the media in 1934 was an earlier, and successful, kidnapping directed at the Carling Brewery. Overlooked, because it was never officially reported.

Charles A. Burns, Carling's president, was the man who had organized the tragic flight of the *Sir John Carling*. His home was at 835 Richmond Street, at the southwest corner of Richmond Street and College Avenue (now the Ambassador Apartments). The Detroit gang kidnapped one of the Burns children, a little handicapped girl, and held her for a ransom of $25,000. The ransom was paid, the child was returned to her parents, and the London public was none the wiser.

In September, 1934, labour leaders from London, Toronto, and London England paid tribute to the Tolpuddle Martyrs, the English farm workers who were banished for starting a trade union. The group made a pilgrimage to Siloam Cemetery in London Township where George Loveless, leader of the movement, is buried. The date marked the 100th anniversary of the banishment. In attendance were descendants of the men who settled in London. They included George Loveless, great grandson of George Loveless, Dr. O.I. Cunningham, J.W. Cunningham, and George Stanfield, grandsons of George Stanfield, and John Brine of St. Mary's, son of the martyr James Brine, along with Phillip and James Brine, grandsons. A representative from the British labour movement, John Marchbank, sprinkled some Dorsetshire earth on Loveless's grave.

By the mid-1930s everyone had become accustomed, perhaps inured is the better word, to the prolonged depression. Its effects were not all bad. People were driven in upon themselves and forced to rely on their own resources, for entertainment, for instance. The cinema and the ra-

1936
King George V dies; Edward VIII abdicates; King George VI becomes monarch.

*"Many victims were
crushed to death when the
decks and machinery
fell onto them."*

**THE WRECK OF THE
VICTORIA, MAY 24,
1881**

*The most frightful disaster
ever to befall London,
the wreck of the steamer
Victoria brought about
tremendous outrage.
Newspapers from across
the continent justly claimed
that the loss of 182 lives
could have been entirely
avoided if the boat had not
been overcrowded. This
lithograph, published in
June, 1881, by Hugh John-
ston, recreates the horror
of the tragedy.*

"British was the Empire on which the sun would never set. And, of course, 'the Maple Leaf, our emblem dear' would likewise be forever."

CIGAR BOX LABEL, c. 1900
At the turn of the century, London was Canada's second largest cigar manufacturing centre. Combining the romance attached to the expanding Canadian west with a young nation's rising feelings of patriotism, the London Cigar Company marketed the "Jack Canuck" brand to the smoking public.

LABATT BREWERY POSTER, c. 1895

Effective promotion has always been paramount in the brewing industry. In the mid-1890s, the Labatt Brewery distributed this handsomely lithographed poster across the country.

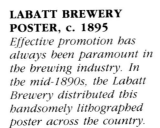

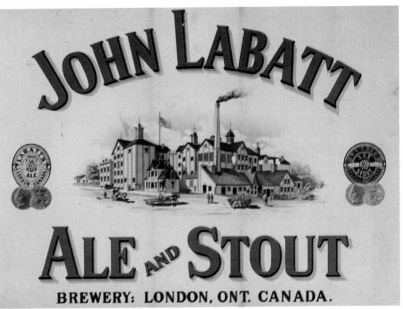

QUEEN VICTORIA, c. 1890

For most of the nineteenth century, Londoners fondly looked upon Queen Victoria as their beloved monarch. During her reign (1837-1901), London grew from a small frontier village to a thriving city commanding an entire region.

SPRINGBANK PARK, 1909
Acquired by the city in 1878, Springbank Park has charmed Londoners ever since. As this post-card view illustrates, "Merrymaking" at the park's pavilion was immensely popular with city residents during the Edwardian Era.

Merrymaking, Springbank Park, London, Can

". . . London had become a fully modern city, ready to take its place among Canada's Metropolitan centres."

McCORMICK'S N
BI
THE LARGEST, MOST MODERN AND MOS
"THE FACTORY IS PURE WHITE BOTH INSI
TERRA COTTA, AND ON THE

NEW HOME OF JERSEY CREAM SODAS AND HUNDREDS OF VARIET
THE McCORMICK MANUFA
LONDON, CA
BRANCH WAREHOUSES: MONTREAL   OTTAWA   HAMILTON   KINGSTO

POSTCARD VIEWS OF
LONDON, 1907
*The innocence that was
the Edwardian Era gave
rise to the postcard
rage. Street scenes were
especially popular with
Londoners who sent
postcard messages across
the entire continent. Note
the misspelt street name
in the lower card.*

Creig Street, South London, Ont. Canada.

NOW WHITE SUNSHINE
T AND CANDY FACTORY

ARY FACTORY OF ITS KIND IN AMERICA.

, FINISHED ON THE OUTSIDE WITH WHITE
WHITE ENAMEL AND TILE"

GH CLASS FANCY SWEET BISCUITS AND CANDY
G CO., LIMITED

CALGARY   ST. JOHN, N.B   PORT ARTHUR

**McCORMICK PLANT,
1156 DUNDAS ST. E.**
*When constructed in 1913,
this plant, central to
McCormick's operations,
was the largest confec-
tionery factory in Canada.
Thousands of windows lent
effect to the nick-name,
"The Sunshine Palace,"
bestowed upon the build-
ing, whose enamelled
exterior still gleams with
pride after eighty years.*

LONDON LIFE CALENDAR, 1914
With the first design appearing in the early 1890s, beautifully illustrated calendars were an advertising trademark of the London Life Insurance Company until well into the twentieth century. Such innovative promotion helped London Life grow to become one of the city's most enduring corporate enterprises.

"WHY! IT'S ME"

London Life Insurance Co.
London, Canada
POLICIES "GOOD AS GOLD"

1914

TOURIST BROCHURE, c. 1925
Port Stanley, billed as "the most popular and complete summer resort on Lake Erie's north shore", was a favourite with Londoners during the "Roaring '20s". Colourful brochures invited the pleasure-seeker to enjoy the village's sandy beaches by day, and dance to the latest big band sounds into the night.

"During the 1920's, London lived up to its reputation as the biggest small town in Canada."

KITCHENWARE ADVERTISEMENT, 1927
Famous for its line of heavy appliances, the McClary Manufacturing Company also found success producing very durable kitchenware. As this advertisement suggests, McClary's "Bonnie Blue" cook-set was an ideal gift for the bride-to-be.

"Innovation has marked the city's industrial efforts."

HUNT CLUB ORANGE

Silverwood Dairies, Limited

MINIMUM CONTENTS 30 FLUID OUNCES

SOFT DRINK LABEL, 1938

Though noted for its milk and creamery products, in 1938, the London-based Silverwood Dairies expanded into the soft drink business. Under the "Hunt Club" label, the dairy produced orange pop, dry ginger ale, and lime rickey. Second World War sugar restrictions, however, abruptly ended this venture.

SUPERTEST GAS STATION, c. 1935
Growing from small beginnings as a single gasoline depot established in the early 1920s, the Supertest Petroleum Corporation, based in London, was among the largest independent fuel companies in Ontario. Pride in Canadian ownership was often reflected in the company's advertising.

dio, as the wireless was now called, provided cheap amusement. The ornate picture palaces allowed all but the very poorest among us to pretend, briefly, that we "dwelt in marble halls," sipped champagne, and supped on caviar. The Gothic designs of such radio sets as the popular Philco helped us to dream that we lived amid medieval splendour as we listened to the clowns of the twentieth-century royal courts — Jack Benny, Fred Allen, and Abe Burrows.

As the people of London struggled through the economic strictures of the Depression era, the future appeared to be an uncharted wilderness, with little hope of change. Only the past was certain. In this atmosphere local history came into its own. Nostalgia became organized. The London and Middlesex Historical Society had dwindled into obscurity as senility and death overtook its members. In 1936, a year that saw the Art Deco Dominion Public Building erected at the intersection of Richmond Street and Queens Avenue and a new Canadian National Railway station opened, was also marked by the reorganization and revitalization of the historical society. The people involved were Dr. Edwin Seaborn, Fred Landon, and Orlo Miller. These three men were responsible for uncovering an immense mass of documentary material, long considered lost, in Middlesex, Huron, Norfolk, and Elgin counties. These discoveries made possible a whole new approach to the social history of southwestern Ontario, based on contemporary records.

The dramatic history of the past was overtaken by the even more dramatic history of the twentieth century, when the tortured Thames River once more revenged itself on its tormenters. Heavy spring rains, falling on a still-frozen watershed, filled creeks and rivers to overflowing. In the late afternoon of Monday, 26 April 1937, floodwaters twenty-three feet (7m) above normal levels poured over the breakwater above the forks. With both north and south branches of the river in flood, all of London West, as well as low-lying sections to the north and south, was inundated. One life was lost and some thousand houses damaged. Total losses were

1938
Orson Welles' radio production "War of the Worlds" causes widespread panic.

THE FLOOD OF 1937

Rising 23 feet above its normal level, on April 26 and 27, 1937, the Thames River once again reminded Londoners of its wrath. The torrent left one fatality, damage to about 1,000 houses, and nearly $1,000,000 in losses. Here we see the havoc the Thames played in front of E.G. Nichols' grocery at the corner of Blackfriars and Napier Streets.

estimated at slightly less than one million Depression dollars.

In spite of this renewed reminder of the power of the river and warnings from environmentalists like Edward G. Pleva, University of Western Ontario geographer, it took ten years and another flood threat (in 1947) before any practical steps were taken to control the capricious Thames.

As the bad times went on and on, London's poor and unemployed suffered ever more intensely. The long struggle against crushing odds took its toll on the mental and moral as well as the physical health of the victims. The most devastating effect was the loss of self-esteem. This in turn led to a decline in personal morals and a blurring of ethical standards generally.

An experiment in what would now be called "workfare" was launched at this time by the city administration, the university, and the London and Middlesex Historical Society, acting cooperatively. A number of men were on the city's welfare rolls, who had had previous clerical experience, were given an opportunity to "work out" their welfare cheques and make a little cash in addition by helping the Historical Society to sort and index some of the thousands of documents found in an attic at the Middlesex Courthouse. The University and the Society between them provided the funds to employ a director for the project, Orlo Miller, who was paid the Depression wage of fifty cents an hour.

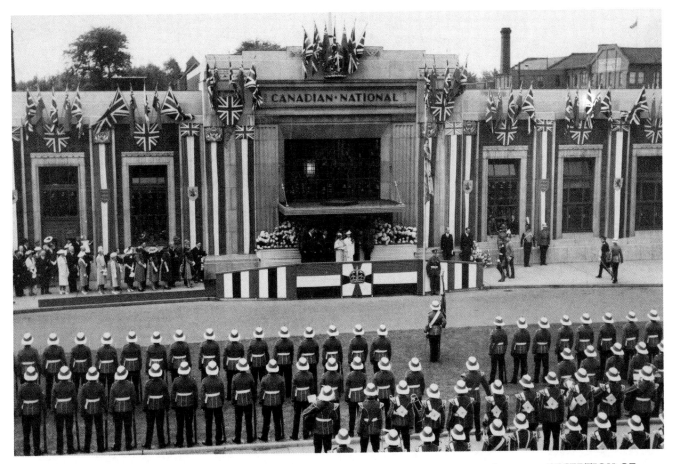

The outbreak of the Second World War gradually brought an end to the endeavour, but the indices are today a useful research tool in the Regional Collection of the D.B. Weldon Library.

On Wednesday, 7 June 1939, the city, no stranger to royal tourists, greeted its most important visitors of all — His Majesty King George VI and Her Majesty Queen Elizabeth. They were given an ecstatic welcome by an estimated 300,000 persons.

Many of those who lined Richmond Street in front of the offices of the London *Free Press* to see the royal cortege had stood at the same spot two and a half years earlier to listen to the abdication speech of King Edward VIII over the newspaper's radio station, now bearing the call letters CFPL.

On Sunday, 3 September 1939, Britain and France declared war on Germany. A week later, Canada followed suit. For the second time in a generation, the youth of Canada were offered up as a sacrifice on the altar of freedom.

Compared to the euphoria that gripped the city in August 1914, London's mood was sombre.

RECEPTION OF THE ROYAL VISIT, 1939
On Wednesday, June 7, 1939, London beamed with pride and graciously welcomed King George VI and Queen Elizabeth [now the Queen Mother] as its honoured guests at the recently completed Canadian National station on York Street. The visit, the first by reigning British monarchs, drew 300,000 well-wishers from across the region.

1939
World War II begins with German invasion of Poland, Sept. 1st.

CHAPTER ELEVEN

Growing Pains

Canadians who can think back to the Great War will recall the amazing difference in the reception of the news of the two conflicts. In 1914 Great Britain had not been engaged in a major struggle for over one hundred years. There had been so many years of peace that the world had come to believe that a war on a large scale was almost impossible. Only a few people imagined that Great Britain and Germany would come to blows — they were regarded as pure jingoists. ...

There are no illusions today as to what war means. Canada is just as determined and patriotic as in 1914, but Canadians of 1939 know the horrors of war. It is a more serious Canada which faces this crisis. ...
— Arthur R. Ford in "Over the Week End,"
London *Free Press*, 4 September, 1939.

At the beginning of the Second World War London was still recognizably the city to which the veterans of the First World War had returned. The corner of Dundas and Richmond streets was still the commercial hub, and the Smallman and Ingram department store still dominated the intersection. The cottage in which Sir James Alexander and his talented wife lived in the 1840s stood where it had for at least a century, at the southeast corner of Richmond and Horton streets, north of the frame house in which the artist Paul Peel was born in 1860.

Socially, London was still the tight little community where, it was said, "everyone knew everyone else," which was hyperbole, and "everyone knew his place," which was not. The lines between the classes, which had been established after the American Civil War and the oil boom, remained firm. Membership in the Establishment was based on money, rather than church affiliation, as it had been earlier. There were two kinds of money — Old Money and New Money. Socially, the Old Money tended to practise philanthropy; the New Money practised expansion and development, which was called "progress."

The most visible minority continued as before to be the black population, who retained significant presence in the community. Canada's only black newspaper, *The Dawn of Tomorrow* was published here by the Jenkins family. Started in 1921 by James Jenkins, with the help of the black business community and Walter Blackburn of the London *Free Press*, the paper continued to be published in the 1990s.

The invisible minority — London's Jewish community — continued

KING STREET, c. 1952
Looking east from Talbot, this stretch of King Street, like much of London, was forever to change during the 1950s. A new market and parking building replaced the old market hall (to the left) in 1956, and shortly after, the street was widened to accommodate increasing amounts of automobile traffic.

1940
Lascaux caves discovered in France: prehistoric wall paintings approx. 20,000 BC.

LONDON AIRPORT, JANUARY 23, 1941
Constructed near the tiny crossroads of Crumlin, the London Airport was officially opened by C.D. Howe, the federal minister of munitions and supply, in June of 1940. Rebuilt in 1965, and still serving the city, passenger service at the airport was inaugurated two months after its opening.

1941
Women's divisions of Army and RCAF established.

to be respected in business and finance, but socially proscribed. Membership in the London Club, the London Hunt and Country Club, and the private golf courses continued to be the exclusive privilege of the city's accredited Gentiles.

One "club" where everyone was welcome, regardless of ethnicity, was the new Elsie Perrin Williams Memorial Library, built in 1940. Funded through a bequest from Elsie Perrin Williams, heiress to the Perrin Biscuit fortune, the new library on Queens Avenue also housed the London Art Gallery for many years. In 1942, another bequest from a London woman, Wilhelmina McIntosh, led to the opening of the McIntosh Art Gallery on the campus of the University of Western Ontario. The Hume Cronyn Observatory also opened at the university in the early years of the war.

Economically and physically London had stagnated during the years of the Depression. Since the major annexations at the turn of the century, there had been only small changes in the city's boundaries. In the ten-year period ending in 1940, the population had grown by a little more than 5,000. Indeed, between 1937 and 1939 London actually lost 325 people, entering the first year of the war with a population of 76,099.

Income-tax statistics showed that London had many wealthy citizens, but records of bank clearings indicated little movement of entrenched capital. In 1925 the figure for the year was $136,640,609; in 1940 it was $137,393,049 — an increase of a little more than one half of 1 per cent.

All this changed in the six long years of the most terrible war in human history, but the changes were slow and subtle. The world was on fire, but the conflagration was too immense for comprehension. Today's students know far more about what happened in the Second World War than the civilians who lived through it. Tight censorship prevented the average Londoner from knowing how close to home it all was. The Holocaust was not even a rumour here, but there were families in London who lost relatives to Hitler's ovens. The war in the Pacific seemed far off, yet Japanese-Canadians were interned as though they were active enemies

THE CANADIAN BANK OF COMMERCE, 1942
Constructed in 1905, and reflecting a liberal inerpretation of classic Greek architecture, the Canadian Bank of Commerce building firmly stood at the northeast corner of Dundas and Richmond Streets for nearly fifty years. The stability offered by such solid financial institutions helped cushion the Great Depression's effects on London.

of the Canadian state. The war at sea reached Canadian territory on both the east and west coasts.

In spite of the fact that the Second World War was longer, bloodier, and deadlier than the First, the effect of the conflict on London and Londoners was very different. The hysteria of the First War was missing. There were thousands of soldiers moving in and out of London; airmen of many Allied nations received their training at bases in and around the city; there were casualty lists and rationing — but in the main these things were taken in stride. People no longer believed everything they heard or read; the media reported to an audience that was more sophisticated, more cynical.

Perhaps a measure of this sophistication can be found in Londoners' practical responses to the calamity. Citizens rallied to the cause on a scale never known before. One area that received considerable effort was civil defence. The Canadian government warned people that attacks by air on southwestern Ontario were a possibilty, and they should be ready in case it happened. So, over 1,000 Londoners aligned themselves with the Civilian Defence Committee (CDC), which provided civilians training in firefighting, police work and first aid. Beginning in 1943, the CDC staged a number of mandatory "blackouts" and air warning tests. Newspapers ran these instructions on what people should do in the event an air raid siren began to wail:

1) All persons shall immediately take cover.
2) All street lights shall be extinguished.
3) All lights of every kind, both indoor and outdoor, of occupied, unoccupied, or untenanted premises shall be extinguished except those behind adequate shades so that light is not permitted to be seen from outside.
4) All lights on outdoor signs of every kind shall be extinguished.
5) All buses shall be stopped and their light extinguished; all other vehicles, including motor cars, motorcycles, horse-drawn vehicles and bicycles, shall be driven to the right-hand curb or right-hand side of the roadway and in rural municipalities shall be driven off the travelled part of the highway, stopped and their lights extinguished.

1942
Persons of Japanese origin on West Coast are relocated to interior camps.

CWACs PARADE, DUNDAS STREET, 1943
Hundreds of London and area women expressed their support for the Allied effort in the Second World War by joining the city's detachment of the Canadian Women's Auxiliary Corps. Though they never saw combat, these women served with dignity and honour in war-torn Europe.

1944
Nearly 30,000 Canadian troops take part in the D-Day invasion of Normandy.

Not all of these mock air raids, were taken seriously by the public. A London *Free Press* account the first half-hour "blackout" on May 31, 1943 suggests that war-weary Londoners took the opportunity to have a little fun during the exercise. "London's Crowds Turn Blackout Into Carnival of Songs, Merry-Making," ran the headline. It continued:

> ...The downtown crowds passed the blackout period in varied ways. Those on roof-tops shouted at those on the ground, and those on the street level yelled back. Full advantage of the darkness was taken by many members of the younger generation and authorities refused to give even a conservative estimate of the amount of "woo" that was pitched between 9:45 and 10:15 pm. ... For the first 15 minutes the CDC injunctions against smoking were generally obeyed by the merry-makers, but toward the end of the period glowing cigarettes and flaring matches cast pools of light on the pavements, making perfect targets for hypothetical bombs.

Perhaps the most energetic and dedicated contributors to the war effort were women. Women played their part in a number of ways: by volunteering for active service, by working in London's war materials factories, and by serving in the countless local volunteer organizations.

World War II marked the first time that women were organized into separate military units. Most of the women went into what would be called support services — clerical work, food services, technical assistance, driving ambulances and supply vehicles. Although they did not have combat roles, the women were, nevertheless, often quite close to the front lines. London's first office for the Canadian Women's Army Corps (CWAC) opened on September 1, 1941, and Helen Brownlee became the first woman to enlist. She went overseas in 1942, and later followed the male soldiers after they landed on the beaches of Normandy on D-Day. Said Brownlee in an interview with the *Free Press* after she returned:

> When we first went to the continent we were three-quarters of a mile from the front line, but that was a mistake and we were moved back. We were with the Second Echelon, Montgomery's headquarters, and were known as the 'ten-mile snipers'.

The first CWAC officer at the London division, Second Lieutenant Margaret Newman, said of the female soldiers: "The girls are of all the same mind. Everyone would like to go overseas." Hundreds of London and area women did make it overseas, and their active participation in the war, although often overlooked, was certainly a factor in the conflict's outcome.

London also had its own versions of the American "Rosie the Riveter." As the city's male factory workers left to enlist, their places were taken by hundreds of young (and not so young) women, who received crash courses in putting together airplane parts and other war materials. Some of the factories making war materials that employed large numbers of women were General Steel Wares Plant, Sparton of Canada Ltd., Webster Air Equipment Company, and the E. Leonard factory, by then London's oldest.

London women also took part in the war effort by performing thousands of hours of volunteer work. The Local Council of Women coordinated much of this work by setting up the Central Volunteer Bureau, which matched potential volunteers with appropriate organizations. Many of these women's groups worked closely with the Red Cross and St. John's Ambulance, providing food, medical supplies, clothing and bedding to be sent overseas. In the course of the war, London women knitted thousands of socks and turtleneck sweaters, sewed hundreds of miles of sheets and pillowcases, rolled endless strips of bandages, and put together countless numbers of "ditty bags" — cloth bags filled with such goodies as soap, socks, combs, and razors for the soldiers. Besides the Local Council of Women, other women's groups that helped in this area were the Imperial Order of Daughters of the Empire, Hadassah (Jewish women's club), Catholic Women's League, Home and School Associations, the YWCA, and any number of church groups.

Providing recreation for the soldiers stationed in town was another activity to which London women gave their time. On December 7, 1940, the Active Service Club opened its doors to the young men who wanted some light-hearted diversions before being sent to the unknown dangers overseas. There to entertain the new recruits were young women who had been trained as "hostesses" by the YWCA. This course, taken by hundreds of London women, was held at the London Life building and the old public library building on Wellington Street. A questionnaire given to all the graduates of the course reveals some of the duties that these hostesses were expected to perform:

> What age group are you in? — 18-21, 22-25, 26-30, or 30 or over — Occupation? — Do you play piano a) for community singing b) for dancing? — Can you call off square dances? Can you lead a conga line or coke-oke? — Can you square dance? — Can you folk dance? — If not, would you like to learn? — Do you play ping pong well? — Do you play any musical instruments? — If so, what? — Do you play bridge? — Would you like instructions in social dancing? — Have you any special ability? — If so, what? Are you doing any other war work? — If so, what? — Are you willing to do canteen work? —

GUY LOMBARDO
Born in 1902, Londoner Guy Lombardo gave his first concert in 1914. By 1920, he was headlining at London's Winter Gardens and the Port Stanley pavilion. An established reputation carried him to the ballroom glitter of New York City, where he and his Royal Canadians became world famous for their New Year's Eve performances of "Auld Lange Syne". He died in 1977.

1945
US drops atomic bombs on Hiroshima and Nagasaki.

HUME CRONYN, 1944

No other Londoner can match the acting accomplishments of Hume Cronyn, the great-grandson of Bishop Cronyn. Born on July 18, 1911, he began on the stage, and found later success in Hollywood. Nominated for an Oscar for his performance in 1944's The Seventh Cross, *Hume Cronyn currently lives in New York where he is married to actress Jessica Tandy.*

1945

Xerography process invented by Chester Carlson.

Are you willing to abide by the regulations? — Has this course been any help to you? — Would you suggest any changes? — If so, what? — Can you dance once a week? — If not, how often?

One thing they were not expected to do, however, was leave the Active Service Club with any of the soldiers. In fact, it was repeatedly stressed that the hostess program was not a ''dating bureau.''

These were some of the things that London women did to support Canada's war effort. Yet, as F. Beatrice Taylor said in an article in the *Free Press*:

> ... it is not possible to give in figures, or even in words, any concept of the faithful and often inspired effort which has marked the participation of London women in the struggle of the long years of war, an effort multiplied a thousandfold across the Dominion.

On Tuesday, 6 June 1944 — D-Day — Allied forces landed on the beaches of Normandy, and the push toward Berlin was on. Eleven months later, Germany surrendered. The articles of peace in Europe were signed on Tuesday, 8 May 1945, and cheering mobs went mad in all the major cities of the western world. A new phenomenon presented itself. It might be called ''victory vandalism.'' Celebrants turned to violence and the destruction of property as a way of expressing their feelings. London escaped the vandals; Halifax did not.

With the change in the fortunes of the war the media began to direct the attention of their audiences to the technological marvels that were to emerge from the womb of war. It is no coincidence that the years of the Second World War marked the rise to popularity of science fiction, in which the scientific developments of the day were extrapolated into the wonders of tomorrow.

The prophecies achieved substance very quickly. A terrifying catalyst speeded up the technological machines. The atomic-bombing of Hiroshima and Nagasaki opened the gates of hell to the stunned gaze of a world that would never again know the benefits of an easy conscience.

However great the impact of these technical discoveries proved to be, post-war London was faced with the more immediate task of re-integrating returned soldiers into society. Education proved to be a priority for many. The Department of Veterans Affairs paid tuition for any returned soldier who wished to enter university, and the University of Western Ontario was swamped with applications. In 1945, Western accepted 700 first year students — many of whom were returning soldiers — compared to a total of 297 new students the year before. Even though space was limited, the university decided that it would not turn down any returned soldier, and made do by holding classes at night, and at other city locations. Despite the initial hardships, Western seemed to benefit generally by this forced expansion. Many new professional schools were added in the post-war years, and Western's sports program grew by leaps and bounds. Legendary Johnny ''the Bull'' Metras was coach of the football Mustangs, and between 1945 and 1959 they won nine league championships. Women's sports, too, benefited by the expanded facilities, and the swimming team under the direction of Mrs. H.H. McKellar won wide acclaim.

**DUNDAS STREET,
VE DAY**
*Upon news of
Germany's surrender,
on May 8, 1945,
Londoners staged the
largest spontaneous
celebration in the
city's history. That
day, Dundas Street
was quickly filled
with a relieved
majority of London's
citizenry. With
Japan's defeat three
months later, a new
era was christened.*

BOYS' BAND, 1946
*Smiles were all
around when the
London Police Boys'
Band posed for the
camera on May 4,
1946.*

INTERIOR OF THE WOLCOTT SHOE COMPANY, JUNE 6, 1952
Founded in the late 1940s, the Wolcott Shoe Company, Limited, at 285 Ashland Avenue, was representative of the dozens of medium-scale manufacturing industries that located in post-war East London.

1947
Paris designer Christian Dior introduces the "New Look" in women's fashion.

Finding housing for the returned veterans and their quickly-growing families was another problem for the city. The London *Free Press* reported that, in 1947, approximately one in six returned soldiers did not have his own place to live. After some minor complications, the city expropriated some land north of Oxford Street East and built London's first subdivision for veterans. Named "Bellwood Park" by Mayor Fred McAlister for City Treasurer James Bell, who had served the city for sixty-one years, the housing development contained 186 new, modestly-sized homes. These were sold to veterans for from $6,750 to $8,600.

Medically, the soldiers' needs were met by Westminster Hospital, built after World War I, in 1920, at the southeast corner of Commissioners and Wellington Roads. Serving all of southwestern Ontario, this Department of Veterans' Affairs hospital provided rehabilitation and treatment for those injured overseas. Some were treated and released. Others, sadly, went to Westminster soon after coming home, and are there to this day, along with a very few still surviving Great War vets. It was here, in the post-war years, that London artist Selwyn Dewdney and his wife Irene pioneered the use of art therapy in Canada.

The physical and social face of London began to change, slowly at first. The city's street cars were discontinued early in the war. Their rails were ripped up and the steel was directed to Canada's war effort. Gasoline-powered omnibuses came into service, more efficient and more flexible than street cars, but lacking the charm. There was a camaraderie in the electric trolleys that has largely disappeared in the business-like buses. No one who ever rode the tiny "Toonerville Trolleys" of the North Belt Line will forget those monstrous little machines. The roadbed on Cheapside Street was an ill-kept one, and the little carriage or trolley that fed

electricity to the cars would often bounce off the overhead wires. Usually the motorman or the conductor would manoeuvre the trolley or troller back on to the wire with a long stick; sometimes one of the passengers would be allowed to do it.

That was all a very long time ago, of course. In the last days of the trolley service the street cars were long, large affairs running smoothly on fine steel rails on a well-maintained roadbed, but they still retained much of the old neighbourhood feeling. Despite the improvements in equipment and service, fewer people were travelling by public transit. The automobile became the acceptable mode of moving from place to place for anyone who could afford one. Businessmen took to driving the family car to work, and little by little rush-hour traffic, morning, noon, and night, came to consist of a mass of automobiles, each often with only a single person inside — the driver. During the war "car pools" became the accepted thing, but we were all anxious to get back to our own chariots, our own enclosed space.

On December 14, 1946, London city council marked the ascendence of the automobile age by installing the first 500 parking meters downtown, on a trial basis. Apparently, the trial was successful, as the ubiquitous meters are still the bane of every downtown driver's existence.

A by-product of this changing pattern was the increasing isolation of the middle and the Establishment classes from their environment. A move to the suburbs by those people began long before. Now the businessman and the industrialist moved between his house and his office in the privacy of his mobile carapace without coming into contact with the residents, permanent or temporary, of the core area. He did not meet them; therefore, for him, they did not exist.

Being thus insulated from reality, such people became increasingly difficult to convince of the existence of poverty and deprivation in London. On occasion they or their wives might shop in one of the prestigious luxury businesses on Dundas or Richmond streets without being aware that above the brilliantly-lighted storefronts, rabbit warrens of tiny drab rooms and sleazy apartments housed another London population of alco-

OXFORD AND RICHMOND STREETS, c. 1959
As evident in the photograph, this intersection has undergone considerable change in almost forty years. By the 1950s, the automobile had become an inseparable part of Canadian life. Note the many signs advertising products that are still familiar today.

1948
Mackenzie King resigns; Louis St. Laurent becomes Prime Minister.

HAMILTON ROAD DOMINION STORE, MARCH 2, 1941
Arriving in London in the early 1920s, the Dominion Stores supermarket chain was one of several national syndicates that guaranteed the demise of the neighbourhood grocery stores. Though a few independent groceries managed to survive into the 1960s, by the early 1950s, it was clear that they were a vanishing breed.

1949
Communist Peoples Republic takes over China under Chairman Mao Tse-tung and Premier Chou-Enlai.

holics, dope-users, drifters, prostitutes, and just plain poor people. The affluent Londoner picking out a gift of jewellery, lingerie, or furs for his wife or girlfriend would have been horrified to learn that the employees of the premises who put out the firm's garbage at night at the back of the building had best be equipped with a piece of wood or similar weapon to drive off the rats that had infested the downtown area for generations.

In this, of course, London differs scarcely at all from any North American community of more than village status. But Londoners have generally preferred not to know of such conditions.

There have been exceptions to this purblind insularity. Many such exceptions have come from the old established families — the Carlings, Labatts, Cronyns, Bechers, and others. The late Edward E. Reid, vice-president and managing director of the London Life Insurance Company, used to walk daily to and from work from his home, as also did J. Allyn Taylor, the then-president of the Canada Trust Company. The late Colonel J. Innes Carling, descendent of Sir John, used to do likewise, as did the Ingrams (Gordon J. and Kenneth H.) of the Smallman and Ingram Department Store. So did Walter J. Blackburn as a young man in the forties. These men and others like them knew their city in all its aspects, good and bad.

One of the first casualties of the war years in the business field was the long-established department store Smallman and Ingram. Perhaps there were no interested family members prepared to carry on the tradition. For a time the controlling shares were held by U.W.O. under a Smallman family bequest. Eventually the firm received an offer it could not refuse and the store was taken over in 1944 by the Robert Simpson Company of Toronto. Although this was a Hogtown takeover, local people could derive some satisfaction from the fact that the Burton family who controlled Simpson's had relatives in London and the surrounding area.

This was the first of the major changes to affect the London business community. Other changes in the immediate post-war years came more slowly and more subtly. A feature of London's business life for more than a century began to disappear — the independent grocery store. The Great

Atlantic and Pacific Tea Company (A & P) was among the first of the big grocery chains to enter the competition for the shopper's dollar. Loblaw's, Dominion Stores, and Red and White stores quickly followed. In an effort to match the bulk buying-power of the big chains, many of the independents formed a cooperative organization, the Independent Grocers Association (IGA). The number of autonomous corner-grocery ventures steadily declined. In later years they metamorphosed into the so-called "convenience" or "variety" stores, many of which in their turn have been gobbled up by chains like Mac's Milk, Becker's or Seven-Eleven.

In the past London had had little in the way of heavy industry aside from the two foundries, McClary's and Leonard's. The Leonard foundry eventually closed (the London *Free Press* building now stands on the site of the foundry), and McClarys became General Steel Wares Limited. In 1950 the Diesel Division of General Motors of Canada located in London, on Oxford Street East, to engage in the glamorous business of building diesel-locomotive engines and the not-so glamourous business of producing tanks and other military vehicles for use in Canada and abroad. Another major industry that came to London in 1952 was the Minnesota Mining and Manufacturing Company (3M).

Romantics among us deplored the passing of the hugely beautiful steam railway locomotives and their never-to-be-forgotten whistles, whose mournful wail represented for generations the magic of travel and the lure of a world beyond. The raucous hoot of the diesel horn can never elicit the same nostalgia or evoke the dreams of Xanadu. One locomotive remains as a monument outside Western Fair Grounds on Dundas Street.

The diesels, they said, were more efficient. Efficiency became the new god of the market-place. While atomic energy was efficient as a killing device, scientists were quick to point out the peaceable uses of atomic power, in medicine and in the production of electrical energy.

It was in medicine that Londoners first saw the new energy source demonstrated. It had early been discovered that certain by-products of the atomic-bomb experiment could be useful in treatment of some forms of cancer. A radioactive isotope of cobalt was used in what the media dubbed the "cobalt bomb." The cancer clinic at London's Victoria Hospital installed one of the new treatment contrivances. Under the direction of the late Doctor Ivan H. Smith the clinic became famous throughout North and South America for its advanced method of treatment.

In fact it is in the field of medicine that London has long occupied a pre-eminent position among the cities of the western hemisphere. For instance, Doctor George Edward Hall, of the Royal Canadian Air Force, carried out special research in aviation medicine at the University of Western Ontario that earned him decorations from the Canadian and American governments. Dr. Hall's pioneering study on the effects of gravity on the human body led to the development of "pressure suits" basic to the future of aeronautics and astronautics. In this work Dr. Hall was associated with the late Sir Frederick Banting, who was a lecturer at Western's medical school when he made his initial discovery of insulin in 1921; and also with the late Walter J. Blackburn, publisher of the London *Free Press*.

After the war Dr. Hall became dean of medicine at Western and, in

THE LONDON HUMANE SOCIETY TRUCK, SEPTEMBER 24, 1952
Established in 1912, the London Humane Society has been the city's leader in the field of animal welfare ever since. A new truck, purchased in 1952, greatly helped the organization's inspectors carry out the task of preventing cruelty to animals.

1950
Antihistamines become popular remedy for colds.

JOHNNY P. METRAS, 1952
From 1940 to 1969, Johnny "The Bull" Metras coached the University of Western Ontario Mustangs to 119 victories, seven Yates Cups (Ontario title), and one Vanier Cup (national championship). Here we see Metras being hoisted in victory after shading the University of Toronto Blues 8 to 1 on November 15, 1952.

1951
J.D. Salinger publishes "The Catcher in the Rye."

1947, president and vice-chancellor. Under his direction the University, and especially its medical faculty, greatly enhanced its reputation. The medical school became one of the top institutions on the continent, in the same league as McGill and Harvard.

Another medical pioneer in London was Dr. Evan Shute, who, along with his brother Wilfrid, founded the world famous Shute Institute for the study of Vitamin E. Evan Shute began experimenting with Vitamin E in the 1930s, but later began studying broader applications — for treatment of diabetes, heart disease, and burns, for example. Reaction among Canada's medical community was negative, however, and Dr. Shute was forced to finance his work mainly on his own. In September, 1948, he bought the Morgan-Smallman mansion on Grand Avenue, or "Waverley" as it was commonly known, for use as a clinic. Cars of patients in the parking lot regularly had license plates from most provinces and several US points like Texas and California. His struggle for recognition and acceptance from the medical community continued for many years, but his research and the work at his clinic has proven invaluable to Vitamin E research today.

In 1947 the Thames River once again reminded London of its presence and its threat to life and property. It was Sunday, 5 April, when the unruly river came a-knocking at the door. For two days the flood waters lapped at the London West breakwaters as they had ten years earlier. Lon-

**"ROMPER ROOM",
1960**
*As an affiliate of the
Canadian Broadcast-
ing Corporation,
CFPL began televised
transmissions in
1953. One of the sta-
tion's most popular
and enduring
programmes was
"Romper Room", a
favourite with chil-
dren. Here we see
Constance Kensing-
ton, Mary Jane
Graham, and Billy
Paul receiving their
"Good Do Bee"
diplomas from Miss
Dorothy, the show's
hostess, on June 3,
1960.*

doners didn't need a house to fall in upon them — not quite. It had been ninety-six years since the first serious flood struck the city, in 1851.

Action was now taken, finally. The city moved with commendable speed. On Thursday, 8 April, a special meeting of city council authorized an expenditure of $134,999 for local flood-control measures. On Wednesday, 7 May, the Upper Thames Valley Conservation Authority was established at Woodstock. Their first meeting was held at Stratford on Monday, 20 October. The Fanshawe Dam on the north branch of the river was the first stage of the flood control system. It was opened in 1953.

1953 was also the year the television age was ushered into London. CFPL, then an affiliate of the Canadian Broadcasting Corporation, began broadcasting over channel 10 on November 28, 1953. The "baby boomers," children of the post-war period, became the first generation to be raised on the "boob tube."

1953 was a momentous year for another reason — the Local Council of Women succeeded in getting Margaret Fullerton, a former Central Collegiate teacher and London's first female alderman, elected to city council. Making sure that women were represented in municipal politics had long been a goal of the LCW. In 1949, they gave this goal an extra push when they organized a committee to nominate women to run for civic elections. "It is about time that London had more than one woman (Miss Evelyn Harrison, K.C., a member of the Board of Education) representing this city's 50,000 voters," said Mrs. F.E. Underhill, committee member. Their hard work paid off on election night in November, 1953. Said the *Free Press*: "More than 250 enthusiastic women from all parts of the city 'got behind and pushed' Mrs. Fullerton to victory in one of the most highly organized feminine campaigns London has ever experienced." Of course, several women had tried to break the male blockade before. One of the more colourful was Lucy Cole, who knew the growing labour political code well, from London East, who tried a number of times in the 1940s.

1952
*Popular song, "I
saw Mommy Kiss-
ing Santa Claus"
the hit of the
season.*

MARGARET FULLERTON, 1953
Margaret Fullerton rejoices after becoming London's first female city councillor. Sponsored by the Local Council of Women, her successful election in 1953 ushered in a new era of local politics.

1953
Hilary and Tenzing become the first to climb Mount Everest.

Although she never won, she occasionally came close, and certainly gave her opponents a run for their money.

A lesser-known political incident also occured in 1953 — a near-riot during a speech at the Masonic Temple by Dr. Hewlett Johnson, the so-called "Red Dean" of Canterbury. The "Red Dean," who obtained his nickname because of his socialist views, was invited to London by the London Soviet Friendship Committee, and the London Peace Congress, of which labour leader Arthur Mould was the chairman. In the year when the anti-Soviet paranoia of "McCarthyism" was coming to a head, the Dean's message that the Russians were decent people who did not want war, was unwelcome. As soon as he rose to speak, a group of people wearing "Western" sweaters and jackets jumped up and started clanging cowbells, bursting paper bags, and shouting. The Dean left the stage, saying "They are not quite adult in London." Ten years later, the *Free Press* reported:

> At the time, Western students were accused of starting the disturbance, and charge and counter-charge flew back and forth for days. At least one of the main ringleaders was not a student; he was an ex-paratrooper nicknamed "Airborne" Fairbairne who subsequently ran for city council.

Whoever the perpetrators, a few Londoners were disgusted by the display. Said Rev. George Goth of Metropolitan United Church, who attended the meeting: "It wasn't the dean who was humiliated last night; it was a thousand years of Anglo-Saxon tradition of freedom and fair play."

Two years later the city celebrated its hundredth birthday with great fanfare. Among the many special events was Orlo Miller's play *This Was London,* staged at the Grand Theatre, and directed by Roy Irving, formerly of the famous Abbey Theatre Players of Ireland. A Toronto newspaper reported that this was the first time a Canadian municipality had commissioned a stage play.

London's one hundredth anniversary was marked by a complex game of musical chairs in the mayor's office. The first occupant was Allan Rush, a former city police officer. He was mayor from Monday, 1 January 1951, to Tuesday, 29 March 1955, when he resigned to become superintendent of the newly-built Dr. John Dearness Home for Elder Citizens. The home was named for one of the city's most distinguished educators. The job at the municipally-operated residence must have been an attractive one. When Superintendent Rush died suddenly on Tuesday, 9 July 1955, he was succeeded as superintendent by his successor as mayor, George Beedle. Mayor Beedle, the self-proclaimed first labour mayor of London, was succeeded in turn by Alderman Ray Dennis, who thus became London's third mayor in one year, a record even for this city.

In keeping with centennial celebrations: the Roman Catholic Diocese of London celebrated its first one hundred years in 1956. The Anglican Diocese of Huron had its centennial the year following.

The 1950s were also a time when another religious group, the Mennonites, began looking for ways to help the destitute men who wandered the streets of London. In 1950, a group of mission-minded Mennonite farmers near Nairn, 25 miles northwest of London, took the proceeds of 100 acres of wheat they had grown and used it for a downpayment on a house

THROWER'S

WHARNCLIFFE AT COVE ROAD

Groceries - Fruit - Meat - Vegetables

These Specials For Thurs., Fri. and Sat., October 27-28-29

Extra Special! **BUTTER**   FIRST GRADE   1 lb. prints   **24½c**

FREE! LUX KNITTING BOOK

49 Tested Instructions when you purchase **2 lg. pkgs. 47c**

ARVA IMPERIAL PASTRY FLOUR

3½ lb. **12c** | 12 lb. **32c**
7 lb. **19c** | 24 lb. **59c**

A HIGH GRADE SELF-POLISHING FLOOR WAX

Pint tins **59c**

OLD DUTCH CLEANSER "CHASES DIRT"

2 tins 19c

A Finer Cake Flour

27c pkg.

A TABLE SYRUP OF THE FINEST QUALITY

2 lb. tins, each **16c**

HALLOWE'EN SPECIALS

HALLOWE'EN WRAPPED KISSES	lb.	**15c**
HALLOWE'EN JELLY BEANS	**2** lbs.	**25c**
Rosey Red McIntosh Eating Apples	**5** lbs.	**25c**
Choice Emperior Grapes	lb.	**10c**
Fresh Potato Chips FOIL BAG	ea.	**5c**
Christie's Carmel Cookies	**3** doz.	**13c**
Florida Grapefruit LARGE SIZE	**6** for	**23c**
EATMOR CRANBERRIES	lb.	**19c**
SUNKIST ORANGES med. size	dozen	**25c**
WAXED TABLE TURNIPS	ea.	**5c**
Real Good! OLD CHEESE	lb.	**25c**
CHOICE CAULIFLOWER	ea.	**10-15c**
FINEST CARADOC POTATOES	peck	**19c**
SEEDLESS RAISINS	**2** lbs.	**23c**
DISCO bag **15c**	Charcoal	**2** bags **25c**

Telephone - - - Metcalf 5160

GROCERY FLYER, 1955
Unbelievable — one pound of butter for 24-1/2 cents, or a dozen "Sunkist" oranges for 25 cents! Such were the bargains to be had at Arthur Thrower's neighbourhood grocery store in the mid-1950s.

1954
Marilyn Bell swims Lake Ontario.

at 536 Talbot Street. This house, known as the Goodwill Rescue Mission, became the flagship institution for what was to become Mission Services of London. Alvin and Madeleine Roth traded the known world of their Nairn area farm for the unknown world of street missions when Alvin became the first director of the house and opened the doors to the public in January, 1951. A report of their first month of operation is a testament to the great need that the mission was filling:

9 hospital visits
A quantity of tracts distributed
4 house visits
631 meals served
350 nights lodgings
75 gospel services
25 confessions for Christ of Salvation

COVENT GARDEN MARKET, SEPTEMBER 6, 1954
Two years after this photograph was taken, this site, the western edge of the Market Square running along Talbot Street, would support the new Market Garden and Parking Building.

DR. WILFRID JURY
Through the untiring efforts of Dr. Wilfrid Jury, Fanshawe Pioneer Village was established at Fanshawe Park in 1956. Here we see Dr. Jury, familiar pipe in hand, discussing London's early newspaper history at the museum's recreated nineteenth century printing shop.

PLAQUE UNVEILING, ELDON HOUSE, OCTOBER 1, 1960
On hand for the ceremony commemorating Eldon House, generously given to the city by the Harris family, were from left to right: B.S. Scott, the Very Rev. R.C. Brown, Lucy Harris Little, Dr. Robin Harris, Margaret Fullerton, Hon. John P. Robarts, and Leslie R. Gray. In front: David Harris, George Little, and Mary Harris.

In 1960, the men's mission moved to its present location on York Street. Over the years, Mission Services expanded until it became one of London's largest social service agencies, encompassing a women's mission (later the Rotholme Women's and Family Shelter), Quintin Warner House for recovering alcoholics, and the Teen Girls Home on Wharncliffe Road. That one hundred acres of wheat certainly went a long way in serving those Londoners who had "fallen through the cracks" of society.

The pace of development quickened in the 1950s and downtown landmarks began to disappear. The beautiful old Covent Garden Market building, once the subject of a sunny painting by Paul Peel, was knocked down and replaced by a truly prosaic cement parking building and a very popular enclosed market. The old firehall on King Street was razed and the site became yet another parking lot. The city's first public library building was torn down and replaced by an architecturally uninspired addition to the soaring old "Victorian pile" building of the YMCA, by now combined with the YWCA. (1951)

Local history was now beginning to find a place in London's social life. In 1958 the city established a temporary museum, "Victoria House," on Wellington Street opposite Victoria Park. This was a typical London achievement: such a museum had been proposed a mere fifty years earlier. Perhaps a more lasting tribute to London's past had been the establishment, in 1956, of Fanshawe Pioneer Village. A pet project of Dr. Wilfrid Jury, curator of museums at UWO, the village was to be a piece of living history, where visitors could see first hand how the early settlers lived. It started off small, with only an authentic log cabin and a rail fence, but over the decades that followed, a barn, artisan shops, an Orange Lodge, a store, a church, and the original Paul Peel house, amongst many others, became part of the village.

Further impetus was given to the promotion of the city's history when the Harris family, descendants of Captain John Harris, RN (1782-1850), one-time treasurer of the old District of London, and his wife Amelia Ryerse (1798-1882) made a gift to the city of the family home, "Eldon House," together with much of its contents. This magnificent donation included the estate grounds and the river parkland below them.

These were matters of special interest to a relatively small group of citizens. Bigger fish were frying. Mercantile history was being made with the building of a one-block-square enclosed shopping mall and parking garage in the downtown area. Wellington Square, as it was called, was the first such structure to be built in a midtown setting in North America.

The most talked-about event of the 1950s, however, was not London's claim to mercantile fame, Wellington Square, but the odyssey of Slippery the Sea Lion. The grand opening in June, 1958, of London's children's theme park, Storybook Gardens, was eclipsed by the escapades of one of the zoo's sea lions, who quietly slipped into the Thames River by Springbank Park and headed into the Great Lakes. Over the next ten days Slippery was sighted first in the Thames River, then in Lake St. Clair, then in the western portion of Lake Erie. Phil Skeldon, director of the Toledo Zoo, took up the chase and eventually cornered him in an empty boathouse near Sandusky, Ohio. A minor brouhaha erupted, however, when Skel-

1956
Prince Rainier of Monaco marries US actress Grace Kelly.

STORYBOOK GARDENS, 1958
The premier children's attraction in Springbank Park, Storybook Gardens was opened in June 1958. Still a delight with its nursery rhyme themes, the park within a park continues to draw thousands of youngsters of all ages through its gates each summer.

don declared his intentions to keep the animal. Petitions circulated, including this one sent to Toledo: "Slippery come home. London needs you, 100,000 Londoners await your arrival at Storybook Gardens. P.S. Don't swim, transportation has been arranged." Even London's M.P., Ernest C. Halpenny, showed his support:

> I don't think Canada will withdraw its diplomatic corps from Washington or anything as drastic as that, but if they don't give it back I'll get my secretary and a few others and we'll picket the U.S. embassy.

The righteous indignation subsided, however, when the Toledo zookeeper announced that Slippery would return to London after some rest and relaxation. (Years later, Skeldon admitted that his threat to keep the sea lion was a joke he and London PUC assistant chairperson Earl Nichols, a long-time alderman, controller, and PUC member, cooked up.) As a token of esteem, Slippery was given the keys to the city of Toledo before his journey home. In London, thousands of people lined the streets as Slippery received a hero's homecoming. Slippery became a North American celebrity, even making an appearance on the CBC television show, Front Page Challenge. Slippery and his Storybook Gardens home was a favourite subject of London *Free Press* cartoonist Merle "Ting" Tingley.

RETURN OF SLIPPERY THE SEA LION, 1958
An estimated crowd of 200,000 turned out to welcome home Slippery the Sea Lion after his adventures in Lake Erie. More interested in renewing his acquaintance with his mate Lonesome, Slippery graciously ignored the fanfare surrounding his return to Storybook Gardens.

Walt Disney couldn't have come up with a better story, and the London PUC couldn't have asked for a better promoter for their fledgling children's park.

Triumph and tragedy marked London's wresting of the Harmsworth boat racing trophy from the Americans on August 27, 1959. The *Miss Supertest III*, driven by Bob Hayward, and owned by London resident James Thompson, shattered previous records for the race run annually on the Detroit River. A few years later, however, Londoners were stunned by the news that Hayward had been killed in a racing accident. The Bob Hayward branch of the YM-YWCA on Hamilton Road was named in his memory.

As a fitting climax to this year of frothy promise, London was host on Friday, 3 July 1959, to an official visit by the head of the Commonwealth of Nations, Her Majesty Queen Elizabeth II, and her consort, His Royal Highness Prince Philip, Duke of Edinburgh. It had been a little over twenty years since the Queen's parents had visited the second London. On both occasions, royalty was officially greeted by Mayor J. Allan Johnston, the only mayor in London history to be accorded this honour twice. There had been great changes in those two decades.

No longer could it be said of London, even half-truthfully, that "everyone knew everyone else"; nor could it be said, as it once was, that everyone knew his or her place.

The late Mrs. Edna Cleghorn, daughter of William M. Gartshore, president of the McClary Manufacturing Company, once complained wistfully of the passing of those days as she sat beneath a portrait of herself as a young woman painted by Paul Peel. She told her visitors that she had gone uptown with her companion on a recent Friday night. Window-shopping on Dundas Street, she had not seen a single person whom she knew.

1958
Henry Moore, famed 20th century sculptor, creates "Reclining Figure" for Paris UNESCO building.

CHAPTER TWELVE

Greater London

In the years since the Second World War, the London area has experienced its period of greatest expansion. The urban area has spread out to embrace old centres such as Byron and Lambeth. This new suburban belt, together with the city, is known as Greater London.
— Urban Renewal London Ontario: A Plan for Development
and Redevelopment 1960-1980. (London: 1960)

The early 1960s were heady days for staid old London. The population was soaring; industries were racing with each other to expand, build, hire more workers; schools were bursting at the seams; hospitals launched ambitious building campaigns. Nothing seemed impossible. The London *Free Press*, attempting to capture some of the excitement of the age ran several special inserts documenting the tremendous growth of the city. The very titles of these special sections reveal something of the unbridled enthusiasm of the day: *Greater London* (1961), *This is London: The Only Thing That's Constant is Expansion* (1962), *Dynamic London* (1963), and *London Unlimited: Pacemaker of Western Ontario* (1964).

In 1960, the city of London set the wheels in motion to direct some of this growth with its official plan: *Urban Renewal London Ontario: A Plan for Development and Redevelopment*. It prophesied:

> In the next twenty years London may become a city with a population of some 350,000 persons, an increase of 200,000 persons. The area of Greater London will be extended to nearly three times its present size and many more public services will be demanded. New express routes will have to be developed to handle the traffic moving into and out of the central area, and around and through the city. The city will grow towards the east and southeast attracted by easy access to Hamilton and Toronto via Highway 401. As the city population approaches half a million in the next quarter century, the provision of large areas of parkland and playgrounds will be imperative. Open agricultural land will be farther removed by new urbanization and the river valley will be threatened with sporadic development. The river valley should be conserved for recreational use and parks. ...

As it turned out, these words were eerily accurate. Yet, amid these promises of growth and prosperity were sounded a few ominous notes. The report hinted that a modern city could not be achieved without a few sacrifices:

> With dramatic growth and change there will come challenging problems. These are linked with the damage of physical decline of part of the central commer-

CITY HALL, 1971
A symbol of London's dramatic growth during the 1950s and 1960s, city hall on Dufferin Avenue was opened in 1971. Like many large municipal expenditures of the time, the building's $5-1/4 million price tag was the source of some controversy.

1960
Major films include "Exodus," by Otto Preminger, and "Psycho" by Alfred Hitchcock.

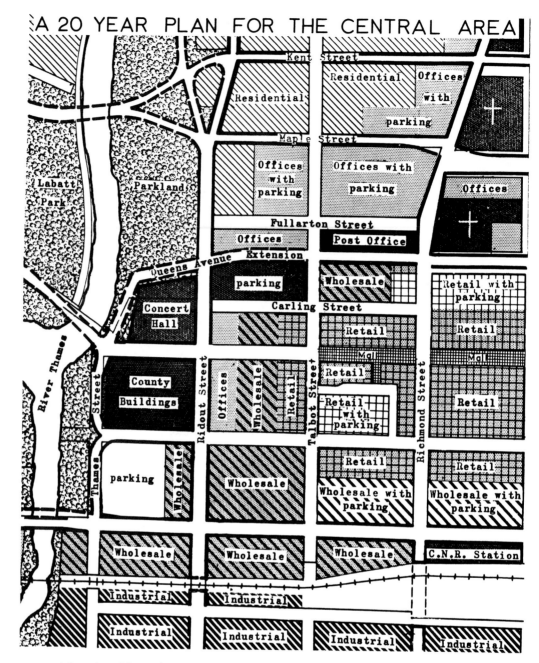

URBAN RENEWAL PLAN, 1961

In an attempt to revive a downtown ravaged by the rise of suburban shopping centres and malls, an urban renewal plan was projected for the city in the early 1960s. As of today, a cohesive development strategy has yet to be successfully implemented.

1961

Soviet cosmonaut Yuri Gagarin becomes first man in space.

cial and residential areas. Many structures near the city centre are between 70 and 100 years old; some should have been replaced long ago. Large buildings and high property values make changes in the road pattern very difficult. A dynamic approach must be taken to solve the present congestion and to establish the central area firmly as the heart of Greater London.

Clearly, the powers-that-be felt that preserving the past was incompatible with "progress." To be modern was to look forward, not backward. So, in this way, the stage was set for the next twenty, nay, thirty years. Almost as soon as this out-with-the-old-in-with-the-new way of thinking became part of London's development strategy, small, but dedicated groups of Londoners began to fight back. The struggle between these two visions for the city has been a characteristic of civic life in London ever since.

Annexation in 1961 was the first step towards the entrenchment of Greater London. Citing the need to find the "greatest common good,"

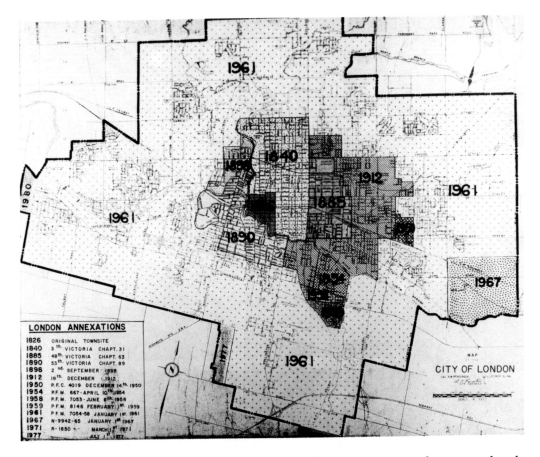

LONDON ANNEXATIONS

1826	ORIGINAL TOWNSITE
1840	3ᵗʰ VICTORIA CHAPT. 31
1885	48ᵗʰ VICTORIA CHAPT. 63
1890	53ᵗʰ VICTORIA CHAPT. 89
1898	2 ⁿᵈ SEPTEMBER 1898
1912	19 ᵗʰ DECEMBER 1912
1950	P.F.C. 4019 DECEMBER 14ᵗʰ 1950
1954	P.F.M. 667 - APRIL 10ᵗʰ 1954
1958	P.F.M. 7053 - JUNE 6ᵗʰ 1958
1959	P.F.M. 8146 FEBRUARY 1ˢᵗ 1959
1961	P.F.M. 7054-58 JANUARY 1ˢᵗ 1961
1967	N-9942-65 JANUARY 1ˢᵗ 1967
1971	R-1650 - MARCH 1 1971
1977	JULY 1 1977

CITY OF LONDON

ANNEXATIONS
Originally drawn in 1962, and subsequently updated, this map illustrates the 14 annexations made by London from 1840 to 1980. The largest of these land acquisitions occurred on January 1, 1961, when the city, with the blessing of the Ontario Municipal Board, secured 42,550 acres from London and Westminster Townships.

the Ontario Municipal Board granted the city its request for more land. The new city broke, once and for all, the confining limits of the river valley, leaping the north branch of the Thames into London Township, and the main branch southward into Westminster Township. The population of the city increased by 63,072 to 165,815. As a means of gauging this increase, it may be sufficient to point out that the number of people absorbed by the annexation was almost equal to the total population of the city in 1924 (63,369). Even more startling, however, was the physical size of the new metropolis of southwestern Ontario. Previous to the 1960 land-grab the city contained 12.37 square miles (32.03 square kilometres). On 1 January 1961, London's area ballooned to 66.37 square miles (171.84 square kilometres).

Before annexation, much of the land in Westminster and London townships that was absorbed by the city was already drawing a steady stream of "immigrants." New Veterans Land Act subdivisions (housing developments set aside for returning World War II vets) in the south, and lands around the university to the north were filling rapidly. Some of the areas, like Byron and Broughdale, were older settlements with long histories. Ironically, in the ten years prior to annexation, it was the townships, not the city, that experienced the greatest growth. While the populations in Westminster and London townships doubled and trebled, respectively, London's population had increased by only 10%. A list in the London *Free Press* of the area subdivisions engulfed by the act of 1961 reveals how developed these lands already were (i.e. farmers' fields do not usually have names such as "Stoneybrook"):

1962
Marilyn Monroe, screen goddess, dies, age 36.

JOHN P. ROBARTS, 1963
Upon succeeding Leslie Frost as leader of the Ontario Conservative Party, John P. Robarts served as Ontario's premier from 1961 until resigning in 1971. Here we see Robarts and his wife, Norah, celebrating an election victory at campaign headquarters in the Hotel London on September 26, 1963.

Byron, the Beck San, part of the Hunt Club, Oakridge Park, Oakridge Acres, Hickory Heights, Orchard Park, Medway Heights, Masonville, Stoneybrook, Hillcrest, Huron Heights, parts of the airport, the "Golden Mile" of London Township, Fairmont-Trafalgar Heights, Pond Mills, the V.L.A. subdivisions in both Westminster and London townships, Wilton Grove, the Westminster Township offices and the Northern Electric plant, the Ontario and Westminster Hospitals, the Dearness Home, Mountsfield, the Highland Golf Club, Southcrest Estates, Kensal Park, and the London Ski Club.

Annexation year also saw the election of London Conservative M.P.P. John Robarts as Ontario Premier. Actually the second London member of the provincial legislature to hold the premier's reigns (W.H. Draper, in the nineteenth century was the first), Robarts led the province throughout London's "growth spurt" of the 1960s. He resigned in 1971, but continued to contribute to community life.

Another politician who entered with gusto upon the London scene in annexation year was Mayor F. Gordon Stronach, the pipe-smoking, sports-minded former chief of police for London Township. Stronach, who lost his job as police chief in the annexation shuffle, floated into office on waves of sympathy for the underdog battling entrenched bureaucracy, and new voters getting a degree of revenge for the annexation most of them did not want. Londoners have often been partial to anyone seen to be fighting city hall.

1963
President John F. Kennedy assassinated in Dallas Nov. 22; Lyndon B. Johnson becomes President.

FANSHAWE DAM, JULY 6, 1961
As part of its flood control mandate, the Upper Thames River Conservation Authority constructed the Fanshawe Dam across the North Branch of the Thames in 1950-53.

CONSTRUCTION OF FANSHAWE COLLEGE, MARCH 1964
One of nearly two dozen community colleges built in the province during the 1960s, Fanshawe College opened its doors in 1967. Enjoying a well-deserved reputation for excellence in teaching and program offerings, today the college is one of Ontario's largest.

City hall itself underwent another major change that year with the addition of a new tier of government — a Board of Control. Recommended by the Ontario Municipal Board annexation report, this new city-wide elected body of five persons including the mayor, was to be in charge of finances, property, and personnel. The election of controllers Bentley I. Baldwin, Norman Bradford, Margaret Fullerton, and Earl Nichols marked the city's second experiment with a second tier of government — London had had a Board of Control briefly during World War I.

One of the things immediately affected by annexation was the city's education systems. In one fell swoop, the London Public Board of Education gained thirty-four elementary schools, two high schools (Oakridge and Clarke Road), and 391 new teachers. Likewise the London Roman Catholic Separate School Board gained twenty-five teachers and seven schools. Enrolment for the Separate Board jumped from 1,500 to 4,500. One year later there were 6,000 pupils registered.

Throughout the 1960s, enrolments rose in staggering amounts (in the early 1960s yearly increases in the public schools ranged from 800 to 1000). Millions upon millions were spent in building new schools and enlarging old ones. Portable classrooms made their debut in this period as well. Physical increases, however, were not the only changes in the 1960s. New classes for children with special needs — either physical, or intellectual — became a part of the education experience. New ideas concerning what and

1964
The Beatles take North America by storm, playing in Montreal, Toronto and Vancouver.

how children should be taught circulated. The comments of W.D. Sutton, Director of Education for the London Board, reflect some of these changes:

> The young people in our schools must be taught to be world citizens; it is no longer enough to indoctrinate them in the customs and attitudes of the nation's adults. ...
>
> Educational leaders are challenging ideas that have long been regarded as safe and sound, such as the ideal size of the class, the inflexible organization by grades, the time for the introduction of a second language study, the age of admission to school for the first time and the age of graduation, the limitation on how much and how well children learn. There are other ideas to be challenged, but there has been a breakthrough. The future appears brighter.

Higher education also underwent some drastic changes in the 1960s. In 1966, the provincial government passed an act that created the "community college" system in Ontario. This consisted of post-secondary vocational training colleges which were to provide an alternative to university education, and continuing education for those already in the workforce. Londoners had been campaigning for such a centre for many years, and in September, 1967, Fanshawe College of Applied Arts and Technology opened. Situated at the site of the former Ontario Vocational Centre on Oxford Street East (opened 1964), Fanshawe first offered courses in Agriculture, Applied Arts, Business, Health and Welfare, Social Services, Humanities, and Technical and Technological Studies. It also offered extension courses on a part-time basis in centres in Elgin, Oxford, Middlesex, and Norfolk counties.

The University of Western Ontario also had the expansion bug. In 1962, the president of the university, Dr. Edward Hall, announced a $30 million dollar expansion program, which would replace an earlier, less ambitious plan. Aiming for a student enrolment of 9,000 by 1970, and a staff three times its 1962 size, the university cited an increase in demand for post-secondary education for the change. Said Colonel D.B. Weldon, chairman of the Board of Governors:

> Careful as our planning has been and justified as we may be to our desires and hopes to keep Western a fine university of relatively small size, it is imperative in the light of new information that we examine once again our policy of enrolment and size limitations.

This "new information," made available by the province, included the revelation that approximately 20% of young people between the ages of eighteen and twenty wanted to attend university, compared to only 9% a few years before. The "baby boom" generation, raised in the relatively affluent post-war years, had a different set of expectations than their parents. They made an indelible mark on the education system. And, indirectly, they made more than a few changes to the campus of the University of Western Ontario. In the 1960s, Western's buildings mushroomed to include two new arts colleges (Middlesex and Talbot), the Natural Science Centre, the Kresge Nursing School, a cancer research lab, the law school building, the School of Library Sciences, Alumni Hall, and three student residences.

One of the changes at Western that helped put London on the inter-

LONDON KNIGHTS HOCKEY, 1973
For more than 25 years, the London Knights Junior "A" hockey club has supplied the professional ranks with raw talent. These Knights' players were drafted by the National Hockey League on May 18, 1973. The defunct World Hockey Association also expressed an interest in their abilities. Left to right: Lou Nistico, Reg Thomas, Larry Goodenough, Dennis Vervegaert, Steve Langdon, Peter Crosbie.

1965
Paris designers shock the world with the mini-skirt.

national map was the expansion of the medical school and its linkage to the new University Hospital. In 1965, Western's medical school moved from its cramped quarters at Victoria Hospital to a new four-storey building situated between the cancer research lab and the Kresge building. The decision to move the school, however, was made back in 1948. Said the Board of Governors at the time:

> We have an added opportunity to give our medical students the benefit of university life rather than an isolated professional existence. We have an opportunity of giving added leadership in education in Canada. An existing building, personalities, and present lack of funds should not becloud our vision when looking toward the future of this University.

Just three years after Premier Robarts opened the medical school, Western's new School of Dentistry, built near the medical school, opened its doors. Also on the drawing board were plans for a new teaching hospital to add the final touch to the medical centre. President Hall had long wanted a teaching hospital on campus, but the university itself was not interested in getting into the health care business. So, the London Health Association, which ran the former Beck Sanatorium, decided to take on

AERIAL VIEW OF U.W.O., MAY 1967
The 1960s witnessed the most dramatic expansion in the history of the University of Western Ontario. Continually rising enrolment figures compelled the school to grow from a tightly-knit campus focused upon today's University College (centre) to a sprawling complex dotted with a myriad of new faculty buildings.

UNIVERSITY HOSPITAL, MARCH 21, 1972
Administered by the London Health Association, University Hospital, situated on a site adjacent to Western's campus, opened in the fall of 1972. Since opening, the hospital, which counts neurosurgery and organ transplants among its specialties, has maintained an international reputation for both research and teaching.

1967
Dr. Christiaan N. Barnard performs world's first human heart transplant, Cape Town, South Africa.

the project. Several successive presidents of the Association, including V.P. Cronyn, J.H. Stevens, and Walter J. Blackburn provided much of the leadership in this drive. The money came mainly from the provincial government, but the London Hospital Association and the Richard Ivey Foundation also made generous contributions. A site to the north of the medical and dentistry buildings was agreed upon for "University Hospital," and the ground-breaking ceremony was held on June 2, 1969. Over the years University Hospital has gained a reputation for excellence in research and clinical practice. Dr. Charles Drake and Dr. H.J.M. Barnett in Neurological Science, and Dr. Murray Barr in cell research are just a few of the doctors and researchers who have helped make Western one of the best places in the world to study medicine, and to receive treatment.

The 1960s saw many other developments in health care in London. Because tuberculosis was no longer a major health problem in Ontario, the London Health Association relinquished guardianship of the Beck Sanatorium to the province in 1960. In its place, the Children's Psychiatric Research Institute, opened as an 'outpatient clinic' for children with developmental handicaps. Founded by Dr. Matthew Dymond, the Ontario Minister of Health, and Dr. Donald Zarfas, a psychiatrist who was to become the first superintendent, the centre was designed to help keep children out of institutions. During the mid-1970s, in response to community needs, CPRI expanded to become a regional children's mental health centre. Now known as the 'Child Parent Resource Institute', it has become a diagnostic, assessment and short-term treatment centre for children with developmental handicaps, psychiatric, emotional or behaviour problems, and more complex, multiple handicaps from all over southwestern Ontario. CPRI is a major teaching institute, providing students from the University of Western Ontario, the University of Waterloo, and Fanshawe College

WELLINGTON SQUARE, NOVEMBER 5, 1964
Opened in 1960, Wellington Square was unique for two reasons; it was the city's first mall, and it was the first enclosed shopping centre in Canada.

a chance to learn first-hand about children with special needs.

All of London's health care centres underwent major expansions in the 1960s. Victoria Hospital launched a $16 million building project, St. Joseph's added 180 beds to their facilities, and Westminster Hospital built a seven-storey, $6.5-million addition.

London's retail and industrial sector grew at a record-breaking pace. By the early '60s London had over 328 manufacturing plants, 80 whole-sale businesses, and 70 construction supply companies. Older companies such as Labatt's and Kellogg's made substantial additions. Northern Electric was one of the larger new plants to locate in London. During this time, the London Chamber of Commerce was credited with doing much to create a favourable climate for business to come to London.

It was in the retail sector that the most visible changes were made. London began its love affair with shopping malls in 1960 when Wellington Square opened on the site of the former General Steel Wares plant. Many suburban shopping centres servicing the growing population in the newly-annexed areas soon followed. These "plazas" usually featured a grocery store, a department store and a few other shops, along with acres of parking spaces. In fact, the automobile probably made the most impact on retail patterns in the 1960s. In 1950, 21,000 vehicles were on London streets; by 1961, there were 45,000. Consequently, the London retail landscape became dotted with service stations, car washes, and the ultimate symbol of a culture in love with its cars — the drive-in restaurant.

Indirectly, the automobile posed the first real threat to London's heritage in the early 1960s. A large-scale traffic study by A.D. Margison and Associates called for, among other things, the construction of a freeway along the river valley. This posed a demolition threat to both the courthouse and jail, and London's first financial district, a group of buildings

1968
First of 10,000 Czech refugees arrive after Soviet invasion of their homeland.

on Ridout Street built in the 1840s. The ever-outspoken Mayor Stronach was all for tearing down the "monstrosity" of a courthouse, saying "As long as we perpetuate junk we are encouraging others to do the same." Some fierce opposition in the community soon quelled ideas about tearing down the courthouse, but the Ridout Street buildings were the subject of a more protracted debate. A "Save Ridout Street" campaign, supported by the University Women's Club, the London branch of the Architectural Conservancy of Ontario, and the London and Middlesex Historical Society, held the wrecker's ball at bay for several years. Finally, John Labatt Ltd. offered to restore the buildings and use one of them for a head office for its corporation. As for the top brass at city hall, they were glad a solution was found without having to shell out any money.

London's river, on which its citizens had turned their backs for so many decades, was slowly becoming, once again, a place of beauty. Without fanfare, the Public Utilities Commission, with the help of the Kiwanis Club, transformed the banks of the river, wherever feasible, into parkland. The river flats below "Eldon House" became Harris Park. The old Dennisteel foundry was demolished, some aging and deteriorating buildings on Ridout Street were razed, and, for the first time in more than a century, Londoners could see the forks of the Thames much as they had appeared to John Graves Simcoe and his staff in 1793. The development of parkland along the river continues to the present, a gracious presence, an antidote to the urban blight that threatens other parts of the city.

Surprising to some, London became an important art centre in the 1960s. Said art critic Barry Lord in an article in *Art in America:*

> London, Ontario, is admittedly hard to believe. Situated midway between Detroit and Toronto in a pastoral river valley called the Thames, home of insurance and trust companies and the province's Conservative premier, this town of two hundred thousand is also one of Canada's four major art scenes. Younger than Montreal, livelier than Toronto, vying with Vancouver in variety and sheer quantity of output, it is in many ways the most important of the four.

The breeding ground for London's artists in the 1960s was the art department at H.B. Beal Technical School, which had been set up by Vera McIntyre (Mackie) Cryderman in 1927. Artist Herb Ariss was in charge of the department while such promising students as Jack Chambers and Greg Curnoe went through the program. Known for their energy, enthusiasm, and use of the southern Ontario landscape for inspiration and subject matter, these London artists made the national and international art world take notice. Continued Barry Lord:

> What London has that everywhere else needs is an understanding that provincialism in art today is a false problem. Plugged into the world but conscious of the necessity to produce their own work out of their own experience, London artists are indelibly Canadian, and perhaps among the first global villagers.

Other artists producing work in London at the time were Bernice Vincent, John Boyle, and Murray Favro, along with recently-arrived out-of-towners Tony Urquhart (first "artist-in-residence" at U.W.O), Kim Ondaatje, and Patterson Ewen. Ironically, for a city of such importance

1969
Neil Armstrong, US astronaut, becomes first Man on the Moon.

artistically, it was yet to build a permanent art gallery.

The really big show of the 1960s, of course, was the centennial of Canadian Confederation in 1967. Every community in the nation pulled out all the stops, suitably to commemorate the occasion.

In retrospect it may be said that the effect of the celebrations on the Canadian public's perception of, and interest in, the history of the country and its communities, big and small, was beneficial. On the other hand, the attempts physically to cement the occasion in memory by buildings and memorials were not universally successful.

A small community in Alberta, with a large sense of humour, built a landing pad for visiting Unidentified Flying Objects (UFOs). London's project, Centennial Hall, is still looking for UFOs, or *anything* animate or inanimate, to land on its largely uninhabited formal plaza facing Victoria Park. In attempting to please everyone, the city, in commissioning this combined concert hall and convention centre, pleased no one. But, the hall was built within budget, a rarity in political circles.

Oblivious to the white elephant behind it, the new Canadian flag flapped proudly in front of Centennial Hall as Centennial year drew to a close, and a December twilight settled over a community of some 205,000 people.

Increasingly, after 1967 the long-established White Anglo-Saxon Protestant (WASP) majority in London became diluted by exotic ethnic minorities. The number of black people rose, for instance, but the voices were different now; the accents were African or Caribbean instead of entirely North American. There were dark-skinned Pakistanis and sari-clad Indian women. There were Sikhs, with their beards and distinctive turbans. There was a growing Muslim community with its own Mosque.

Then, there were the refugees. The Hungarians, the Czechs, the Viet-

THE LABATT RESTORATION
Generously restored by John Labatt Limited in the early 1970s, these buildings, some of London's oldest surviving commercial structures, materially add to the west side of Ridout Street immediately north of Queens Avenue.

1970
Pierre Laporte, Quebec Minister of Labour, is assassinated by FLQ terrorists; War Measures Act proclaimed.

CENTENNIAL HALL
Built in tribute to Canada's 100th birthday, Centennial Hall was officially opened on June 21, 1967. A storm of controversy surrounded its construction, and the facility's adequacy has been questioned ever since.

1971
Cigarette advertising is banned from U.S. television.

namese, and the young Americans fleeing their country's participation in what they saw as an unjust war. It seemed that half the world was in flight from political systems, from oppression, from poverty, and malnutrition.

London received its share of the globe's shifting populations with commendable compassion, for the times were reasonably good. It is usually when jobs are scarce and the newcomers are seen as competition for one's daily bread that skin colour and language difference become a source of friction.

Evidence of the changing face of Londoners was found in the first Holiday Festival held at the Ukrainian Club in 1968. This festival gave members of the various ethnic groups in the community a chance to show to the roast-beef-and-potatoes set (i.e. London's majority ethnic group, the WASPs) as well as to other ethnic groups, their native crafts, music, dances and food. The annual event was sponsored by the London Folk Arts Council, which was affiliated with the Canadian Folk Arts Council. Led by Pegi Walden, the organization helped people of different ethnic groups to form clubs, provided translation services, and gave informative talks to school children, among other things.

The Cross Cultural Learner Centre, another sign of the changing ethnic make-up of London, was founded in 1968. Originally set up as a resource centre for Canadian university students who planned to work in developing countries, the founders soon discovered that people from a wide range of backgrounds were using the centre. This unique organization, now located in the city's storefront core, evolved over the years to include a range of services for new immigrants and refugees, providing counselling and information to those unaccustomed to life in a North American city.

**SNOWSTORM
OF 1971**
Beginning on Tuesday, January 26, 1971, a monstrous snowstorm pounded Southwestern Ontario for six days, leaving in its wake two feet of snow, and drifts of up to 12 feet. Here we see Dundas Street looking east from Talbot Street a day after the blizzard had subsided. Seven years later, an even more crippling winter storm hit London.

A popular winter pastime, hockey, underwent some changes. In the 1960s, "Junior A" hockey became a mult-million-dollar business. In 1965, the "Junior B" "London Nationals", who played at the new "London Gardens" just south of the city, paid $30,000 for the privilege of joining the "Junior A" league. In 1968, it was decided that the team needed a new name, a new colour scheme, and a new image. The *Free Press* sponsored a "name-the-team" and "pick-the-colours" contest. The winning name entry was the "Knights" and their new sweaters would be henceforth adorned with green, gold and white. Londoners have been following the careers of former "Knights" such as Daryll Sittler, Brad Marsh and Rob Ramage ever since.

After much heated discussion a site was chosen for a new city hall. One proposal not taken seriously would have placed the municipal headquarters in Victoria Park, with a parking area underneath it among the tree roots; an impossibility in any event because of the water table. This, one of many such assaults, before and since, on the integrity of the city's cherished open space, aroused the anger of the citizenry. The proposal was hastily dropped and a site nearby was chosen, on Dufferin Avenue. It was completed in 1971.

The new city hall was "broken in" to the sometimes rough world of

1974
"Streaking" becomes a fad in North America and UWO.

JANE BIGELOW, 1975

Jane Bigelow served as London's first female mayor from 1972 to 1978. Her administration was marked by an increased awareness of social issues and shrewd financial management.

1975

Anglican Church in Canada approves ordaining women to priesthood.

municipal politics when a replacement had to be found for the ailing new mayor Fred Gosnell, who had been forced to retire because of ill health on March 6, 1972. Jane Bigelow, as Deputy Mayor, was set to win by virtue of heading the polls for Board of Control, but she was opposed by a group on council who were wary of her reportedly "socialist" and feminist leanings. Tensions built while a meeting to hold the vote by secret ballot was heatedly debated. At the last minute, Alderman Judy Gay, who had been hurriedly summoned from a vacation in South America, returned just in time to elect London's first female mayor. It was rather an anti-climax when the *Free Press* reported that Mrs. Bigelow spent the next morning doing her grocery shopping. Bigelow's trademarks during her seven-year stint as mayor were her concern for human issues — child care, the arts, services for seniors, neighbourhood improvement programs and public transportation. London also received its first "Triple A" credit rating during her time in office.

Mayor Jane Bigelow became the centre of a mild tempest in a millinery teapot when she declined to wear a hat to meet Queen Elizabeth II during the Queen's third visit to the city in June, 1973 (her second as reigning monarch). Yet, this breach of royal etiquette did little to dampen the spirits of the enthusiastic crowd of 30,000 who attended the Queen's "walkabout" in Victoria Park. "They came wrapped in garbage bags and raincoats," recounted the London *Free Press*,

carrying umbrellas, cameras, children and lawn chairs they hung on with a fierce determination to see the tiny regal woman in the spring-green coat and matching hat and her tall, handsome husband, the Duke of Edinburgh.

A lucky 500 guests chosen by the city administrative staff and advisors sat down with the Queen and dined on pheasant and champagne in Centennial Hall. The more observant among the crowd milling around outside would have seen a small brigade of catering staff wheeling coffee urns across Civic Square from City Hall to Centennial Hall. It seemed enough electrical outlets that worked could not be found in the banquet hall to do the job. All in all, it was an expensive couple of hours (to the tune of $30,000) but complaints from loyal Londoners were not too loud.

As the expansion-obsessed days of the 1960s gave way to the new decade, leisure time became more of a public focus. Two perennial entertainment favourites, the Home County Folk Festival and the London International Air Show appeared in the 1970s. In August, 1974, the newly-formed Home County Folk League invited the London public to Victoria Park for a weekend of music, folk art, and fun. 20,000 took them up on the invitation, and every year since, Londoners have been entertained by the talents of Valdy, Colleen Peterson, Jackie Washington, David Bradstreet and the Dixie Flyers, among others. The first London International Air Show got off to a rougher start in 1975, when weather was poor. Organizers persisted, however, and thousands of London and area residents continue to put up with sunburns and cricked necks to watch the Canadian Armed Forces' "Snowbirds" and the rest of those "crazy young men (and women) and their flying machines."

Londoners bid "auld lang syne" to a favourite son, Guy Lombardo,

THE AIR SHOW, 1982
Since its inauguration in 1973, the London International Air Show has annually drawn thousands to the city's airport to view "flying machines" from all corners of the world. Here we see Canadian "voodoo" jet fighters impressing the crowd with precision routines at the 1982 air show.

on November 5, 1977, when he died in Houston, Texas. Earlier in the year, Lombardo and his Royal Canadians had returned to the Stork Club dance hall (it burned down in 1979) in Port Stanley to play a concert celebrating his fiftieth anniversary in show business. A music scholarship was named in his honour, and the following year, the Guy Lombardo Bridge joining Wonderland and Hutton roads (it had the unfortunate reputation as being the "bridge to nowhere") was opened.

The grand old lady of London entertainment, the Grand Theatre, re-opened for the 1978-1979 season after undergoing a $5.5 million face lift. A few Londoners were somewhat disappointed, however, when the skeleton of former owner Ambrose Small who mysteriously disappeared in 1919, did *not* turn up. Much less disappointing, to say the least, was the showpiece of the theatre, the restored proscenium arch which was painted by London artist Eva Bradshaw in 1901. The Grand Theatre Company, which had turned professional in 1972, has established a reputation for excellence. Two particular London favourites, actors Hume Cronyn and Jessica Tandy, have made appearances at the theatre from time to time. Hume Cronyn is a great grandson of the first Bishop of Huron, Benjamin Cronyn.

Not so entertaining to Londoners in the 1970s was the weather — the blizzards of 1971 and 1978 in particular. The January 1978 storm, saw

1976
Gases from spray cans discovered to cause damage to the atmosphere's ozone layer.

"CONDEMNED" COURTHOUSE, 1971
When the new Middlesex County Courthouse was built at the northeast corner of Dundas and Ridout Streets in 1971-74, the future of the old courthouse came into question. Merle R. "Ting" Tingley, the London Free Press cartoonist, added some humour to the dilemma. Luckily, the Gothic landmark was given a reprieve when the County of Middlesex agreed to maintain it as an administrative centre.

1977
President Jimmy Carter grants a pardon to American draft evaders of the Vietnam War era.

London virtually crippled by the howling white winds from Lake Huron. The *Free Press* reported that:

> The north winds stranded thousands in homes, autos and businesses, turned downtown hotels and highway service stations into refugee camps, and closed city and area schools yet again, blew down trees, demolished store signs and high rise apartment windows, and left thousands without heat or light.

The timing of the storm was unfortunate, because most of the 1st Battalion RCR, who had done much of the rescue work in the '71 blizzard, were out of town on manoeuvres. They did manage to get a few armoured vehicles out on the road to assist those who needed help. Eight London area residents lost their lives in the storm, most from carbon monoxide poisoning caused by sitting in stalled cars waiting for rescue.

London's most enduring landmark, the Middlesex County courthouse, was also in need of a rescue mission. Once again, it found itself in the midst of a heated, long, yet always passionate debate over its future. By the mid 1960s, it became clear to everyone that the building was just too small and the jail was a veritable disgrace. Said one grand jury: "If it were used to house animals rather than human beings it would still be inadequate." The province of Ontario solved the problem of space by taking over the costs of administering justice and building a new concrete edifice on the Ridout-Queens-Dundas-Talbot block, opened 1974. The question remained, however, — what to do with the old courthouse? Several groups representing competing visions began to mobilize. In one corner were those who supported the idea of a "Middlesex Court Centre" — a combination museum, library, recreational oasis, tourist attraction, educational facility and art studio. In another corner were those who would have preferred to bulldoze the thing and build an arts centre. Still another group favoured simply restoring the courthouse and jail. Finally, in 1977, thanks to Middlesex County Council's initiative, in partnership with the federal and provincial governments, a $2.5 million courthouse restoration was approved for county council offices. City council, for its part, agreed to support the building of London's first permanent art gallery, right across from it at the northwest corner of Ridout and Dundas streets, overlooking the forks of the river.

Probably no other building in the history of London has been the subject of so much conflict, concern, controversy, and passion as the courthouse. "It's too small; It's too smelly; The door faces the wrong way" are just a few of the refrains heard over the decades. Despite all, however, it has always managed to escape with most of its integrity intact, and none the worse for wear. At the close of the 1970s, the plans for restoration in the works, the future of Talbot's castle seemed secure. And perhaps, finally, it had achieved a dignified, and peaceful, old age.

1978
*First "test-tube"
baby born in
England.*

CHAPTER THIRTEEN

The Greening of London

To be modern is to find ourselves in an environment that promises us adventure, power, joy, growth, transformation of ourselves and the world — and at the same time that threatens to destroy everything we have, everything we know, everything we are."
— (Marshall Berman, *All That Is Solid Melts Into Air.* New York: 1982.)

By the 1980s, London's days of light-speed development were over. The mushrooming of houses and industries in the periphery of the city had slowed. The London *Free Press* no longer ran special development supplements full of articles enthusing on the number of factories being built per month. Growth was still evident in the gradually increasing population and in the development of subdivisions in the south and north of the city, but things were moving at a steadier pace. In this time, there was a perceptible change in attitude among many Londoners to the way the city was growing. The values of development at any price were being questioned from a number of quarters. Instead, Londoners began to focus more on things that enhance the quality of life in the city — the arts, recreation, the environmental and architectural heritage, and community services.

A sunny May 3, 1980, saw the official opening of the London Regional Art Gallery at the northwest corner of Dundas and Ridout streets. In a typically cautious fashion, London's permanent art gallery was built only one hundred years after members of the Western Art League began arguing for one in the 1880s. It was almost inevitable, then, that such a long-awaited building be somewhat controversial. A brochure on the gallery describes the building designed by Toronto architect Raymond Moriyama in rather dramatic terms:

> On the outside, its blue barrel vaults cascade toward the Thames while the canopied entrance invites visitors into a world of images and ideas, colours and imagination.

Yet the new building also invoked more than a few not-so-complimentary comments — comparisons with silos, horse barns, and boiler factories, for example. There was noticed, moreover, a striking similar-

THE FORKS OF THE THAMES RIVER, 1984
This aerial photograph presents a striking contrast with "The Forks" familiar to John Graves Simcoe. Nonetheless, the city still radiates from the honoured point of its civic genesis.

1980
Mount St. Helens, Washington State, erupts.

**INTERIOR OF THE
LONDON REGIONAL
ART GALLERY,
APRIL 22, 1980**
*Inviting "visitors into
a world of images
and ideas, colours
and imagination"
the London Regional
Art Gallery at the
northwest corner of
Dundas and Ridout
Streets officially
opened its doors on
May 3, 1980.*

1980
*Ex-Beatle John
Lennon murdered
by Mark David
Chapman.*

ity to the existing gallery in Fort Worth, Texas. The 7,000 visitors who trekked through on the first day, however, didn't seem to mind.

Just one short year later, London gained another new cultural landmark. On May 21, 1981, Wilfrid and Elsie Jury opened the Lawson-Jury Building, the new home of the Museum of Indian Archaeology on Attawandaron Road. This event, too, was the result of many years of hard work, diligence and campaigning. In this case, the main proponent was Wilfrid Jury, the first curator of the museum. As a young boy on a Lobo Township farm, Wilfrid and his father Amos began collecting and cataloguing various Indian artifacts they found in the area. By 1930, the collection, which they stored behind their barn, had grown to 3,000 items. When the Lawson Memorial Library opened at Western, the university invited the Jurys to bring their collection to the library. This led to the creation of the Museum of Indian Archaeology and Pioneer Life. In 1948, Wilfrid married Elsie McLeod Murray, an historian and librarian at Western. Together, the husband and wife team embarked on many archaeological excavations which included Ste. Marie-Among-the-Hurons at Midland and the Moravian village at Fairfield near Chatham.

The new museum in the Lawson-Jury Building features the Wilfrid Jury Collection, some 40,000 items, which represents fifty years of work. It is also one of the best archaeological research and training centres in Canada. Next to the village is the Lawson Prehistoric Indian Village, a recon-

**LONDON REGIONAL
CHILDREN'S
MUSEUM**
*Unique in South-
western Ontario, the
London Regional
Children's Museum
offers the young
mind a "hands on"
approach to learning
about the world.
Opened in 1982, the
museum was the first
of its kind in Canada.*

struction of a 15th century village on its original site. Wilfrid Jury died just a few months after the museum opened, at the age of 91.

The London Regional Children's Museum, the first children's museum in Canada, found a permanent home in the old Riverview School on Wharncliffe Road South in 1982. Inspired by a visit to a children's museum in Boston, founder and director Carol Johnston used a "hands on" approach to learning in the creation of the museum in rented quarters in 1975. Visitors crawl through tunnels to learn about "Things in Caves," play Inuit games in the "Inuit Gallery," try on old clothes in the "Child Long Ago Gallery" and other fun things.

Although the building of these galleries and museums was an achievement, most artistic and cultural groups in the city went through some lean financial years in the 1980s. Orchestra London came up with "Interiors," an innovative approach to fundraising that also brought a part of London's past to the public. Every year, one of London's mansions built by merchants and doctors and lawyers long ago is loaned to the Orchestra. Local interior designers redecorate each room of the house and the public is invited to view the result. Some of the houses used over the years have included "Windermere," the Elsie Perrin Williams Estate, "Hylands," the former Ivey Estate, and "Idlewyld," the former home of Charles Smith Hyman.

1981
*Terry Fox, one-
legged cancer vic-
tim raised millions
by attempting a
cross-country run,
the "Marathon of
Hope," dies age 24.*

While these grand old buildings were being refurbished and renewed, dedicated groups of Londoners were fighting to save other pieces of London's architectural heritage. After several landmarks, such as the Benjamin Cronyn mansion, the 1872 Federal Customs House, and the "Beechwood" estate were demolished by developers in the 1970s, several groups of heritage-minded citizens began organizing to make sure important historical buildings could not be destroyed at the owner's whim. They pressured for a committee to advise city council on heritage matters. Leading this drive were: the Urban League, the Council of Women, the local chapters of both the Architectural Conservancy of Ontario and the Ontario Association of Architects; the London and Middlesex Historical Society, and the London Public Library's Historic Sites Committee. The result, in 1973, was the Local Architectural Conservation Advisory Committee. In 1989 Mark Gladysz was appointed the city's first Heritage Planner.

The Talbot Streetscape, a block of Victorian commercial buildings on the west side of Talbot Street between Dundas and King streets, became a rallying point for these heritage groups in the 1980s. The streetscape was the last unbroken stretch of Victorian storefronts in the downtown area, and was considered by some to be the finest example of such architecture in Ontario. It was threatened with demolition when Cambridge Leaseholds Inc., owner of the properties, announced plans for a shopping and residential complex on the site. At first, city council supported the developer, but public pressure, and the newly-formed Talbot Coalition, made many council members reconsider the project. City council held off Cambridge's attempts to obtain a demolition permit, while the empty Talbot buildings slowly began to deteriorate. In the end, however, Cambridge won. The divided council finally voted to issue the permit. Cambridge, who from 1979 had patiently assembled an entire city block, quickly tore down most of the streetscape buildings in the fall of 1991. Whilst the battle had raged, Campeau Corporation, in 1989, opened its own shopping complex, Galleria London, on the enlarged site of the former London Eaton Square. The Cambridge site in 1992 remained a windy parking lot dotted with uneven outlines of its former structures. The whole experience left many Londoners bitter, but it did inject them with the belief that a more comprehensive heritage plan needed to be developed. Said Peter Desbarats, dean of Western's Journalism School in a *Free Press* column:

> As one of the combatants, I'm keenly aware of our failure to attract widespread support in the community. Saving the Talbot Block has remained an elitist issue despite our best efforts to popularize it. Unfortunately, the elite in this case didn't represent the real centres of money and power in the community, but only a small band of artists, intellectuals, historians, activists, a smattering of independent-minded architects, and a couple of unorthodox developers. We were unable to persuade a significant minority of Londoners that saving the Talbot streetscape made sense, not only historically and culturally, but commercially.

1981
Prince Charles, heir to the British throne, weds Lady Diana Spencer.

London's environmental heritage also became a focus for Londoners in the 1980s. When PCBs (polychlorinated biphenyls) were discovered in Pottersburg Creek, London residents began to realize that some of the parks and waterways they had always thought were safe places for their chil-

TALBOT STREETSCAPE DEMOLITION, SEPTEMBER 26, 1991

Though temporarily halted by the discovery of London's first town hall (framework of which is pictured), the demolition of the Talbot Streetscape forever obliterated the city's most complete row of Victorian storefront architecture.

THE "BLUE BOX" PROGRAM, 1989

In response to growing concern for the environment, the City of London adopted the "blue box" household recycling program in the late 1980s. Fully implemented by January, 1990, the effort has helped to reduce demands on municipal landfill space.

PANORAMA 1990
Friendly smiles have been an inseparable part of the ambassadorship associated with London's cultural festivals. This children's dance troup greeted visitors to the Chinese-Canadian Club during Panorama 1990.

1982
Falklands Islands war between Argentina and Britain lasts 10 weeks, costs $5 billion.

dren to play, weren't. In the wake of the cleanup project carried out by the provincial government, citizens groups began organizing for change. People such as Western professor Joe Cummins, Dawn Erskine, who later became a city councillor, and Diane Whiteside, who also entered municipal politics as a member of the PUC, came to the public forum to address health hazards in the community. There have also been campaigns to save natural areas in the city limits by such groups as the McIlwraith Field Naturalists, the Thames Region Ecological Association, and the Upper Thames River Conservation Authority. The Sifton Bog (formerly Byron Bog) is one such area that has been protected from development since 1962, but others that have had to be "saved" include Westminster Ponds/Pond Mills, and Meadowlily Woods in southeast London.

The health of the people living in the community got a "shot in the arm," so to speak, when all three hospitals expanded. University Hospital added the Robarts Institute, which specializes in immunology, and heart and stroke research. Work began on a new St. Mary's Hospital, part of the St. Joseph's Health Care Centre. Victoria Hospital expanded a century of life on South Street when it began moving, in 1985, to new quarters on the Westminster Campus, at the corner of Wellington and Commissioners roads. London's position as the medical centre of southwestern Ontario was firmly established.

During the devastating famine in Ethiopia in the 1980s, Londoners and the medical community worked on a joint project to help alleviate the suffering. In a campaign spear-headed by the local Kinsmen, $175,000 was raised in just a few months to send a medical team to Camp Bete, a camp for the starving refugees of the long civil war. Two teams comprised of doctors, nurses and administrators went to Bete in 1985. Several team members remained well beyond their scheduled three-month stay to help set up a permanent clinic, and form a tree-planting program called "Future Forests".

In education, the 1980s were a time when the school boards were able to reach out to those they had not been able to serve before. The G.A. Wheable Centre for Adult Education, formerly a regular secondary school, opened in September, 1987 for adults who, for some reason or another, had not been able to complete their schooling. Likewise, francophone secondary school students were given the opportunity to receive full instruction in their first language at the Ecole Secondaire Monseigneur Bruyere operated by the London and Middlesex County Roman Catholic Separate School Board.

Two long-time havens for London's young people burned to the ground and rose again from the ashes in the 1980s. On a cold January 5, 1981, the YM-YWCA building at the southwest corner of Wellington Street and Queens Avenue was destroyed by fire. Spray from the fire hoses left the remains of the 85-year-old building looking like a gothic ice palace. Two years later, a brand new facility opened at the corner of King and Waterloo streets. Similarly, the Memorial Boys and Girls Club, housed in a wildly painted former warehouse on Horton Street, was damaged by fire, torn down, and born again on the same location in 1986. As always, London's United Way continued to get Londoners involved in raising funds for projects such as these.

London's ethnic balance shifted more noticeably in the 1980s. In 1980, between 25 and 30% of London's population was of non-British origin. The largest minority ethnic groups were still the Germans, Dutch, Italians, and the Portuguese, but some of the fastest growing groups were refugees from southeast Asia, Central America, Poland, and Africa. The Cross Cultural Learner Centre (CCLC) began operating the Immigrant Settlement and Adoption Program to help newcomers adjust to life in their new country. CCLC also provided advice and guidance to church and other community groups who "adopted" refugee families. In 1987, Global House, a transition accommodation centre, opened at 719 Dundas Street for new arrivals. Before, many ended up staying in government-rented rooms in

DAVID PETERSON, 1987
The third Londoner to sit as an Ontario Premier, David Peterson, representing the riding of London Centre, carried his Liberals to a coalition government in 1985, and to a landslide victory in 1987. He and his administration, however, were swept out of power in 1990 by Ontario's first New Democratic Party government.

1983
In the Caribbean, Grenada's Premier Maurice Bishop is assassinated and the U.S. invades the country.

the Esquire Hotel. Because of these programs, London has been considered one of the best refugee settlement centres in the province.

The Folk Arts Council's Holiday Festival evolved into "Kavalkade" in 1980. From 1980 to 1987, this ethnic festival was held annually at various ethnic clubs around the city. Each participating club provided entertainment, displayed their arts and crafts, and served their traditional food and drink. In the final year of its existence, 25 clubs took part, and 250,000 "passports" were sold. For various reasons, Kavalkade in its existing format was not continued after 1987, but a number of the ethnic clubs in the city carried on the tradition with "Panorama," which continues to be held every fall.

Women, still considered a "minority" even though they comprise 52% of the population, were also active in organizing to improve the lives of women in the community. Joining the long-standing Council of Women was a new organization with a more specifically feminist orientation, the London Status of Women Action Group (LSWAG). Founded in March, 1978, LSWAG acts as a lobby and action group, committed to social change. They also organize activities for International Women's Day, and the annual "Take Back the Night" marches.

Violence against women in society is one such issue that LSWAG has been bringing to the public's attention. London has had its share of this social problem, and several agencies have been helping women and children caught in a cycle of violence. The Battered Women's Advocacy Clinic opened in 1983 to provide counselling for abused women. The Women's Community House shelter first opened in 1978, and because of increasing demand for its services began building a second shelter in 1991.

Violence of another sort — in this case the destructiveness of a tornado — had Londoners hiding under tables and in doorframes on September 2, 1984. The tornado that touched down in South London that afternoon caused $5 million in damages to 600 houses and 50 businesses. Thirty people were injured. Southwestern Ontario is a frequent target for tornadoes, the most destructive incidents being the Sarnia tornado of 1953, the Woodstock tornado of 1979, and the demolition of Reeces Corners in 1983.

The political scene, fortunately, was slightly less chaotic. In 1985, Mayor Al Gleeson, who had replaced Jane Bigelow in 1978, was defeated by Ward 6 Alderman Thomas C. Gosnell, son of former mayor Fred Gosnell. That same year London sent yet another local MPP to the premier's office, Liberal David Peterson. First elected to the Ontario legislature in 1975, he captured the Liberal Party leadership in 1982.

The London "Mall Wars" broke out in the 1980s when two of the largest suburban malls, Westmount and Whiteoaks, announced major expansions. Meanwhile, a new Cadillac-Fairview centre, Masonville Place, opened its doors and parking lots to shoppers at Richmond Street and Fanshawe Park Road in 1985.

London added a few more summer festivals to its annual calendar of events in the 1980s. Colonel Tom Lawson and London teacher Tyrone Traher organized the first Big Band Festival on the Canada Day Weekend in 1984. A special feature of the event was Guy Lombardo's Royal Canadi-

1986

Explosion at Ukraine's Chernobyl nuclear power plant exposes millions to radiation danger.

ans. Also in 1984 the first London Hot Air Balloon Fiesta was scheduled to take off at Harris Park. Although poor weather kept the balloons grounded that year, organizers persevered and the event had been a success ever since.

The "Old Boys' Reunion" which was held at erratic intervals between 1897 and 1938, was resurrected in 1988, on the fifthieth anniversary of the last, as "Reunion London". The original "Old Boys" were former pupils of London educator Nicholas "Old Nick" Wilson. Held during the busy Canada Day weekend, the recent version featured parades, sidewalk entertainment, the Big Band Festival, and the RCRs' 105th anniversary celebrations.

Baseball has long been a favourite summer pastime in London, ever since the days of the World Champion London Tecumsehs. In 1936, the Labatt family bought and refurbished the old Tecumseh playing field at the forks of the Thames. It was in Labatt Park that another favourite London team, the London Majors, won the North American Sandlot Championship in 1948. In 1989, professional baseball returned to London (the original Tecumsehs, among others, were a professional team) with the arrival of the London Tigers, a "Double A" farm team of the Detroit Tigers. Labatt Park, which is one of the oldest still-functioning sites for amateur

LONDON TIGERS BASEBALL GAME, JUNE 4, 1990
In keeping with London's time-honoured tradition as a fanatic baseball town, the London Tigers professional club came to the city in 1989. Affiliated with the Detroit Tigers, and calling Labatt Park their home, the London Tigers captured the Eastern "AA" League title in 1990, downing New Britain 2 to 1 in the final game.

THE JOHN GORDON HOME, AUGUST, 1992

Acquired Immune Deficiency Syndrome (AIDS) has been the most misunderstood disease of the 1980s and 1990s. Intended to provide dignity and comfort to those dying from the devastating illness, an AIDS hostel was opened at 414 Dufferin Avenue in the fall of 1992. The facility is named in memory of John Gordon, who campaigned tirelessly for such a home.

1987

Vincent Van Gogh's painting "Irises" sells for record $71.5 million at auction.

baseball in North America, also won the Bean Clay Professional Field Award for 1989-90.

The Londoners who flocked to the Tigers' games in the summer of 1989 were generally a contented lot. The *City of London Annual Report* of that year boasted that London offered to its citizens:

> A world class medical community; well-established educational facilities; a vibrant downtown; a good commercial and residential mix; including a broad manufacturing base and a large retail sector, clean streets and well-maintained sidewalks, riverbank parklands; a myriad of entertainment, history and cultural activity; a shopping mecca; and a caring and accessible social services network all add up to a quality of life that is second to none.

Most would say that London is a good place to live, but maybe a few exaggerations crept into the above passage. "Vibrant," most would say, is too strong a word to describe the downtown area. In fact, many were concerned about the growing number of empty storefronts that were left in the wake of the arrival of Galleria London. Those who witnessed the battle over the Talbot Streetscape were not reassured that the city was able to preserve the valuable architectural heritage. Despite London's traditional reputation as a "fat cat" city, approximately one-quarter of the population was classified in the "low-income" bracket. Clearly, London still had a way to go before it was as perfect a place as the *Annual Report* described it.

The city's first "Official Plan" in eighteen years appeared in 1989, spik-

ing the guns of critics who had long claimed London didn't really have a plan for development and growth. With the theme of "Taking London into the 21st century," the plan advised:

> As the economic, institutional, administrative and cultural centre for southwestern Ontario, London has experienced consistent growth and development in the past decade. The growth is expected to continue and a policy plan is necessary for continued orderly urban development which will allow London to remain one of the most beautiful and prosperous cities in Canada.
>
> The New Official Plan is based on a 25 year growth period for the city and replaces the 1971 Official Plan. The Official Plan outlines City Council's planning objectives and policies for the short and long term development of London. It also establishes a review process for dealing with applications for development and contains a detailed implementation section which explains how plans will be put into action.

Time has yet to prove how well this new "Official Plan" will keep London "beautiful and prosperous," and whether or not its guidelines concerning development have any "teeth". Unlike previous "Official Plans," however, it at least acknowledged the importance of heritage buildings and the natural environment in the city. The thinking at city hall had come a long way since the early 1960s when it seemed that building more shopping plazas in the suburbs was all that really mattered.

CONVENTION CENTRE
London's long-awaited Convention Centre began construction Nov. 1991 and anticipates completion Sept. 1993. Its civic promoters proclaim. . .: London. . . a city committed to making your convention an outstanding success. Meeting your needs! Exceeding your expectations."

1989
Pro-democracy demonstrations in China start in April; crushed by brute force with many deaths in June.

CHAPTER FOURTEEN

Celebration and Challenge

(Edward Phelps, with research by Miriam Wright)

Approaching the 200th anniversary of its founding, the City of London looks toward a future filled with promise and hope, never losing sight of its rich heritage. Recognizing that its greatest resource is its citizens, London is wise in its support of the age-old adage — "the future lies with the people!"
City of London Annual Report (London: 1991)

As the 200th anniversary of the visit to the forks by John Graves Simcoe is marked in 1993, London has many reasons to celebrate. Perhaps few but the visionary Simcoe would have imagined that the meeting of the branches of the Thames River in the midst of a large forest could ever evolve into a healthy metropolis of more than 300,000 people. Yet, many challenges lie ahead for the city and its region. In the first instance, many Londoners are pre-occupied with sheer economic survival during a prolonged business recession beginning with a severe stock-market decline in late 1987. Indeed, by the summer of 1992, despite glimmerings of recovery, it appeared that the area was enduring its most critical challenge since the Great Depression of 1929-1939.

London's economy was very much beyond Londoners' ability to influence or control, as many major head offices had now left the city for Toronto or elsewhere. (Symbolically, perhaps, Labatt's, in 1992, moved its annual meeting to Toronto.) The multi-national nature of business, together with the emergence of powerful continental trading blocs, placed major decision-making outside the region. Locally, some plants have migrated to the United States and Mexico as a result of North American free trade. Such phrases as "GST", "Cross-border shopping" and "free-trade agreement" dominate concerns both at the breakfast table and in the board room.

Taking up the challenge to adapt and survive into the next century, the business community, in various co-operative associations with federal, provincial, and municipal governments, and sometimes with the University of Western Ontario and Fanshawe College of Applied Arts and Technology, has brought forward a number of innovative programs. The

GREG CURNOE AND J.H. MOORE, 1992
The special relationship between renowned London artist Greg Curnoe (left) and John H. "Jake" Moore has resulted in Mr. and Mrs. Moore generously donating 53 of Curnoe's works to the London Regional Art and Historical Museums. Such good will has provided the city's artistic community with fertile ground in which to flourish.

1990
Mikhail Gorbachev becomes first executive president of USSR amidst crumbling of the Soviet federation.

EMPLOYMENT LINE, FEBRUARY 1992

The recession of the early 1990s brought about a sudden end to what were occasionally termed the "acquisitive 1980's". A hard time for many including the highly skilled, the years saw the employment lines swell.

1990

US invasion of Panama ends with capture of General Noreiga.

London Community Small Business Centre starting in 1987 at the former Proto Tools plant in London's east industrial section, is a "business incubator" providing new ventures with a network of expertise, and information, together with affordable rental space. Twenty-six companies were tenants in 1992, whilst another sixteen had "graduated" to set up on their own. Adjacent to their premises the City of London plans its first High Tech Park of 35 acres tailored to specialized business needs. Northwest of the UWO's main campus is now located the UWO Research Park, housing firms engaged solely in research. Its centre-piece is London's second-largest private mansion, the former Smallman home on Windermere Road, now renovated and preserved. Also on Windermere Road, London's largest mansion, the former Spencer home, which was Western's original women's residence, became a major business conference centre in recent years in partnership with the Bank of Nova Scotia.

The London High Technology Association was formed in 1987 "as a chance for the small operations that are so common in the world of high tech to establish some professional connections, as well as building on their individual strengths by working together;" as an influence group, it had 175 members by mid 1992.

In 1967, members of Junior Achievement of London and District proudly watched Hon. John P. Robarts, Ontario's premier, open its headquarters at Dundas and Wharncliffe, which was primarily funded by 92 local businesses. Its plaque echoed the pride of this group which was founded in 1962 under Jack Mahoney, a Victoria Cross winner who became their first Executive Director. It reads,

This building, Canada's first permanent Junior Achievement Business Centre, is a Centennial project, created by the members of the business community of greater London. It is dedicated to the preservation of Canada's economic free enterprise system through the "learn by doing" education of youth.

SUBURBAN FARMLAND, SPRING 1991
The prime farmland surrounding London, the target of countless development schemes, has become especially threatened since the city annexed large tracts of acreage from neighbouring rural areas of Middlesex County, in 1961 and again in 1993.

Now in its 30th year of operation, the London program enrols about 3,000 youths from area elementary and secondary schools, between the levels of Grades 5 and 13, in a wide variety of programs.

Federal government activity profoundly affected London in the 1990s. During 1989 it was announced that, owing to a nation-wide military restructuring program, London's Royal Canadian Regiment contingent would be relocated at Petawawa; by mid-1992 the entire 750 personnel had vacated their base. However, the popular and well-established RCR Museum, located in hallowed old Wolseley Hall, is designated to continue for the foreseeable future. In its hands rests many relics of 150 years of military history in London dating back to 1838 when the 32nd Regiment of Foot marched into the settlement to secure order after the Upper Canada Rebellion. A number of proposals are under active consideration for the use of the military property for community enhancement purposes. In a positive contrast to London's loss of a major economic bulwark, the Ontario Command of the Royal Canadian Mounted Police, involving about 250 positions, relocated from Toronto to London during 1992. Clyde Kitteringham, the Force's planning officer for Ontario, declared that two deciding factors in the move were London's superior airline connections, and the variety of courses available at UWO, such as law, business, and psychology, which would motivate the personnel to enhance their qualifications. He said, "I've been a strong proponent of London from day one; it's one of the classiest cities in Canada."

Federal, provincial, and municipal governments co-operated from 1988 onward in securing for London a long sought first-class Convention Centre. Senior governments each contributed $10 million, and in 1990 the city secured the site, the former Bridlewood Inn owned by Commonwealth Hospitality Ltd., east of Wellington and between York and King Streets. The civic project, valued at $69 million, commenced November 1, 1991 and was targeted for opening on September 1, 1993.

1990
VIA Rail cuts end Canada's trans-continental service. "The Canadian" went west Jan. 14 for the last time - three hours late.

The greatest challenge facing the London of the next few years is clearly annexation which takes effect January 1, 1993. About every thirty years, or once in a generation, London, like many other growing cities surrounded by a generally rural hinterland, breaks its bounds in a giant leap. The last growth spurt, effected in 1961, was, like that of 1992-3, the product of intense negotiations and controversy.

Many years of negotiating with its Middlesex County neighbours saw the growth of valuable co-operative programs, such as suburban roads, water resources policy, waste management, school board adjustments, and more. All, however, fell short of meeting London's demand for more growth space under its direct control, eventually, by 1987 the City felt ready to assert and to ensure its predominance in the region. Early in 1988 Council passed the necessary by-laws giving forth its intent to annex. Boundary adjustment negotiations by committee followed, reaching a stalemate in early 1992. At that point, the government of Ontario, with a backlog of other pending annexation requests province-wide, took the innovative step of appointing John Brant, a city businessman, as the "Greater London Area Arbitrator."

Two months of intensive speculation followed on the possible outcome of Brant's work, as he stoically endured uncounted hours of meetings, and reviewed thousands of pages of written submissions and research data. His report, entitled, "Co-opportunity: success through co-operative independence," was released April 3, 1992, to a standing-room-only audience at the Middlesex County council chamber. For municipal personnel from both city and country, and for the media, it was a dramatic moment. Brant's findings appeared virtually to grant the City of London its full "wish list." He stated:

> My recommendation is that the City of London be granted much of its annexation request and be challenged to develop a future city with a vision that includes the most creative environmental and social planning while the County will receive substantial compensation in the form of a capital fund which will allow it to develop as the financially strongest county in Ontario. ...

> "... Effective January 1, 1993, the London PUC responsibilities will become the responsibility of the City of London Council. The London Council will create a Hydro-Electric Commission of appointed officials and may want to appoint the present elected PUC members as the first Commission."

Under this scenario, London will grow by 26,000 hectares (64,220 acres) at the expense of five of its municipal neighbours. It will be nearly three times its present size, and, by comparison, will swell to eighty percent of the area of Metropolitan Toronto. Annexed lands include London Airport, and the highways 401 and 402 corridors. The Town of Westminster (formerly a township to 1988) will cease to exist; its distinctive communities such as Lambeth and Glanworth will become London neighbourhoods, albeit with continuing local identity, as was the case with Byron after 1961. Middlesex County will lose 35 percent of its tax base but be paid $20 million in compensation over the next decade. London will border directly on Elgin County, to the south; on the west, north and east perimeters of the enlarged city there will be a three-kilometre-wide buffer zone, aimed at discouraging fringe development and preserving farmland.

1990

Nelson Mandela released from South African prison after 27 years in jail.

TIM TINDALE WITH THE BALL, SEPTEMBER 28, 1991
Playing for the 1991 Western Mustangs, a team renowned for its punishing running backs, sophomore Tim Tindale set a new Canadian rushing record with 1208 yards. The Saunders High School graduate also broke another national mark by scoring an amazing 17 touchdowns. In a game against McMaster University, three defenders were required to haul down a determined Tindale, who led his team to a 32 to 7 victory.

Two of the three parties to the new arrangement were highly displeased: the County of Middlesex and the London Public Utilities Commission; they appealed for public, civic, court and legislative support to overturn or amend the Brant report, which in the meantime had formed the basis for provincial legislation.

An interesting historical sidelight, was a thoughtful proposal submitted to John Brant by two former county wardens, William Galbraith and Douglas Reycraft. Their brief suggested a serious study of consolidating the counties of Middlesex and Elgin, which would more evenly balance the urban and rural mix of the combined area — the same region divided into these two counties 140 years previously, in 1853.

In the midst of its greatest expansion, London's city administration saw a number of its familiar personages take their leave. Police Chief LaVerne Shipley, a 40-year veteran of the force, retired in the fall of 1991. His successor, Julian Fantino, was London's first chief to come from outside the ranks of the local force; he was recruited from the Metropolitan Toronto Police Force where he had served over twenty years.

Popular fire chief Robert Barr, a 36-year veteran of the department, retired August 1991 after ten years at the helm. Deputy Chief J.F. (Jim) Fitzgerald was appointed late in 1991 to head the force of 300 professional fire-fighters based at ten stations. It was away back in 1873 that the force went over from a volunteer group to a paid professional force. Chief Fitzgerald carries on a unique four-generation tradition in London fire-fighting. Grandfather Fred began in 1909, father James H., in 1925, his own career started 1955, and his son Shawn began in 1986.

Two senior London administrators finished their civic careers in 1992:

1990
Sept. 6th - Ontario's first NDP government is elected under Premier Robert (Bob) Rae.

"PEOPLE AND THE CITY", 1992
In tribute to those who have helped shape London over the last two centuries, in 1991, the City of London erected this bronze sculpture on the Wellington Street median just north of Queens Avenue. A timely project, the monument commemorates the 200th anniversary of John Graves Simcoe's arrival at "The Forks".

1991
"Gulf War" involving U.S., allies, on behalf of Kuwait, against Iraq, lasts several weeks.

Maurice Engels, City Administrator, retired and was replaced by John Fleming, who had been Chief Administrative Officer at the Regional Municipality of Halton, City Engineer D'Arcy B. Dutton retired in August, 1992. John W. Jardine, his successor, started October 1992; he came from the London PUC, having been manager of waterworks and engineering. Long-time Middlesex County Clerk-Administrator Ronald F. Eddy was elected to the Legislature of Ontario as the Liberal member for Brant, following in the footsteps of Ontario's longest-serving elected member Robert F. (Bob) Nixon. His office was filled by Donald Hudson, the Treasurer, pending the resolutions of the city's annexation procedure.

London's civic pride showed itself in two major developments: its first major public swimming facility, and its first venture into "public art."

For years, every time a major competitive national or international sports event was touted for London, the lack of Olympic-standard facilities had been a problem. In August 1991 the London Aquatics Centre was opened on Wonderland Road north in the Sherwood Forest community area, with the assistance of one of London's best known philanthropists, Colonel Tom Lawson, a nearby resident. Colonel Lawson donated one million dollars in memory of his late sister, Mrs. Jean Kennedy, but died himself in February 1991 while the project was under way.

"People and the City," a monument for the city of London "honouring men and women of London whose contributions in various fields have enriched and developed the life of this city," was unveiled by His Worship Mayor Thomas Charles Gosnell and the Council on Monday, August 5, 1991 on Wellington Street at Queens Avenue. Commissioned in 1990, created by Toronto artists Stuart Reid and Doreen Balabanoff, the slim bronze opus bears the profiles of fifty prominent Londoners of the past two centuries, headed up by a dramatic rendering of John Graves Simcoe. Textual material was supplied by London commentator and essayist Herman Goodden. Attractively mounted on a recessed granite pediment, the work, at a cost of $200,000, rests on the median of London's broad central boulevard, Wellington Street, as it widens to its most spacious promenade. Public art in most Canadian towns, large or small, has traditionally generated a healthy degree of controversy, London's being no exception.

In its patient, effective way, around the same time, the Public Utilities Commission replaced the ageing Kiwanis bandshell in Victoria Park with a state-of-the-art concert structure widely admired by the public. In the summer of 1992, with the help of dedicated volunteers, the Parks and Recreation department produced a new guide to cycling and hiking routes within the city. Said Ben Gomberg, a volunteer who co-ordinated the community efforts to put the map together, "It's beyond a dream come true." Retired Professor Gordon Winder, who teamed up with Gordon Jackson to personally trek out the trails, added,

> Right in the middle of the city, people can go out and contemplate nature. There are places out there where you would think you were in the middle of the wilderness. People can go out and walk along a trail and sit on a tree trunk or grass and watch nature in progress.

Amid the patchwork quilt of ancient downtown buildings, some quite decrepit, a few lovingly restored and maintained, interspersed with endless acres of parking lots where bustling streets of human-scaled shops and businesses once flourished, great monuments of stone, cement, glass and steel arose. Among these were Old Oaks Properties' glittering Talbot Centre occupying five acres bounded by Richmond, Fullarton, Talbot, and Dufferin erected 1989-90; lost to history here was London's oldest useable downtown building, the Western Hotel (ca. 1853) a solid structure known in lore and legend as the terminus of the Donnelly stage coach routes. "Station Park" was the name given to a series of hotel/office/commercial towers erected on derelict railway lands on the north side of Pall Mall between Richmond and Waterloo. The London Chamber of Commerce is an anchor tenant in one of these fine buildings. The original late Victorian CPR station is a picturesque reminder of the days of steam transport, and awaits a redevelopment in fitting character. One London Place, a joint project of Sifton Properties Limited and London Life Insurance Company at the southwest corner of Wellington and Queens (once the site of the YM-YWCA and the original public library) was announced in 1989, and by 1992 its gleaming 24-storey steel-blue tower, London's tallest, was completed. Since 1989 plans have been under consideration for the refurbishment, replacement or relocation of Covent Garden Market and its ob-

1991
The GST (Goods and Services Tax) takes force in Canada on January 1st.

ONE LONDON PLACE, SPRING 1991
The construction of the city's tallest skyscraper, the 24 storey One London Place, was an irresistible attraction for the curious onlooker. Taken from atop the Canada Trust tower, this photograph gives the "sidewalk superintendent" a much better view of the building's foundation work.

1991
Dec. 31 USSR (Union of Soviet Socialist Republics) formally dissolved; the CIS (Commonwealth of Independent States) is organized.

solete parking facilities. The crowded, picturesque farmers' and fresh food market is a vital drawing card to the business core of London, just as its century-old antecedent was until the mid-1950s. The market's historic near neighbour, the Smallman and Ingram building, latterly Simpsons, finally The Bay, left vacant when the famous store decamped eastward to Galleria London, was overhauled, a striking corner clock tower added, and opened to a variety of business uses under the name of Market Tower.

Despite nearly thirty years of constructive heritage preservation activity, marked in recent years by the London Downtown Facade Improvement Program, numerous historical designations under Ontario heritage legislation, and latterly a voluntary Heritage Designation Program, there yet remains an uneasy truce between heritage concerns and development interests, be it over the built environment or the preservation of natural sites, with city planning considerations and standards an "uncertain trumpet."

Orlo Miller, London's senior city historian wrote recently:

> The face of London, especially in what is now called 'the old city,' has changed almost beyond recognition. Buildings that have benignly observed the passing scene for fifty, seventy-five or a hundred and more years, are being gobbled up by the developers' bulldozers, or starched, prettified, and 'gentrified' ... Many projects, if fully realized, may turn the streets of the core area into canyons of high-rise steel, concrete and glass mediocrities. This is highly unfortunate since many of the older structures are capable of being turned into attractive retail shops and boutiques of the kind that in other communities have charmed and attracted not only visitors but suburban shoppers as well. ... The needs of the automobile and its symbiotic driver have led to the development of massive shopping malls in London's suburbs, where shoppers may dawdle in a protected environment after parking their vehicles free on huge, paved prairies. These gigantic bazaars, strategically located at all the major points of the compass, have siphoned off a good deal of the trade traditionally attracted to the city's core..."

Despite the apparent prosperity indicated by the mushrooming of new buildings and shopping malls, poverty took its toll as social agencies such as the Children's Aid Society, social services, and food banks of London and its region all found their facilities and resources taxed beyond afford-able limits. In 1992, London had over 200 such helping and supporting organizations.

There were bright spots. Several years of patient yet intense lobby-ing by the AIDS Committee of London and its associates, notably Dr. Iain Mackie, paid off in June, 1992, when a spacious Dufferin Avenue home owned by Councillor Joe Swan, was offered for use as London's first AIDS hostel. When it opens in September, nursing and social support systems will come from community agencies and groups, according to Mackie, president of the John Gordon Home board of directors. (John Gordon was the first person in the region to publicly discuss his AIDS; he died January 1, 1992.) Plans are to convert it to a hospice with support services located in the building by March, 1993, provided money is available.

In the late summer of 1991 the AIDS Committee of London, mindful of the needs of the ever-increasing number of homeless street youths in London, opened the "Street Connection" in a rented core-area basement. This round-the-clock drop-in centre, under the caring, yet firm, manage-ment of Leone Wesby and a host of volunteers, was soon displaced by water damage caused by a fire elsewhere in their building. Their second location was sold to developers and the peripatetic group left "on the street," so to speak, in June 1992, but planning a come-back.

Years in planning, the new Women's Community House (SEMJA

RESURFACING CENTRAL AVENUE, JUNE 1992
The City of London undertook several large-scale works projects during 1992, including major repairs to stretches of Central Avenue.

1992
Home mortgage rates in Canada fell to a 35 year low.

UWO ORIENTATION WEEK, SEPTEMBER, 1992

UWO Orientation Week, Sept. 1992, included this enthusiastic tour of the campus by hundreds of "Frosh," who later helped in the struggle to beat cystic fibrosis in their Shinerama fundraising blitz. The annual event, started in 1968, reached a 25-year record in 1992, also topping the $1-million mark in total donations collected from Londoners over the quarter-century.

Incorporated) opened in the late summer of 1992, better equipped to fulfil its mandate: "to offer emergency shelter for physically, emotionally, and sexually assaulted women and their children," followed up by counselling programs, advocacy information, and public and professional education. The $2 million home at Wellington Road and McClary Avenue is an impressive landmark in its neighbourhood.

On London's cultural scene, its Art Gallery, for years a financial "white elephant," was administered under painful and at times controversial cost-cutting measures by its director Nancy Poole, until budget stability was finally achieved. A celebratory 50th anniversary dinner in the fall of 1990 was marked by three note-worthy events: the unveiling of an outstanding Paul Peel opus, "The Reluctant Model;" the publication of a magnificent pictorial volume entitled "The Collection," and by the announcement of the gift of the Wolf Sculpture Garden through the kind generosity of The Norton and Bernard Wolf Foundation. In 1988, The London Foundation, as a gesture to improve attendance and draw people into the little-visited downtown west end, provided funds to ensure free admission to the gallery. Programs involving the young and the old in gallery activity, the re-establishment of the Western Ontario Art exhibitions, all served to en-

TEA BOX, c. 1940
For many years a land-mark at the southwest corner of Dundas and Richmond Streets, the L-shaped Smallman and Ingram department store building was a prominent feature found on the company's tea box labels.

FOOTBALL PROGRAM, 1957
In the days before the dominance of the Canadian Football League, the city cheered on the London Lords football club. Competing in the Ontario Rugby Football Union's senior division, the Lords were joined by the Kitchener Dutchmen, the Sarnia Golden Bears, and the Toronto Balmy Beaches.

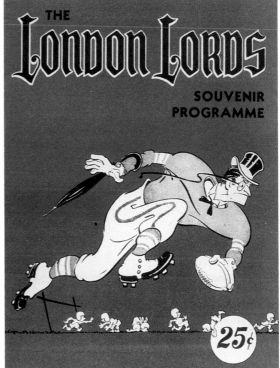

**VICTORIA PARK,
1980**
*The spring colours of
Victoria Park have delight-
ed generations of Lon-
doners and visitors alike.*

*"The 1960s brought
about dramatic
change in the city."*

BREWERY MUSEUM, 1968

Recreated by John Labatt Limited in the mid-1960s, John Balkwill's pioneer London Brewery museum pays tribute to the early beginnings of the city's oldest surviving industry.

HOTEL LONDON, SEPTEMBER 16, 1961

When a gala banquet marked its official opening on Monday, July 25, 1927, the 350-room Hotel London was the largest in Southwestern Ontario. For nearly the next 45 years, the grand building was the premier accommodation offered by the city. Today, its site supports the Canada Trust towers at Dundas and Wellington Streets.

DUNDAS STREET, 1966

This scene, looking west from Clarence Street, shows the glittering lights of a night-time Dundas streetscape.

*"Heritage is important
to a community's
sense of identity."*

**THE GRAND THEATRE,
1985**
*The faithful 1977-78
interior restoration of the
1901 Grand Theatre build-
ing on Richmond Street
revealed this magnificent
proscenium arch.*

**THE BYRON MILL,
c. 1910**
*A modern recreation, this
nostalgic painting by Ron
Nickles provides an historic
glimpse of the Byron mill.
Founded in 1836, and
demolished in 1936, the
mill gave rise to the
community of Byron.*

**GROSVENOR LODGE,
1987**
*Built in 1853 as the Gothic
residence of Samuel Peters,
and later housing the
Lawson Historical Museum
during the 1980s, Gros-
venor Lodge at 1017
Western Road currently
serves as The London
Regional Resource Centre
for Heritage and the
Environment.*

*".. . Londoners began to focus
more on things that enhance
the quality of life in the city."*

**CHILDREN'S FESTIVAL,
JUNE 9-13, 1992**
*A celebration of the une-
qualled spirit of childhood,
the second annual London
International Children's
Festival was a joyous success. The festival, which
draws performers from
across the world, offers a
diverse variety of enter-
tainments for the young,
and the young at heart.
Here we see some of the
activities at Victoria Park.*

**DOWNTOWN LONDON,
JUNE 1987**
*As viewed from a distant
point on the Thames River,
the city's downtown core
presents a tranquil, late
evening scene.*

"For many Londoners, the withdrawal of the military has been a sad parting."

REMOVAL OF THE R.C.R., JUNE, 1992
The thunder of the cannon marked the beginning of the tattoo at the Wolseley Barracks on Wednesday, June 17, 1992. The day witnessed the last official act in London of The Royal Canadian Regiment whose removal to Petawawa came by order of the federal government.

GRAND THEATRE
Artistic director of the Grand Theatre, Martha Henry, announces the offerings for the 1992-93 season, its twentieth, overshadowed by the ghostly visage of Ambrose Small (1867-1921) the theatre's greatest historical character.

GREG SALMELA AND ONTARIO'S 1992 QUARTER
Proudly seated next to his creation, London graphic artist Greg Salmela was chosen as the designer of the Ontario quarter issued in 1992 by the Royal Canadian Mint in honour of Canada's 125th birthday. Salmela's winning submission was selected from over 700 entries.

THE GOVERNOR'S LADY, ELIZABETH SIMCOE
Vigorously represented by educator Jane Barrett; her period costume was designed and created by Lisa Wright.

1992
August's Hurricane Andrew cuts across Florida and the Gulf states; over $25 billion damages.

large the sphere of activity and the degree of public participation. In 1989 a merger of the London Regional Art Gallery and the Historical Museums and Eldon House (formerly administered by the London Public Library board) was finalized; the new organization is known as the London Regional Art and Historical Museums (LRAHM). Completion in 1992 of a much needed storage, conservation, and research facility greatly enhanced the ability of the LRAHM to preserve the culture and history of the area.

A community highlight was the opening on June 24, 1992 of the new London Regional Resource Centre for Heritage and the Environment, located at Grosvenor Lodge, on Western Road. The mansion was built in 1853 for Samuel Peters, a prominant merchant. This imposing, Tudor-Gothic white brick building was designed by the owner's nephew, also named Samuel Peters, a talented architect. In 1972 the last resident family member Leila Peters Dunn sold the house and grounds to the University of Western Ontario. In 1977, UWO donated the house to the London Public Library Board to ensure its preservation. In 1981 it was opened as the Lawson Museum, and closed in 1989 because it was greatly under-used. After two years of civic responts and public hearings, Grosvenor Lodge was entrusted to the stewardship of the Heritage London Foundation in the spring of 1992. The Foundation, organized in 1981, had successfully managed another of London's public trust houses, the Elsie Perrin Williams Estate, "Windermere," and was ready to use its considerable expertise and enthusiastic membership for a new challenge.

Grosvenor Lodge has again become an active historic site, cherished and maintained by its ten founding member organizations, who are dedicated to the enhancement of the quality of life in the region. Four are heritage groups: The London & Middlesex Historical Society, and the local chapters of: the Architectural Conservancy of Ontario, the Ontario Association of Archivists, and the Ontario Archaeological Society.

Six environmental groups participate, the senior being the McIlwraith Field Naturalists, founded in 1890. Five are of more recent origin: Environmental Awareness of Greater London Education (EAGLE); Global Action Plan for the Earth (GAP); London Sports Fishery Inc.; Thames Region Ecological Association (TREA); and Thames Trail Association.

By the early 1990s, summer in the city was never so much fun. Summers came alive with the ever-popular Big Band Festival, the Canada Day festivities (highlighting the 125th anniversary of our nation in 1992), Home County Folk Festival, the Balloon Fiesta at Harris Park, the Memorial Boys' and Girls Club Rib Cook-off, and a new event that burst upon the scene in '91 — the first annual London International Children's Festival held in Victoria Park and other sites around the city. Sponsored by area school boards, the London Regional Children's Museum, and the Public Utilities Commission, the festival brought together singers, theatre, dance, and hands-on activities such as painting and tie-dying, all geared towards children. Said organizers of the philosophy of the event:

> By surrounding children with a plethora of arts experiences of the very highest calibre from around our country and around the globe, the festival encourages young people to come to understand the world around them while celebrating the arts which unite them.

As always, the summer comes to an end with the Western Fair. A reminder of the agricultural roots which were behind London's rise to prominence in the region, the fair has been held almost continuously since 1868 (the fairgrounds were used by the military during 1940-47). Despite out-of-town attractions such as "Canada's Wonderland," near Toronto, the fair remains the region's most accessible and affordable family seasonal entertainment. A kaleidoscope of displays, competitions, commercialism, loud music, rides and barely concealed "hucksterism," cotton candy, and schmaltzy grandstand shows, the Western fair, like Old Man River, just keeps rolling along. A great variety of year-round indoor and outdoor activity, and its eternally popular racetrack, keep London's Western Fair a vital meeting place for Londoners all year round. In 1991, under the guidance of President Gerry Long, Western Fair was named Major Fair of the Year by the Canadian Association of Exhibitions.

A whole year's celebration was developed to commemorate the 200th anniversary of the arrival of John Graves Simcoe at the Forks of the Thames. The "London 200" Committee, whose program appears elsewhere in this volume, is preparing a four day Festival at the Forks extravaganza for the Canada Day weekend of 1993. The good governor and his lady, decked out in period costumes, researched and created by Lisa Wright, a local designer, have made numerous colourful appearances in and around London. John Graves Simcoe is portrayed by Woody Lambe, and Elizabeth Simcoe by Jane Barrett.

What of the future? London, as its history has shown, will meet the future with courage. In the past we have survived and risen above natural disasters and the problems created by humankind. We have developed and grown. We have welcomed newcomers with open arms. We, the citizens, are slowly learning to value humanity over technology; we continue to care for our poor, our lonely, our elderly, and we owe a great debt of gratitude to that long line of selfless volunteers who carry on their works of compassion for the needy.

The secret lies in working together. It lies in an awareness of the past, and being able to profit from both our past victories and our defeats. It lies in having the courage to take the knowledge of the past and use it to build a brighter future.

We have reason to be proud of our city and its citizens. We will maintain that pride and take it with us into the coming years.

London — we salute you, and may your next 200 years be as fruitful, as exciting, as interesting, as the first!

LT. GOVERNOR JOHN GRAVES SIMCOE
Eloquently portrayed by Embro, Ontario teacher Woody Lambe; his period costume was designed and created by Lisa Wright.

1992
Barcelona Summer Olympics a great success; Canada had its best results ever.

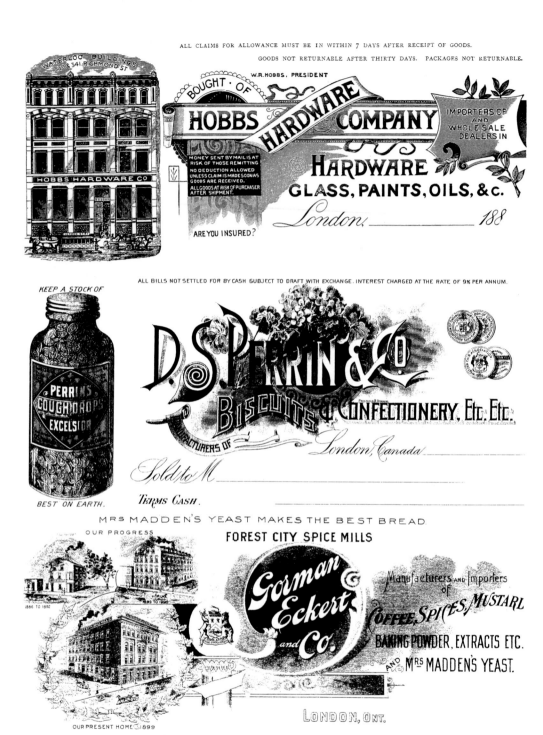

ALL CLAIMS FOR ALLOWANCE MUST BE IN WITHIN 7 DAYS AFTER RECEIPT OF GOODS.

GOODS NOT RETURNABLE AFTER THIRTY DAYS.   PACKAGES NOT RETURNABLE.

WATERLOO BUILDINGS
339 & 341 RICHMOND ST.

W.R. HOBBS, PRESIDENT

BOUGHT OF

HOBBS HARDWARE COMPANY

IMPORTERS OF
AND
WHOLE SALE
DEALERS IN

HOBBS HARDWARE CO

MONEY SENT BY MAIL IS AT
RISK OF THOSE REMITTING
NO DEDUCTION ALLOWED
UNLESS CLAIM IS MADE AS SOON AS
GOODS ARE RECEIVED.
ALL GOODS AT RISK OF PURCHASER
AFTER SHIPMENT.

HARDWARE
GLASS, PAINTS, OILS, &c.

London, _____ 188

ARE YOU INSURED?

ALL BILLS NOT SETTLED FOR BY CASH SUBJECT TO DRAFT WITH EXCHANGE. INTEREST CHARGED AT THE RATE OF 9% PER ANNUM.

KEEP A STOCK OF

PERRINS
COUGH DROPS
EXCELSIOR

D.S. PERRIN & Co.

BISCUITS & CONFECTIONERY, Etc. Etc.

MANUFACTURERS OF

London, Canada _____

Sold to M _____

BEST ON EARTH.

TERMS CASH.   _____

MRS MADDEN'S YEAST MAKES THE BEST BREAD.

OUR PROGRESS

FOREST CITY SPICE MILLS

Gorman Eckert and Co.

Manufacturers and Importers
of
COFFEE, SPICES, MUSTARD
BAKING POWDER, EXTRACTS ETC.
AND MRS MADDEN'S YEAST.

1886 TO 1892

1893 TO 1898

OUR PRESENT HOME 1899

LONDON, ONT.

Bought of

John Marshall & Co.

WHOLESALE
Manufacturers and Importers of
HATS, CAPS, FURS, GLOVES,
MITTS, STRAW GOODS, RUBBER GOODS
AND FANCY ROBES.

68 & 70, DUNDAS AND
65 CARLING ST.

JOHN MARSHALL & CO.

WHOLESALE

VICTORIAN BILLHEADS

London's modern, international business reputation has solid foundations in nineteenth century entrepreneurial success. Some of the province's most prosperous wholesale and industrial enterprises called Victorian London home. These billheads, fine examples of the lithographer's art, broadcast the vitality found in the city's business community of the 1800s.

CHAPTER FIFTEEN

Corporate Profiles

Two hundred years is a long time in anybody's terms — unless you come from a country outside of North America where centuries are the norm rather than decades. We are a young country and London is a relatively young city. But we have packed a lot of progress and excitement into our two hundred years since Lt. Gov. John Graves Simcoe, for military strategic reasons as much as anything else, thought the Forks of the Thames offered an interesting prospect for the future.

The history of a community is made up of the success, or failures, of its businesses and organizations. In this book you will have some nostalgic twinges as you see an old street sign that has long disappeared. That is, if you have lived in London much of your life. But many of today's population of more than 300,000 moved here by choice and considerable numbers of today's businesses are relatively new to London.

But there is a sense of value and comfort that comes with businesses that have not only been long-time employers in the city, but who, over many years, have become an inseparable part of the historic and community fabric of London.

This following section provides an opportunity for London's businesses and organizations to join in marking our Bicentennial. They have reserved space in this book for one of the reasons that they have continued to be successful in London for many years: they care about our community and the future of London.

It is a remarkable coincidence that we are celebrating our Bicentennial in the same year that the most significant expansion in the city's history is about to take place. Cities are living things. The people of cities are like the life blood of an organism. They are always on the move. Their work, how they spend leisure time, and the relationships they build are part of the growth and development of a municipality.

The London Chamber of Commerce, which sponsored this update of the Orlo Miller masterpiece on our first two centuries, was founded in the city in 1857. Originally called The Board of Trade, we were formed to help make London a better place to work and live. That seems to have happened.

The Chamber editorial committee appreciates the commitment of our members to make this project a success. The organizations represented on the following pages reflect a cross-section of the dynamic and forward-looking business community that has helped build and expand London.

by James G. Etherington

Chamber of Commerce

Adam Hope, First President; Arthur W. White, President 1905-6; Samuel Stevely, President 1907.

Gathering of Past Presidents - December 1991. Back row, left to right: Jack Mann, Bob Woxman, Wilf Lamb, Mark Handelman, Ron Dawson, Bryan Thomas, Bill Chizmar, Jim Etherington, John Robinson, Jim Belton. Seated, left to right: Gord Hume, J. Allyn Taylor, Del McLennan, Glenn Irvine.

Non Nobis Nati Solum — Not born for ourselves alone. Indeed, over the course of its 135 year history, the London Chamber of Commerce has come to epitomize its motto, having played an active role in almost every aspect of London's development.

On Wednesday, April 22, 1857, in the midst of an economic depression, 42 pioneer businessmen gathered for the first time at the Mechanic's Institute with their membership fee of one pound in hand. Adam Hope, a former town magistrate, became the first president of the organization, which was then known as the London Board of Trade. Simeon Morrill, the first mayor of the Town of London (1848), and Murray Anderson, the first mayor of the City of London (1855), were among the Board of Trade's founding members, as were John K. Labatt, Lionel Ridout and Sir John Carling. Years later, Carling would be instrumental in bringing George Brown and Sir John A. MacDonald together in the interest of Confederation.

The main objective of these early members was to develop London into a vital commercial and industrial centre, and to promote the city as an ideal place to work and to live. During the early years, the founding members lobbied the government for the abolition of imprisonment for debt, opposed the influx of devalued American coinage in Canada, and petitioned the government for revision of the Bankruptcy Act, and for the need of a British mailbag direct to and from London, without the delay of being re-sorted at Hamilton. Towards the end of the century, the Board of Trade successfully lobbied for the establishment of a waterworks system, secured practical courses of study in schools, supported the construction of the London, Huron and Bruce Railway, and was behind the improvement of facilities at the Port Stanley Harbour.

In 1918 the Board of Trade experienced some restructuring and officially became the London Chamber of Commerce. The need for adequate convention services was identified by the Chamber, which supported the construction of the Hotel London, to which it relocated upon the structure's completion in 1927. The construction of a convention centre is now underway and it will begin operation in the fall of 1993.

The Chamber recognized early the importance of the invention of the airplane, and was instrumental in the development of air transport in London. London Airport began operation in the spring of 1927, and a year later the first air express arrived in the city. The Chamber continued to lobby to put London on the air map, and on May 16, 1932, passenger and express service began between Toronto, London and Windsor. Since these early years of flight, the Chamber has continued to promote the development of London's air services.

Over the years, the Chamber has maintained a close relationship with the agricultural community, through its 75 year involvement with the 4H Club, and with the formation of an agricultural committee in the 1940's, which remains active to this day. The Chamber also recognized outstanding farmers with the annual Farmer of the Year Award.

On September 23, 1947, in the midst of moving the offices of the London and Western Trust Company, a bundle was

found in the firm's safekeeping department. The bundle contained the hand-written minutes of the London Board of Trade from 1857 until the early 1900's. Interestingly enough, it was recorded in the minutes that the Board of Trade, upon hearing of U.S. President Abraham Lincoln's assassination on April 14, 1865, sent a letter of condolence to his staff, and received a letter of thanks from Washington some time later.

By the 1950's, the Chamber expanded its responsibilities to include consumer watchdog, a role fulfilled today by the Better Business Bureau. Files were kept on all solicitations, both charitable and commercial, to protect the community from unscrupulous canvassers and fly-by-night businesses.

A great milestone was reached in 1957 when the Chamber celebrated its centennial year of serving the community. Membership at this time reached an all-time high of over 1000 businessmen and professionals.

From its founding until 1971, the Chamber provided tourism and convention services, now the responsibility of City Hall. Through the distribution of pamphlets and other reading material, the Chamber promoted London as an ideal long-term vacation site, rather than a day-trip on a holiday itinerary. One such brochure, sent to 5000 American tourists in 1940, advertised London as "a little bit of Old England," evoking images of the city's namesake.

In addition to tourism, the Chamber was responsible for the promotion of London's industrial development until 1964, when this area also moved under the control of City Hall. Presently, the Chamber continues to work in conjunction with the Economic Development Office to encourage new business to establish itself in London, and to maintain the current economic standards the people of London expect and enjoy.

During the course of its history, the Chamber has had an involvement in the establishment of the University of Western Ontario, Fanshawe College, Western Fair and Queen's Park, Covent Garden Market, Pinery Provincial Park, and the city's libraries and art museum.

Today, the Chamber is still serving the community in various capacities. It has worked diligently towards the continued development of airport services, the expansion of medical and educational facilities, in-

dustrial development, and the growth of London's downtown core.

Now maintaining a membership of over 2000, the Chamber provides an information service to its supporters and to the public, notably through its monthly publication, The Business Advocate. Municipal, provincial and federal government policies are reviewed regularly by Chamber committees, which voice the concerns of London's business community on issues such as free trade, labour relations, pay equity, and the federal deficit. Events such as Business After Five and Business Before Business, give members of the business community an opportunity to meet and exchange information and ideas. Moreover, companies that have made great strides in their development are distinguished with a nomination for The Business Achievement Award for excellence.

The Chamber continues to live up to its motto by successfully promoting the "fun" in fundraising for charitable organizations in the London area with its Corporate Challenge Event, which provides members with a day of fun-filled competition, and charities with revenue raised from pledges and sponsorships.

After relocating its operations several times over the last century, the Chamber settled into its permanent home in the Station Park Development in 1991. Carrying with it the same optimism for the future its founders possessed, the London Chamber of Commerce continues to exercise its mission to be the voice of business, committed to the enhancement of economic prosperity and quality of life in London.

Grand Opening 244 Pall Mall Street - February 19, 1991. Left to right: Jack Mann, President; Bryan Thomas, Chairman of the Board; Miggsie Lawson; Mayor Tom Gosnell; Tom Lawson Jr.; Hugh Smith, former Manager of the Chamber.

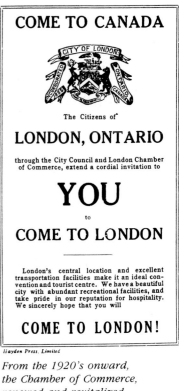

COME TO CANADA

CITY OF LONDON
INCORPORATED 1855

The Citizens of

LONDON, ONTARIO

through the City Council and London Chamber of Commerce, extend a cordial invitation to

YOU

to

COME TO LONDON

London's central location and excellent transportation facilities make it an ideal convention and tourist centre. We have a beautiful city with abundant recreational facilities, and take pride in our reputation for hospitality. We sincerely hope that you will

COME TO LONDON!

Hayden Press, Limited

From the 1920's onward, the Chamber of Commerce, renewed and revitalized, produced a continuous stream of pamphlets and promotional material on London and its attractions.

Sifton Properties

Celebrating 70 years
of service

587 Rosedale Avenue. Harry Sifton's first house.

When Harry Sifton decided in 1923 that he would build quality homes for the people of London, he knew little about the construction business. But in the roaring twenties money was plentiful, and there was a certain sense of business adventure in the air.

Sifton's first three houses still sit on Rosedale Avenue. Harry Sifton had bought the lots, built the houses, and sold them quickly for $4,500 apiece.

From those humble beginnings in 1923, Sifton Properties Limited celebrates its 70th anniversary in 1993 as one of the largest and most respected real estate developers in London. Through those years, Sifton Properties made its name developing subdivisions such as Oakridge and Westmount, and constructing and managing shopping malls, apartments, townhouses, condominiums and office towers. One of the company's recent projects, One London Place, at the corner of Wellington Street and Queens Avenue, is the tallest, most modern state-of-the-art office tower in the city.

After Rosedale Avenue, Harry Sifton was to build many pleasant houses in London, and house building has remained the backbone of this three generation, family run company.

In those days, construction machinery or power tools were virtually unknown. There were no fancy blueprints or development plans. Harry Sifton would sketch his ideas out on a piece of paper and rely on the sweat and talent of his crew, known as the Bull Gang, to build the houses.

But that changed as Harry's son, Mowbray, came to learn the construction business, first as a member of the Bull Gang, and later in partnership with his father. Mowbray Sifton would oversee the expansion and development of Sifton Properties in the 1950s, 60s and 70s, and that modernization would be taken even further after he handed the reins over to his eldest son, Glen, in 1982.

The days of building a few homes on speculation had ended. Sifton Properties became a leader in its field during the post-World War II building boom and began developing entire communities. Oakridge Acres, in London's west end, was one of Canada's first formal subdivisions. It was more than just a series of houses, but a community, with planned parkland, schools and churches.

Mowbray Sifton took these planned community dreams even further with the Oakridge Park subdivision, which included plans for commercial development within the community. The success of those two subdivisions, as well as one in Whitehills, and Sifton's growth in the rental market with the development of Berkshire Village, set the stage for the company's most ambitious land development project — Westmount.

The huge development in London's southwest, built over several stages and two decades, truly became a city within a city, complete with a variety of housing styles, schools, churches, and Westmount Shopping Centre.

In the process, Sifton Properties undertook projects in many other parts of Southwestern Ontario, as well as Ottawa, West Palm Beach and Boynton Beach, Florida. But despite this growth, Sifton Properties remained and still is today a family firm.

As it celebrates its 70th birthday, Sifton Properties Limited is one of London's foremost and best known companies, yet it remains true to Harry Sifton's dream. As company president Glen Sifton says, "we're quality rather than quantity oriented."

One London Place London's finest business address

Kellogg's
Manufacturing in London
since 1924

The roots of Kellogg Company of Canada go back to 1906 when W.K. Kellogg established the Battle Creek Toasted Corn Flake Company. By 1922, All Bran and Rice Krispies were introduced and the name was changed to Kellogg Company. In 1914, the first Canadian cereal plant was opened in Toronto. This was the first Kellogg cereal plant outside of the U.S.A. After ten years of rapid growth the production facilities were moved to the present site in London. In 1924, the Kellogg Company of Canada was established with headquarters in London. These facilities have been modernized and expanded several times over the years to accommodate the steadily increasing market demand for cereal products culminating in the latest significant investment in "Project 2000" during the early 1980's.

This expansion has become a dominant feature of the skyline in the east end of the city. The original factory still remains on Dundas Street with a futuristic glass entrance on Kellogg Lane. Blending the latest in technology with human expertise and a co-operative and informed relationship with employees, this "factory of the future" has served as a test site for the world wide operations of the parent Kellogg Company of Battle Creek, Michigan. The plant has won the Chairman's Cup for Productivity and Quality for the last three consecutive years (89, 90, 91). In Canada and throughout its worldwide operations, Kellogg cereals are renowned for consistent high quality and good value to the consumer.

Kellogg Canada Inc. has its Corporate Head Office located in Etobi-

coke. With a dominant position in the Canadian cereal market today, Kellogg's influence locally and nationally is reflected by a work force of approximately 1,000 and a product line of 24 products. Recently, the plant has begun to manufacture export products for the United States market. In addition, upwards of 57 million kg of southwestern Ontario corn is purchased annually along with other raw materials such as wheat, wheat bran and oat bran.

Kellogg Canada Inc. is proud of its London heritage and will continue to be an economic and social asset to the community.

VISION
At Kellogg Canada Inc., we are a leading innovative team of dedicated people satisfying consumers by providing high-quality, nutritious food products for a healthier life. "The Best to You Each Morning."

C.B.S. Equipment

"Servicing London and area
for over 30 years"

C.B.S. Equipment Limited, a distributor of power transmission parts, has its head office and main stockroom at 145 Adelaide Street South in London, with a branch in St. Thomas.

As a leading distributor of power components and ancillary equipment for various industrial applications, C.B.S. Equipment Limited has enjoyed the distinction of being the only home-grown London business in its field.

Founded by Morley Wilkins in 1959, the company began its operations in a small building on York Street. On July 1, 1968, the firm was acquired by owner/partners Bill Cruden, Lloyd Boughner and Bill Clinton. Cruden acquired controlling interest of the business after Clinton retired as President in 1983 and Boughner retired in 1987.

The business enjoyed a steady growth, and in 1979, after five extensions at its Hamilton Road location, the company was moved to its present operations at 145 Adelaide Street South, more than doubling the capacity to 8000 square feet. A branch was acquired in Simcoe in 1976 and was sold to one of the firm's employees in May, 1992. A second division was acquired in St. Thomas in 1982 and continues to serve a 60 mile radius.

From its head office and main stockroom on Adelaide Street, C.B.S. Equipment's fully computerized operation maintains an inventory of 40,000 parts, and acts as the nerve centre of a network reaching into a large area of south western Ontario.

While C.B.S. mainly distributes power transmission parts, which link the machine with the power source, their vast inventory includes bearings, v-belts, chain, couplings, clutches and brakes, gears, motors, and reducers, as well as conveyor components, material handling equipment and a line of filters. Serving the industrial sector, C.B.S. also distributes parts to an expanding client base in the fields of construction and agriculture.

Over 30 years of business, the sales volume has multiplied almost 25 times to five million dollars annually, and inventory has increased twelve times to a value of $600,000. What began as a staff of six has expanded to 22 employees after the sale of the Simcoe branch. A sales force of two people at head office and one person in St. Thomas support C.B.S. clientele and acquire new business for the firm.

The intensive training of C.B.S. employees in composition and adaptation of the units, in addition to the provision of lines from major manufacturers in Canada, the United States, Europe and Japan, has contributed largely to the success of the business.

In order to generate increased purchasing power, C.B.S. joined with eleven Ontario and two Quebec companies in 1984 to form Independent Distributors Incorporated (I.D.I.). C.B.S. is also a member of the Power Transmission Distributors Association of America, and has been a member of the Bearing Specialists Association (B.S.A.) since 1986.

In 1983, C.B.S. entered a new era of technological sophistication by fully computerizing all of its departments. Recently, this system was completely upgraded and a line of P.C.'s was added. These developments, coupled with the 1985 installation of photo facsimile equipment for instantaneous order processing, have contributed to C.B.S. Equipment's highly efficient operations, and pave the way for future advancement.

The Gallo Group

Proud of our past, excited about our future in London!

A young, energetic company, The Gallo Group Incorporated, founded and managed by Nicolo Gallo, is an enthusiastic participant in the exciting growth of the city of London.

The Gallo Group is dedicated to the development and building of quality, innovative real estate projects within London. The firm is recognized for its creative and practical approach, in addition to its diligent sensitivity to the individual client's requests.

The corporation owns and manages a mixed portfolio of office buildings and retail plazas, and continues to focus on core area development. Of special interest to the firm is the restoration of structures of significant historical value.

As president of The Gallo Group, Nicolo Gallo's commitment to excellence is particularly evident in the quality buildings created for Consumers' Gas Company Ltd. and IST Healthcare Ltd. on Exeter Road.

The firm's team of dedicated consultants and construction professionals provide custom-designed buildings uniquely suited to their clients' needs. For businesses seeking the perfect balance of distinctive architecture and an accommodating work environment, The Gallo Group is the natural choice.

Historical restoration, 320 Princess Ave., London.

Nicolo Gallo.

The Gallo Group office building, 295 Wolfe St., London.

Conference Room, 733 Exeter Road, London.

Matthews Group

A London company competing in the international market

Don Matthews, Chairman and Founder of Matthews Group.

This photo was taken looking east on Princess Avenue towards Adelaide Street during the construction of storm sewers in 1958.

In 1953, Don Matthews decided to go into business for himself. He was 27 years old, the youngest son in a working-class family of 12, and himself a father of two with another on the way.

Armed with a total of $24,500, invested by his father (who mortgaged his house) and a handful of optimistic friends and associates, the determined young man began what was to be a remarkable adventure into the world of business. A $283 watermain connection on Clarke Sideroad was the first job Matthews Construction landed.

By 1958, Matthews was into the land development business. Ridgeview Heights, Northridge, Stoneybrook Heights, Nelson Park, Pond Mills, Windermere Estates, White Oaks, Bonaventure Meadows and River Valley North are some of the London neighbourhoods developed by Matthews Group.

Meanwhile, the construction side of the business continued to grow. Entire mining towns, including roads, sewers, schools, fire halls and houses were built by Matthews in Elliot Lake, Ontario and Tumbler Ridge, British Columbia.

Don was committed to making London a better place to live and raise a family. Perhaps his most tangible accomplishment in London was spearheading the Joint Parks Committee. In 1961, City Council established a committee comprised of members from the Kiwanis Club of London, the City of London and the P.U.C. Their mandate was to plan and acquire land for the riverside park system that now extends the length of the Thames River in London. Matthews was the founding Chairman and continued in that role for the next 12 years. Many battles were fought at council meetings of the day over the wisdom of spending money on such frivolous acquisitions. Today, thousands of Londoners walk, jog and cycle on the paths, secure in the knowledge that future generations will enjoy this natural respite from city life.

By the late 1970's, it was clear to Don Matthews that the greater Toronto area was going to experience unprecedented growth. He purchased a 400 acre parcel of land in Mississauga. Confident that the land bank would return good profits and tightening their belt in the recession of the early 1980's, Matthews held onto that property. Sussex Centre, the acknowledged downtown of Mississauga, now sits on part of that 400 acre acquisiton. Today, Matthews is a well-established developer in the Toronto market.

Matthews Group continues to be a family and employee owned company with operations across Canada and throughout the world, including the United States, Mexico, Germany, Pakistan, Iceland, Kuwait, India, Saudi Arabia, United Arab Emirites, Iran, Ivory Coast, Gabon and Uganda. The company continues to aggressively, but carefully, pursue the international market to ensure its' continuing success.

Labatt

A London tradition for almost a century and a half.

Labatt has always been closely linked with the history of the City of London. In fact, it's difficult to think of one without the other. It was near London that John Kinder Labatt started his brewing company a century and a half ago and it was London that was the base for the company's expansion into other industries and into other countries.

Today, John Labatt Limited is one of the country's largest companies, with holdings in the brewing, dairy and entertainment sectors both in North America and in Europe.

But it is the large Labatt brewery on the banks of the Thames River that is most closely associated with the city. John Kinder Labatt entered the brewing business, and the country's history books, in 1847 when he bought a stake in the London Brewery. By 1853, he was the sole proprietor and its ownership remained in the family for a century.

Labatt found London a good place to develop a market for his English type ales. British troops were stationed there and the city's growth as a judicial and financial centre was attracting great numbers of professionals. Beyond London there were inns along the roads that connected many nearby villages. And the railways soon helped expand Labatt's market to include Sarnia and Windsor to the west, and Toronto and Hamilton to the east.

Son John Labatt, who took over the business in 1866, continued with his father's popular Stock Ale but soon began producing his own recipe, Labatt's India Pale Ale, which is still sold today. His dedication to the brewing and malting industry, combined with his willingness to take risks, made John Labatt one of the most successful entrepreneurs among London's business elite during the next half century.

The company was incorporated in 1911, and within years met its first major test. Prohibition, which began in 1916 and ended in Ontario in 1927, was among the new company's earliest and biggest challenges and one that could have led to its end. But the nine-member Labatt family wisely decided to create a two-tiered operation: One selling full-strength beer to the U.S. and the other selling weaker beer for Ontario consumers. This combination allowed the company to survive through Prohibition and prosper.

The company has never looked back. Labatt became public in 1945, with shares traded on both the Toronto and Montreal stock exchanges. Soon, a brewery was purchased in Toronto, and then later in Quebec, Manitoba and B.C. By 1971, the company owned breweries in every province except P.E.I.

Labatt still retains an active presence in London and is part of the John Labatt Limited family of companies which now employs more than 12,000 people in

Portrait of John Kinder Labatt, founder of Labatt Breweries.

North America and Europe. Along with Labatt Breweries of Canada, which is home to the country's best-selling beer, Labatt Blue, John Labatt Limited also owns controlling interests in Labatt's U.S.A., which includes the Latrobe Brewing Company, producers of Rolling Rock; Labatt Breweries of Europe; Ault Foods; the Toronto Blue Jays Baseball Club and The Sports Network (TSN).

Today, a century and a half after its founding, Labatt is well positioned for continued growth and success in Canada and around the world.

Labatt Breweries as it appeared prior to 1874 (when a large part of the brewery was destroyed by fire).

McCormick Canada

A "spicy" part of London
for over 100 years

316 Rectory Street, London, Ontario.

When W.J. Gorman and D.J. Dyson forged a partnership with $750 in capital and set up business in an old carpentry shop at the corner of Carling and Talbot Streets in London, Ontario in 1883, few people would have envisioned that this small company would grow into a nationwide leader in the food industry. But grow it did, and today it forms the Club House Division of McCormick Canada Inc., a company whose continuing creative responses to its markets figure largely in its success.

The Canadian operations of Club House began in London, Ontario in 1883 under the name Gorman, Dyson & Company. Its original products were coffee, turpentine, liquid ammonia and sewing machine oil; within two years, spices, extracts and baking powder were added to the product line. Partnership changes resulted in renaming the company Gorman, Eckert & Company in 1890, and business expanded to include Spanish olives. By 1900, the company had established itself as the largest olive packer in the British empire. In 1959 Gorman, Eckert & Co. Limited, became a subsidiary of McCormick & Company Inc., based in Baltimore, Maryland, and the world's largest seasoning and flavouring firm. In 1969, the name changed to Club House Foods Ltd., reflecting the major brand, Club House.

But Club House Foods is only half the story behind McCormick Canada Inc., which was formed on June 1, 1989, through the amalgamation with Stange Canada Inc. Canadian operations of Stange began as a joint-venture under the name Stange Pemberton in Toronto in 1952. Stange Co. Ltd. in the United States began in 1905 and had developed a leadership position in seasoning technology and a reputation as the "Silent Partner in Famous Foods". The new Canadian company was the first operation outside the United States. In 1963, the Canadian division became known as Stange Canada Ltd., and business grew steadily through joint-ventures, acquisitions and an expanded customer base. In 1981 Stange Canada became a wholly owned subsidiary of McCormick & Company.

Today, McCormick Canada Inc. is a national leader in the spice, seasoning, flavouring and specialty food industry, with its head office and Club House division in London, Ontario. It has manufacturing, sales and distribution centres in Montreal, Edmonton, Toronto, London and Calgary. The Club House Division serves retail grocery and food service customers with products such as spices, seasonings, salad dressings, sauces, gravy mixes, Spanish olives, and food colourings. The Stange Division serves the fast food industry and industrial customers across Canada with custom seasonings, flavours and ingredients.

McCormick Canada Inc. has recently expanded its London facility as part of a major project that added 25,000 square feet. The expansion is the first major manufacturing renovation in 20 years and became necessary in order to meet the rising demand for its spices and prepared foods.

The company's "Power of People" philosophy, it's versatility and willingness to adapt are easily traced throughout its history and the evolution of its products. Robert G. Davey, the current McCormick Canada President, feels these characteristics provide the foundation for McCormick Canada Inc. to continue as a leader in the food industry.

3340 Orlando Dr., Mississauga, Ontario.

London Life

An institution in London for more than one-hundred years

London Life occupies a special niche in the history of the Forest City as a truly homegrown enterprise. It is a civic asset prized by the community, policyowners and many generations of employees.

Shortly after confederation, London was a small but flourishing community of approximately 20,000. Like today, the city was the financial and distribution centre for western Ontario.

On April 4, 1874, five local businessmen met to launch the London Life Insurance Company with seed capital of $112,500. Three of the founders — William Woodruff, M.D., industrialist John Walker, and banker Joseph Jeffery — were subsequently elected to the first board of directors. The other two founders, lawyers Edward Harris and James Magee were appointed company solicitors.

Joseph Jeffery became the first president of the company and his descendants continued active participation in management and ownership of London Life for more than a century. An unbroken line of Jeffery family ownership lasted until the early '80s, when they joined with Brascan Limited of Toronto in founding Trilon Financial Corporation.

In 1985, Lonvest Corporation — the insurance arm of Trilon — assumed majority ownership of London Life. In 1990, Lonvest changed its name to London Insurance Group, to better represent the company's profile.

The Trilon connection, associating London Life with companies such as Royal Trustco, Wellington Insurance, Royal LePage, and others, has created a comprehensive approach to meet the financial needs of Canadians.

London Life is the nation's largest provider of individual life insurance. A strength of the company is its sales force of 2,900 representatives and managers, the largest in the industry, as well as 2,700 people in administrative jobs. London Life's customers are served in all the provinces and territories of Canada.

London's head office complex takes up one city block south of Victoria Park. This site was opened in 1927, and expanded in 1951 and again in 1964. Head office was also modernized in 1982 at a cost of $18 million. This model office is equipped with state-of-the-art computer technology and electronic communication from coast to coast. It's here that 1,800 staffers comprise the core of London Life's people who operate out of 192 offices across Canada.

In 1992, new expansion was completed on Queen's Avenue. London Life, in a joint venture with Sifton Properties of London, developed One London Place, a modern office complex to include 24-storey and 18-storey office towers.

Through all the decades of growth and change, the underlying philosophy of the five founders of the company has remained intact. London Life counts service to customers as the principle strength for holding and attracting more than 1.5 million policy holders. Intensive training of staff, new product development, and marketing expertise have contributed to substantial gains in sales volume over the years.

The people of London Life are well recognized for participation in the affairs of the community. In all ways, London Life is part of the legacy of the city.

Born in Ipswich, England in 1829, Joseph Jeffery was already a successful businessman when he became the first president of London Life, and remained in that office until his death in 1894.

The imposing front entrance of the company's head office is a London landmark, located on Dufferin Avenue opposite Victoria Park, it was opened in 1927.

The University of Western Ontario

Growing with the Forest City

University College, a splendid example of Western's Gothic architecture, is reflected in the windows of the National Centre for Management Research and Development.

A Western researcher studies the effects of wind on large structures through the use of scale models at the Boundary Layer Wind Tunnel Laboratory, Faculty of Engineering Science.

The University of Western Ontario and the City of London enjoy a partnership dating back to 1878. For more than a century, Western has been a part of London's economic, social and cultural development.

Founder Bishop Isaac Hellmuth of the Anglican Diocese of Huron worked to create an institution of higher learning dedicated to the educational needs of London and southwestern Ontario. As a result of his efforts, the University was incorporated on March 7, 1878 and the present name was confirmed by an Act of Provincial Parliament in 1923. Located on the slopes of the River Thames since 1924, Western's picturesque campus is now an integral part of London.

As a corporate citizen with an annual budget of nearly $246 million, an employee base of almost 4,000 faculty and staff, and home to more than 26,000 full and part-time students, Western plays a leading role in London's financial prosperity. The University ranks as one of the City's largest employers and is a valuable commercial resource.

Education and retraining are vital to our community's economic success and Western is responding with challenging opportunities. Each year, thousands of visitors participate in conferences, special lectures, continuing education courses, athletic camps and off-campus studies.

An important research link is being developed with external groups to ensure Canada's competitive position in a global economy. Research funding totalled almost $57 million in 1991, while fund raising through the Renaissance Campaign surpassed $100 million. Western's faculty and facilities make London an attractive urban centre in which to pursue business. The new Research Park will add to this attractiveness and enhance corporate partnerships.

The University has forged close ties with London's hospitals and health care centres through its medical, engineering and kinesiology faculties. As a result, residents of southwestern Ontario can access a health care system that is one of the most progressive and responsive in the nation.

Athletics and community service are an essential part of the University's tradition. Western athletes compete in a broad range of intercollegiate programs and hold many championship titles. Western students are caring and involved citizens. They undertake charitable projects such as Shinerama, Charity Ball, United Way, Red Cross blood donor clinics and food drives.

For more than 114 years, Western's leaders have strived to establish the University as a world-class educational institution. Today, a tradition of academic excellence continues in seventeen faculties and schools, three affiliated colleges and a library system that holds more than two million publications. The University has 120,000 graduates across Canada and around the world, including 18,000 in the London area.

Western researchers are on the leading edge of discovery in molecular biology, organ transplants, rehabilitative health care, environmental studies and new management strategies to name a few. In addition, internationally recognized faculty teach students to understand the human condition and develop critical reasoning skills through diverse disciplines. A wide range of highly acclaimed research centres, institutes and cultural programs add to the University's distinction.

The University of Western Ontario is committed to the future growth of London and southwestern Ontario, and remains dedicated to preserving Canada's strength and prosperity.

Parkwood Hospital & McCormick Home

The Caring Communities of the Women's Christian Association of London

For more than a century, a dedicated and inspired group of women have been a vital part of London's history and healthcare community. In 1875, long before established social programs, the Women's Christian Association of London began its work; caring for the sick, the poor and the elderly in our community. A tradition of caring through progressive measures continues to guide the W.C.A. in operating programs and facilities that identify and fulfil unmet needs.

Early in its history, the W.C.A. laid the ground work for two of London's oldest and most innovative care communities. McCormick Home celebrates its 100th anniversary this year, and Parkwood Hospital will reach its centenary in 1994. Through these organizations, the W.C.A. provides care and rehabilitation for the elderly and the chronically ill of all ages; a focus which places the W.C.A. at the forefront of today's most pressing care issues.

In 1892, Thomas McCormick donated land and buildings to establish the McCormick Home for the Aged, an environment that has always promoted quality of life and maximized independence for the frail elderly. Still located on the original Victoria Street site, the Home has seen many changes through one hundred years of service to London and surrounding areas. Only twenty-five years ago, McCormick offered a genteel retirement community where meals, housekeeping and minimal care were provided.

Today, that focus has shifted to include programs supporting independent, community living for as long as possible. McCormick's Day Centre Program for the frail elderly reaches out to offer individualized programming for each client's needs. The Alzheimer Community Support Service, another outreach program, offers services which enhance quality of life for patients and their families and delays institutionalization.

Like the Home, Parkwood Hospital is a community within a community; sharing nearly a century of history with London. From its earliest beginning in 1894, the Hospital has moved forward as a regional, specialty teaching, service and research centre and the largest free-standing chronic care facility in Southwestern Ontario.

Located just south of Commissioners Road East, Parkwood offers medical expertise in Rehabilitation, Geriatrics, Palliative Care and Continuing Care; as well as, residential care to the veterans of Canada. A wide range of specialized diagnostic, treatment and rehabilitation services are provided for patients and residents of all ages. In hospital and in the community, programs are aimed at reducing, delaying, or preventing hospitalization, and outreach initiatives bring our specialized knowledge to the community and its care providers.

Through its caring communities, the Women's Christian Association has become part of the fabric of London and region. In the tradition of those first women, who volunteered their time and care so many years ago, innovation and adaptability in a changing world ensures a vital future for the W.C.A. and its caring communities.

In 1875, Mrs. W. Gregsten was the first President of the newly incorporated Women's Christian Association of London. Through more than a century of changes, the Association remains true to its spirit and tradition of care.

Today, Parkwood Hospital, owned and operated by the W.C.A., provides personalized care and rehabilitation for the chronically ill of all ages in an atmosphere promoting maximized independence and quality of life.

Wolverine Tube

Copper tubing for Canada and the World
since 1958.

London Plant of Wolverine Tube (Canada) Inc.

Wolverine Tube London evolved from a small tube redrawing mill built in 1916 in Detroit, Michigan. This company was formed to supply heater tubes to the automotive industry and was subsequently purchased by Calumet & Hecla Consolidated Copper Company in 1942. In 1948, Wolverine expanded by building a huge tube mill in Decatur, Alabama. To accommodate a growing Canadian market, Wolverine began construction of the London Plant in October 1956, and made the first shipment of tubing on April 21, 1958.

The London Plant is a completely integrated facility, starting with refined copper from Canadian mines which is converted to copper and copper base alloy tube in a wide range of sizes. The products are used for plumbing and heating in homes and plants, in the construction of refrigeration and air conditioning equipment, in hydro electric power plants for condenser components, and for a wide number of general industrial uses. Although the Canadian market is the prime outlet for the London Plant, tubing has been shipped to approximately 40 countries throughout the world. For over three decades, Wolverine Tube (Canada) Inc. has flourished and expanded at the London site. Along the way it earned a reputation for a quality product, customer service, employment stability, and community awareness.

Between 1958 and the present, many significant events have taken place in the firm's history. In 1968 Calumet and Hecla merged with Universal Oil Products. A small plant was opened five years later in Ardmore, Tennessee, for the production of Capillary tube products and fabricated parts. The original Detroit plant was closed in 1974 and was moved to a new facility in Shawnee, Oklahoma, which began operation in early 1975. Also in 1975 Signal Companies In-

corporated purchased Universal Oil Products, who owned Wolverine Tube.

The next corporate ownership change occurred in May, 1985, when Allied Corporation merged with Signal Companies Incorporated. These companies in turn spun off a number of divisions, including Wolverine Tube, to a new company called Henley Group late in 1985. Then, in March, 1987, Wolverine Holding Company acquired from the Henley Group, the assets of Wolverine Tube Limited in Canada and Wolverine Tube Incorporated in the United States.

Wolverine Holding Company was owned by senior management, Morgan Stanley Incorporated of New York City, and Drake, Goodwin & Company of London, Ontario. A year later, in October 1988, Wolverine acquired the assets of Noranda Metal Industries, Montreal, including plants in Montreal, Quebec; New Westminster, B.C.; and Fergus, Ontario. In 1989, Wolverine opened a new plant, in Booneville, Mississippi, to supply special tubing to the refrigeration and air-conditioning industries.

The most recent change took place in January of 1991, when Genstar Capital Corporation acquired controlling interest of Wolverine Holding Company.

The London Operation is a story of unqualified success from the original plant employing a total of 82 workers in 1958 to the huge 200,000 square foot plant on the same site today. The intervening years have seen several major expansions and staff has increased to 200 hourly and 80 salaried workers at 1010 Clarke Road. Wolverine employees have been very active in community affairs over the years, participating in many programs with the Chamber of Commerce, United Appeal, University of Western Ontario, and many other professional and charitable organizations.

Quaker State Minit-Lube

"We just want to change your oil"

During the 1970's, many of the major gas retailers moved to the self-serve gasoline station concept. This resulted in the closing of many corner garages and service stations and a void was created; ordinary preventative automobile maintenance was not conveniently or readily available. The Minit-Lube, or "fast-lube" concept was designed to fill the customer's need for speed and convenience. Minit-Lube made what used to be a day long ritual of working out transportation problems, into a brief stop on the way to work, on the way to lunch, or on the way to the grocery store.

In 1977, the original company, Automotive Lube Shop, was founded by two Waterloo brothers, Peter and George Walsh. In 1978, they sold their first franchise located at 623 Wellington Road South in London. The chain grew steadily through the early and mid 1980's and by 1987 Automotive Lube Shop was sixteen stores strong. A year later, Automotive Lube Shop formed a joint venture company with Quaker State Minit-Lube and became part of the large U.S. chain of over 400 outlets.

Presently, Minit-Lube has twenty-two stores in Ontario; ten are company owned and twelve are franchised. In London, the 623 Wellington Road South and 500 Oxford Street West locations are owned by franchisee Ray Falconer. The Minit-Lube located at 1862 Dundas Street is company owned.

In the last five years the number of "fast-lube" concept outlets has more than tripled. Because the industry has grown and competition has intensified, Minit-Lube is constantly re-evaluating its position and developing innovative solutions to the challenges being faced. "Project 2000" is Minit-Lube's most recent innovative solution. A multi-faceted program focused on improving the Minit-Lube systems and its employees. Project 2000's aim is to position the company as "THE PROVIDER OF QUALITY SERVICE" in the fast-lube industry and focus on the most important issue in the coming years: Customer Satisfaction.

To quote the Minit-Lube Mission Statement:

"Our vision is to become the Gold Standard of the lubrication service industry.

To be driven by our desire to provide complete satisfaction and an obsession to continually achieve high standards of excellence that cannot be met by our competition.

To be an organization of outstanding individuals whose pride shows in its commitment to quality.

Our mission is to provide a universally consistent customer experience which is quick, convenient, reliable and error-free.

This experience will be delivered by a team of employees whose technical and professional skills, as well as their desire to exceed customer expectations, will be assured."

Minit-Lube will continue to always provide the finest products available: Quaker State motor oils and Fram filters. The Minit-Lube computer system presently gives the lubrication technicians the most up to date vehicle information available. The operational systems in each outlet, as part of the Project 2000 strategy, is constantly being improved and fine tuned to ensure every customer receives reliable workmanship and courteous fast service. Minit-Lube's employees receive constant on-the-job training as well as seminar instruction.

Minit-Lube, through Project 2000, is dedicated to total customer satisfaction and will continue to be for years to come.

The 500 Oxford Street West location.

Other locations at 623 Wellington Road South and 1862 Dundas Street East.

D.H. Howden

A Canadian hardware
success story

A view of the assembly and repack area in our distribution facility.

Our new PRO hardware store in Guelph Ontario - just the day before it opened.

"Providing customers with quality products at competitive prices with unparalleled service."

A part of the London scene since the turn of the century, D.H. Howden & Co. Limited has experienced significant growth and development to become the franchisor to Canada's largest chain of independently owned retail hardware stores.

It was in 1907, that Howden erected a new warehouse at 200 York Street. Some fifty-three years later they moved to a new warehouse on Southdale Road, serving primarily the Ontario market. Expanding on a national basis, the Company built additional warehousing facilities in the late 1970's on White Oak Road.

On May 25, 1992, Howden opened its new National Head Office and Distribution Centre which Michael C. Tucker, President and Chief Executive Officer of Howden called "an investment in a new generation of retailing excellence for the hardware chain's 1,500 PRO Hardware, Do-it center and independent hardware outlets".

The new consolidated headquarters consisting of 328,000 square feet of distribution facility and approximately 39,000 square feet of office facility includes the latest in warehousing and distribution technologies. It has been designed to look after the Company's distribution needs well into the next century.

Howden, a subsidiary since 1987 of Montreal-based Sodisco Group Inc., which in turn is owned by Unigesco Inc., is franchisor to two of Canada's best known retail banners in the hardware and home renovation sector. Its current list of franchise outlets include 375 PRO Hardware stores and 65 Do-it centers. Howden also services the needs of some 1,000 independent hardware outlets across Canada.

PRO Hardware, one of the best known retail logos in the Canadian hardware industry, was introduced by D.H. Howden & Co. Limited in 1964. It has grown steadily over the last 28 years to its current level of 375 stores.

The central London distribution centre stocks an inventory of over 30,000 products to supply its PRO store requirements. As well as product, Howden also provides full marketing and sales training support for its franchisees. Each and every PRO store is connected to national headquarters by a 24-hour Displayphone system which allows the franchisee instant contact on orders and inventory issues.

What worked for independently owned hardware stores has become the standard for Howden's growing chain of franchised Do-it centers. Strategically aimed at the home project and renovation needs of the busy do-it-yourself, Do-it centers provide a colourful and convenient shopping environment for the widest possible variety of renovation needs — everything from plumbing and power tools to lumber and garden supplies.

Howden introduced the Do-it franchise to Canada in 1986 and currently services the needs of 65 owner-operated stores across Canada.

Howden's London headquarters and distribution centre employs 400 people. In serving our dealer network, Howden's fleet of 45 trucks travel nearly seven million kilometres a year delivering hardware supplies to customers that stretch from Newfoundland to British Columbia and into the Yukon and Northwest Territories.

In reflecting on the past, we do so with pride in our development and accomplishments. As we look to the future we do so with confidence in our ability to meet the opportunities and challenges that lie ahead.

Fanshawe College

Celebrating twenty-five years
in the community

Historically, Fanshawe College may appear young in comparison to other businesses and industries in the London area, but for over 25 years this institution of higher learning has grown and contributed much to the educational needs of the communities it serves.

Since opening its doors in 1967, more than 38,000 students have graduated from Fanshawe and the college can now claim one out of every ten Londoners as a Fanshawe graduate.

The growth has certainly surpassed the expectations of local and provincial authorities.

Arising from a perceived need in the early 1960s, Fanshawe was one of several community colleges introduced by the Ontario government to not only offer career-specific courses but to be an educational alternative to universities.

In London, this vision started to take shape in 1966 when the College set its roots on a suitable site on the Ontario Vocational Centre campus on Oxford Street East. A city-wide contest was held and Fanshawe (meaning a temple in the woods) was selected as an appropriate name.

In its first year, 720 post-secondary day students were enrolled.

Today, as one of the largest colleges in Ontario, Fanshawe educates and trains close to 13,000 full-time students and almost 42,000 part-time registrants annually in a wide range of programs and courses from upgrading and English as a Second Language to post-secondary diploma programs in such disciplines as applied arts, business, health sciences, human services and technology.

Best known for offering combined in-school and paid on-the-job training, Fanshawe continues to provide more cooperative education programs than any other college in Canada.

Students may select from over 85 post-secondary diploma programs and approximately 2000 continuing education courses ranging from personal and professional development and recreation activities to credit courses.

Numerous adult training and apprenticeship programs offered in partnership with the federal government, industrial training councils, employers and other agencies, also help individuals to gain training and job experience in careers outlined on local and provincial critical skills shortages lists.

The value of these programs continue to be proven by the increasing number of students enrolling in them.

For example, in early June 1992, Fanshawe College's 25th anniversary celebration began ceremoniously with the largest graduation in its history. Not only did the college present its first honorary diploma, but over 2500 students graduated during five ceremonies at its Oxford Street Campus in London.

Fanshawe's main Oxford Street campus in London has also expanded over the years. Today, the campus features 100 landscaped acres with nine buildings housing hundreds of classrooms, studios, laboratories and other learning facilities. Three other campuses are also located in the smaller urban communities of St. Thomas, Woodstock and Simcoe plus a number of smaller instructional centres are open to better serve the communities within the College's four county area.

With 25 years of experience behind it, Fanshawe has a firm footing in the past. However, with the recent approval of its first ever strategic plan and with enrolment expected to reach record numbers for the 1992-1993 academic year, Fanshawe is already preparing and adjusting for the rapidly changing needs of tomorrow, reinforcing its "Future Driven" philosophy.

Since opening its doors in 1967, more than 38,000 students have graduated from Fanshawe College.

Fanshawe offers more cooperative education programs than any other college in Canada.

Microtronix Systems

Celebrating the opening of Microtronix's new facility on Aberdeen Drive in London. Official Ribbon Cutting Ceremony, June 1992 Mayor Tom Gosnell, Eric Auzins, President of Microtronix and the Honourable Terry Clifford, M.P. London Middlesex.

Microtronix Systems Ltd. was incorporated in 1972 as an electronics manufacturing company and initially addressed the local market niches of providing telephone testing equipment to Northern Electric (now Northern Telecom) and specialized vehicular electronic modules to General Motors, Diesel Division for use on their off-highway earth haulers and locomotives.

1975 through 1985 were hallmarked by the creation of the firm's own products. Unlike customized products that were built specifically for one customer, Microtronix's own products could be freely promoted to many customers beyond the local marketplace. The first such product was a Rotary Dial Test Set which was sold not only locally but elsewhere in Canada, the US and South America. Next came an Electronic Engine Governor developed for use on derrick digger trucks to control the hydraulics while holes were being dug for telephone or hydroelectric poles.

With the deregulation of the telephone market in North America in the early 1980's, a new opportunity arose. Telephone manufacturers would need testing equipment to verify that the telephones they were producing met certain standards. The Model 60 Telephone Test Set was produced to fill this niche. It was designed to measure all the major electrical and acoustical properties of the telephone and to provide the telephone manufacturer with accurate and repeatable results which were based on international standards.

The ensuing years saw a steady growth of Microtronix. The Telephone Test Set was in demand and it was unique. No one else was making such a product. The market for the product expanded to the United States, Germany and the Far East. Firms such as AT&T, GE, and Siemens AG of Germany were added to the growing list of customers until today over 80 telephone manufacturers use the test set with 85% of sales being exported to 32 different countries.

1987 was the year Microtronix purchased the communications division from Cableshare Inc. and created Microtronix Datacom Ltd. Extensive research and development has produced a full family of products which provide customers such as Unitel, Ford Motor Credit and British Telecom connectivity to the X.25 data communications network.

Microtronix Vehicle Technologies Ltd. was formed in 1991 to focus on the vehicular electronics which had always been a specialty of Microtronix as well as expanding into the new area of automatic passenger counting for the transit industry.

In 1991, Microtronix Systems Ltd. won the Business Achievement Award given by the London Chamber of Commerce and was recognized by the Ontario Chamber of Commerce for its success as an Ontario company competing effectively in the world marketplace.

Victoria Hospital

A vision of caring, teaching and innovation

Victoria Hospital, like the City of London, has a rich history. From a log cabin in a military barracks located in Victoria Park to today's state-of-the-art facilities, Victoria Hospital has provided the community with the finest in clinical services, medical education and research for 118 years.

London's first permanent public hospital opened its doors on August 5, 1875 and was then known as the London General Hospital. From the outset, the physicians' and nurses' dedication to clinical service was paramount. The surgical, general and private wards of the hospital were looked upon with pride by City officials who actually managed the Hospital until 1887 when operational duties were taken on by a Board of Trustees.

Although the term "teaching hospital" was not yet coined, the elements of clinical service, education and research — the elements that make up a modern teaching hospital — were well established. Clinical services were growing at a rapid rate, research was an integral part of medical practice and in 1882 the first six medical students enroled at Victoria's new medical school, followed shortly thereafter by the first nursing students.

To commemorate the Diamond Jubilee of Queen Victoria, in 1899 the London General Hospital changed its name to Victoria Hospital. Staff eagerly looked forward to what the new century would bring in the way of change, challenge and innovation in medical care.

The first half of this century laid the foundation for the Victoria Hospital of today. Victoria's commitment to paediatric care has its roots in the early 1920s when War Memorial Children's Hospital opened its doors. Similarly, Victoria's current focus on cardiac services, cancer treatment and special services began with the first open heart surgery in the region, the establishment of the Ontario Cancer Treatment and Research Foundation, and the development and use of the first artificial kidney machine in Canada.

As London grew, so too did the need for health care. When Victoria Hospital entered its second century of caring in 1975, relocation plans meant Victoria would become the major regional medical centre in Southwestern Ontario. That concept became a reality in 1985 when the first patients were admitted to Victoria's "new" Westminster Campus.

Today, Victoria treats nearly half-a-million patients from across the region, teaches more than 1100 students from a variety of health care disciplines and administers more than $5-million in research grants each year.

As Victoria Hospital reaches for the future it also looks back on its long history with pride. The vision City officials had for Victoria when it first opened its doors — a vision to provide comprehensive medical care, quality research and outstanding medical education characterized by a pioneering spirit — is a vision the Hospital continues to fulfil each day.

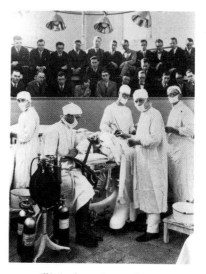

Clinical service and education: As much a partnership in the 1920s as they are now.

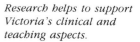

Research helps to support Victoria's clinical and teaching aspects.

Forest City Linen Supply

A London tradition
since 1929.

A tradition spanning three generations of the Cramer Family, Forest City Linen Supply evolved from a small, depression-era operation to become the largest independently-owned textile rental company in Canada.

Founded by Harry A. Cramer, who emigrated from Holland to Canada in 1929, Forest City Linen Supply began as a small domestic laundry operated by his wife, Wilhelmina, in the basement of their home on Richmond Street North. Harry recognized the potential for growth in the business, and began to deliver the finished product to customers in an old Essex car.

In 1934, the business outgrew the basement and was moved to a house and small barn on St. James Street. By 1937, operations were underway at 4 Dundas Street West with the installation of laundry presses, steam dryers and a large flatwork ironer that required four persons to operate. The purchase of the first official delivery truck completed the transformation from a home laundry concept to a commercial laundry.

The Second World War brought about a decrease in domestic laundry and an increase in military contracts, in addition to expansion into the dry cleaning business. In 1946, the original building was removed and sold and the completion of a new building on the Dundas Street site doubled floor space. The end of the war resulted in a return to the domestic laundry service. Harry Cramer became ill and sold the business to his sons Bernard, William and Fritz Cramer in 1950.

The firm survived the devastation of a fire which totally destroyed the 4 Dundas Street plant on November 28, 1953.

Over the next two decades, Forest City Linen Supply expanded rapidly and became a visible face to the region with 28 retail stores in London and Windsor, and 25 delivery trucks on the road. In the early 1960's, the company was a forerunner in bringing the concept of coin-operated laundries to Canada.

By 1965, the introduction of new easy care fabrics and the family-owned washer and dryer created a downturn in the domestic laundry service. The business expanded into the rental of linens to institutions, hotels, restaurants and industry, and extended its service area to include Stratford, Sarnia, and Chatham. The penetration of this new market reaped great success for the firm, and by the late 1960's, the company's trading area included Simcoe, Brantford and Kitchener-Waterloo.

The coin-operated stores were sold by the mid-1970's, and at this time the retail dry cleaning stores were closed. These changes allowed the company to concentrate on its main business of industrial/commercial textile rental. In 1981, a new 40,000 square foot plant was built on Charterhouse Crescent in London, which began production with new state of the art equipment in February, 1982.

In 1986 a third generation of the Cramer family assumed control of the company and increased the company's market share of floor mat services and industrial uniform rentals. The business enlarged its customer base in these markets with the purchase of Tri-City Uniform Limited (Guelph) in 1990.

Presently, Forest City Linen Supply services over 4,000 industrial customers from Toronto to Windsor with the most complete range of textile rental items in the business. The firm has prospered by identifying successful trends, applying the latest technology and providing all employees with a place to do their best work.

The Blackburn Group Inc.

Building for the future
on an historic foundation

Since the first day of 1853, when a resourceful and ambitious Josiah Blackburn assumed control of the weekly paper, The Canadian Free Press, a dynamic interplay of innovation, determination and sound management has prevailed to shape the fortunes of The Blackburn Group Inc. (BGI).

It is less than a decade ago that Josiah's great-granddaughter, the late Martha Grace Blackburn, assumed the chairmanship of The Blackburn Group of companies, but in that short span of time she was true to the legacy of the three entrepreneurial generations that preceeded her: The group of companies has ventured into new businesses and new territories and has established itself as a leader in yet another facet of the communication and information industry — demographic and market analysis.

When Martha Blackburn's father, Walter Juxon Blackburn, died in 1983, the Group was solidly anchored by the daily London Free Press, and the radio and television stations operated by CFPL Broadcasting in London and CKNX Broadcasting in Wingham. Netmar Inc., a network of shoppers which developed from an advertising weekly established in London in 1978, was growing to a new level of maturity and prominence as a nationwide publishing and distribution company. In 1984, the acquisition of Toronto-based Compusearch Market and Social Research Limited, a leader in demographic and market analysis, provided the Group with an entry point into this developing and dynamic new field. In that same year, to reflect the diversity and growth of the organization, the parent company changed its name from The London Free Press Holdings Limited to The Blackburn Group Inc.

Although it was moving in new directions, the Group recognized that the traditional media companies needed strengthening in order to counter aggressive competition in both print and broadcast and to better position them to deal with the complexities of doing business in the 1990's. In 1988-89, The London Free Press underwent a major redesign in response to the changing needs of its customers. In addition to developing better means of providing information to busy readers, the innovative combination of articles and graphics put The Free Press on the leading edge of North American newspaper design. This by no means signalled the end of the change process. The Free Press continues to experiment and introduce innovations to the daily paper that have been admired and copied by others in the industry, both in Canada and the United States.

In 1987, aggressive action was taken to strengthen the Blackburn television holdings in Ontario. Gaining independence from the CBC Television Network in the fall of that year an application was made for an independent station in Ottawa. When this application was unsuccessful CFPL and CKNX continued in their attempt to extend the scale of their operation in order to enhance their ability to purchase quality programming and to secure their entry into the Toronto market. A Blackburn Group bid to purchase CHCH-TV of Hamilton was turned down by the Canadian Radio-Television Telecommunications Commission (CRTC) in 1989, as was a subsequent initiative to form a Southern Ontario television partnership.

Confident in the belief that the television franchise could only survive and prosper as part of a larger broadcasting entity, BGI sold its television holdings to Baton Broadcasting in the

Josiah Blackburn

Walter J. Blackburn

The composing room of The London Free Press in 1922.

The composing room of The London Free Press in 1992.

spring of 1992. That sale awaits CRTC approval.

CFPL and CKNX Radio, the second broadcasting arm of The Blackburn Group, continues to operate separate AM and FM stations in London and Wingham. The reliability of Radio's news and public affairs programming regularly wins awards in the industry, both nationally and internationally.

By the late 1980's, Netmar Inc. was expanding and flourishing as a publisher and distributor of shoppers — it now distributes to one million households — as well as publishing weekly newspapers and distributing advertising flyers.

Headquartered in London, Netmar consists of four operating divisions: Ontario Shopper Group, which includes the London Pennysaver; Ontario Weekly Group, which includes such Southwestern Ontario publications as the Sarnia Gazette, Chatham This Week and The Wallaceburg Courier. The Alberta Weekly Group, includes the Edmonton Examiner and five community weeklies surrounding that city as well as the Mirror, a weekly publication in Calgary. Together the Ontario and Alberta weeklies reach more than 330,000 households. Another facet of this group, Netmedia Enterprises, has the capability to distribute flyers and product samples nationwide.

In 1987 The Blackburn Group identified an opportunity in magazine publishing, and subsequently The Free Press acquired the London regional edition of Ontario Living which it later merged with London Magazine.

With the early success of Compusearch, The Blackburn Group Inc. decided to focus its diversification in the demographic and market analysis industry. In 1989 it established Blackburn Marketing Services Inc. This umbrella group includes Spectrum Decision Sciences Inc., launched a year later to serve the retail, financial and direct marketing industries with state-of-the-art predictive models, and Prospects Unlimited, established a year later, to provide its clients the largest and most comprehensive consumer data base in Canada, covering more than 7.5 million households. In 1991 BMSI made its first major venture into the United States

Martha G. Blackburn

with the purchase of a majority interest in Urban Decision Systems, Inc., an American geo-demographics firm based in Los Angeles and with offices in Washington and Chicago. The company's most recent acquisitions are Infogroup Inc., a national full-service market research firm based in Vancouver, and National Research Bureau of Chicago, publisher of business directories.

It was Josiah Blackburn who established the family enterprise in 1853 when he bought the weekly Canadian Free Press, founded four years earlier by William Sutherland. Josiah Blackburn, 29 years of age at the time, was an English-born printer who previously worked for his brother John at the Paris (Ontario) Star. A flair for business, writing, and politics served Josiah well after he took charge of the weekly Canadian Free Press, housed in a plant on the east side of Talbot Street, a few doors north of Dundas. He accurately perceived a city on the move and he promptly embarked on ambitious planning for the future.

On May 5, 1855, The London Free Press and Daily Western Advertiser made its debut. With the exception of one month in 1857, it has been published continuously ever since. The weekly Canadian Free Press was retained for another 40 years as the daily's financial anchor.

The new daily prospered from the outset, surviving in a period when many other pioneer papers foundered. In his 38 years as editor, Josiah established an enviable record of "firsts" in the newspaper business, among them the distinction of publishing an article from the paper's own war correspondent — Malcolm Brenner's account of the Fenian Raids near Fort Erie in 1866.

In 1868 Josiah and his brother Stephen, who had joined the firm by then, transferred the company to a new building on Richmond Street, where the paper remained until 1931. Stephen Blackburn later sold his quarter share in The Free Press to an employee, William Southam, who went on to establish the Hamilton Spectator. The Southam share was repurchased in 1975, returning full ownership to the Blackburn family.

When Josiah died in 1890, the company was operated by his two sons, Walter J. Blackburn, who served as president, and Arthur S. Blackburn, who was secretary/treasurer. Upon Walter's death in 1920, he was succeeded by his brother Arthur, who applied an abiding interest in mechanical and scientific developments to upgrade production processes at the newspaper. It was Arthur Blackburn's interest in early wireless telegraphy that led to the company's initial foray into broadcasting with radio station CJGC in 1922. In 1933, Arthur opened radio station CFPL in the top floor of the new Free Press building at 442 Richmond Street, but he died in 1935, before the full potential of the broadcasting arm of the company was realized.

It was left to his son Walter to bring the vision to life. Walter J. Blackburn was the first private broadcaster in Canada to place an order with RCA Victor for an FM transmitter and CFPL FM began broadcasting in 1948. In 1953, he established CFPL-TV, only the second privately owned television station in the country. Walter Blackburn further expanded the family broadcasting holdings in 1971, when he purchased CKNX Broadcasting Limited, located 115 kilometres north of London, in the town of Wingham.

During his 47 years at the helm of the family company, Walter Blackburn prided himself in providing his newspaper and broadcasting operations with state-of-the-art equipment and technology. He was particularly proud of the modern London Free Press building that was constructed under his watchful eye at 369 York Street and occupied in July of 1965.

Another facet of Walter Blackburn's life was his unstinting devotion to improving the quality of life in London. His most significant volunteer contribution was his involvement with the London Health Association and his role as chairman of the planning committee for the building of University Hospital.

To continue his work for community service, The Walter J. Blackburn Foundation was established in 1983 and through which today the Blackburn family and companies support charitable organizations focused on the areas of health, education, social welfare, the environment and the arts.

In the entrepreneurial spirit of her father Walter, her grandfather Arthur and her great grandfather Josiah, Martha Blackburn continued the tradition of growth. She firmly believed in the corporate philosophy, "to plough back into the community and the country some of the good we draw therefrom."

At the time of her death in the summer of 1992, she had taken the family companies into international markets and even more importantly had introduced a strong professional management team so critical to the future of an increasingly diverse enterprise. It is this team that continues her work.

The Children's Miracle Network Telethon is brought to London and Southwestern Ontario viewers through the Blackburn television operations in London and Wingham. Shown here are hosts Dinah Christie and Debbie Neufert along with CFPL-TV's Jim Swan and Perry Esler.

The building at 369 York Street in London houses The Blackburn Group head office, The London Free Press and FM-96 and CFPL Radio 98.

Reed Stenhouse Ltd.

Member of the
Alexander & Alexander Group

Senior Vice President and Branch Manager, James E. Bryan (sitting) is flanked by members of the operating team at Reed Stenhouse Limited. From left to right are Geoff Redshaw, Sr. Vice President Marketing; Ronald A. Mousley, Sr. President Sales & Service; and Chris L. Kelch, Vice President Business Development Mgr.

The names of the founding businessmen have long since disappeared from the masthead, but the insurance agency they nurtured to national prominence retains a strong presence in London under the umbrella of one of the world's foremost brokerage organizations, known now as Reed Stenhouse Limited - an international broker of long standing and member of the Alexander & Alexander Group of the United States.

Alexander & Alexander began in 1899 in Clarksburg, West Virginia. A&A gained its first large account - natural gas company — in 1905, a major railroad account in 1914. The Baltimore office was established in 1915, followed by offices in New York (1919), Tulsa (1919) and St. Louis (1920).

A&A was incorporated in Maryland in 1922, went public in 1969 and listed on the New York Stock Exchange in 1982.

The London Branch occupies the entire sixth floor of the City Centre Tower at 380 Wellington Street. With 50 employees, the latest office technology, and a much broader diversity of service, the facility is greatly advanced from the original insurance office opened 142 years ago. Over the intervening years the small firm established at 170 Princess Street by William B. Beddome in 1850 has expanded dramatically, at first through the efforts of astute local ownership and latterly in company with proficient contemporaries via the merger route.

In the early stages Beddome was joined by partner George T. Brown, and new quarters were secured in what was then known as the Prevost Building on Richmond Street. Later it was relocated above the old Boughner's store on Richmond. In 1919 Philip Pocock, a nephew of Brown, entered the business and subsequently acquired control for $45,000. V.P. Cronyn joined the firm in 1921, followed by partner G.W. Robinson in 1931 - at which time the name was changed to Cronyn, Pocock and Robinson.

Through World War II, headquarters were maintained in the Dundas Building; in the late 1940s moves were made to modern offices on Queens Avenue and then to a colonial-style structure at 150 Fullarton Street in 1961. By this time partners G.P. McEvenue and G. Ernest Jackson had taken their seats on a board of well-known Londoners, with Cronyn as president.

A historic merger in 1968, creating one of the larger insurance brokerage firms in the world, cemented an all-Canadian alliance of the London company with Reed, Shaw & McNaught of Toronto (dating to 1872) and Osler Hammond and Nanton of Winnipeg (established in 1883).

Ben Lowry was appointed branch manager of the combined group known as Reed Shaw Osler.

A further merger was concluded in 1973 with the UK-based Stenhouse Holdings Limited, leading to the name Reed Stenhouse Companies Limited in 1978. The largest merger in the history of the insurance brokerage industry was concluded in 1985 with the US-based Alexander & Alexander Group.

Succeeding Lowry as branch manager in 1983 was Bertram Polgrain who was manager till he retired in 1989. Succeeding Polgrain as branch manager in 1989 was James E. Bryan who, with his team of professionals, now offer insurance and risk management facilities on a global basis, while still providing quality service to its local clients as Southwestern Ontario's largest insurance broker.

University Hospital

Finding a better way

On September 21, 1972, University Hospital, a 390-bed tertiary care facility, officially opened to a population of people in need of highly specialized care. The hospital's roots can be traced back to 1909 when a tuberculosis epidemic was threatening the lives of many Canadians. Drawing on a sense of public duty and tremendous compassion, London politician and businessman Sir Adam Beck formed the London Health Association (LHA) to build a facility for the treatment of tuberculosis patients.

In the mid 1960s when tuberculosis was virtually eliminated, the LHA decided to close the 600-bed sanatorium and turned its attention to establishing a new hospital to respond to the changing health-care needs of the community. The building of University Hospital, with its mission of teaching, research and patient care, marked a new era for the London Health Association.

Affiliated with The University of Western Ontario and The John P. Robarts Research Institute, University Hospital's emphasis on excellence, teamwork, innovation and efficiency has enabled it to lead the way in some major medical advancements. Over the years, the hospital has developed outstanding services in such areas as multi-organ transplantation, cardiology, and cardiovascular surgery, reproductive medicine, orthopaedics, and neurosurgery and neurology.

A referral centre for southwestern Ontario, patients from other areas of Canada, North America and the world come to University Hospital for specialized treatment. A few highlights include:

- Performing an average of 200 transplants a year, University Hospital is ranked as one of Canada's leading multi-organ transplant centres.
- University Hospital's Epilepsy Unit is the largest of its kind in Canada, receiving patient referrals from throughout North America.

- The In-vitro Fertilization program is one of the most active programs of its kind in Canada. Between 1983 and 1992 more than 400 babies were born.
- Patients from North America and beyond with severe heart rhythm disorders are treated in the hospital's unique Arrhythmia Monitoring Unit.
- The Department of Orthopaedic Surgery is widely recognized for its innovative work in hip and knee replacements and athletic injuries treatment.

In addition to medical initiatives, University Hospital has taken an entrepreneurial approach to managing hospital finances. The University Hospital Development Corporation and the University Hospital Centre for the Advancement of Medical Device Technology (UH-CAMDT) are just two examples of how the hospital generates revenue from hospital based resources and developments.

University Hospital has experienced a great deal of change since 1972. The staff has more than doubled in order to keep pace with the new initiatives and activities, and the ever-growing volume of patients. Amid such tremendous growth, University Hospital's pursuit of excellence remains constant.

Excellence in patient care, teaching and research has been the primary goal of University Hospital since it opened its doors in 1972.

Bell Canada

Helping Londoners communicate
for over 100 years . . .

When George Edwards was manager of Bell Telephone Company's first London office in 1880, he walked in to find 25 or 30 bells attached to a wall. Those bells alerted operators to calls coming and going between the 40 subscribers of the new "talking" service.

Those bells have long since been replaced by silent computerized switching equipment that can handle thousands of calls per hour from London's 140,000 customers. And Bell is now one of North America's largest and most technically advanced telecommunications providers.

It's all part of Bell Canada's Mission - TO BE A WORLD LEADER in helping people communicate and manage information. That mission is guiding the 2,150 Bell employees who work in London to provide their customers with the best possible services and products whether it's a telephone installation in an apartment or a brand new office telephone system. Many of these 2150 employees are of course associated with Bell's large regional network center located at 100 Dundas.

Bell Canada's long distance service is routed through a high-tech fibre optic (FOTS) network.

Bell employees play an active role in their communities individually and through the Telephone Pioneers. Civic deeds and personal contributions by Bell employees can be found in the archives of local papers. As a company, Bell supports its employees endeavours and itself contributed many thousands of dollars to London and area charitable causes.

Bell is a member of BCE Inc., a corporation that includes Northern Telecom (with its large London-based manufacturing facility), Bell Northern Research and Bell Cellular, among others.

Surveying today's telecommunications technology it's hard to believe it started in London with that simple office more than 110 years ago. The first long distance lines from London to St. Thomas were established in 1882 and a five-minute conversation cost 15 cents. (Today St. Thomas and London subscribers enjoy free calling between their communities.) That original long distance network soon stretched east to Trenton north to Goderich and south to Hamilton.

The first metallic switchboard in Canada was installed in London in 1893.

Customers were advised "not to use their telephones on the approach of or during a thunder storm". Rain and other severe weather could quickly disable the fledgling service. But that didn't stop businesses and individuals from installing telephones. By 1900, there were 1318 subscribers in London. In 1926 there were enough subscribers to justify creation of two telephone exchanges, "Metcalfe" and "Fairmont".

London has always been an important focal point for Bell particularly as new, more efficient technology has been introduced. Many of the changes taking place today are almost invisible to customers.

Fibre Optic transmission for instance, is an advancement that has increased capacity, provided alternate routes and continuous, high quality long distance telecommunications services from London to locations around the world.

By 1994 all of Bell's central offices in the city will be equipped with state-of-the-art digital switching equipment for local calling. The long distance network is now fully digital. Most of this advanced technology was designed and manufactured IN CANADA. These and other modernization projects are expected to cost the company about $40 million in 1992 in London alone. As the network is modernized, advanced

100 Dundas Street, Talbot Square, has been the Bell Canada London Headquarters since early 1980's.

telephone features will become universally available. Call Management Service options, Calling Line Identification, Call Answer, Call Waiting and Forwarding and a wide variety of innovative voice and data services are all made possible with this technology.

1992 was a significant year for Bell Canada. The company created two new administrative units based on the provincial boundaries — Bell Ontario and Bell Quebec. And the national telecommunication providers including Bell Canada realized the need to support their large national clients in the global marketplace. The Stentor Alliance was formed and Signature Service established.

Also, the Canadian Radio-television and Telecommunications Commission (CRTC) made an historic ruling in favour of opening the telecommunications marketplace to full competition. This will mean changes to the company, but not to its commitment to its customers to provide low-cost long distance service while maintaining superb local services at reasonable prices.

A Bell Canada construction crew circa 1905. The early network was vulnerable to the elements.

Avco Financial Services

"To be the best company in the eyes of its customers, employees and shareholders" is the foundation of growth at Avco Financial Services Canada Limited. This corporate philosophy has enabled the company to build itself from a small appliance store arm in early 1954 to what it has become today, an integral and vital part of an international financial services company spanning three continents.

Only a few people worked from Avco's original downtown London location. Today, the company's national home office employs more than 250 Londoners.

These original few employees demonstrated a pioneering spirit that demanded visionary thinking. The attitudes and ethics that early spirit gave birth to are still found at Avco today as the company strives to achieve its vision.

Incorporated in London as Delta Acceptance Corporation, Avco Canada enjoyed tremendous growth during those early years. In fact, by 1964, only a decade after starting the company with a meagre $25,000 capitalization, Avco had grown to a corporation with $250 million in receivables and more than 200 branches in all 10 Canadian provinces.

Following a number of acquisitions and mergers in Canada and the United States, Avco joined forces in 1985 with its current parent organization, Textron, Inc. - one of the world's most successful multi-national companies. Worldwide, including Avco Canada, it employs 72,000 people and has assets of approximately $15 billion.

In Canada, Avco has continued to grow at a rapidly accelerating pace, particularly since joining forces with Textron. Receivables surpassed $1 billion in mid-1990, with nearly half that growth taking place between 1985 and 1990, when the company launched its national drive for Quality Improvement (QIP) and service excellence. Today, the company offers to Canadians innovative financial services products including loans, mortgages, retail sales financing and ancillary products - through more than 240 offices across the country.

Since the QIP process was introduced in 1985, more than 1,450 employee recommendations have been implemented, which has resulted in a corporate savings of more that $10 million and has brought about ever-increasing customer satisfaction levels.

Avco's involvement in London and elsewhere in Canada will not slacken, either in business or human terms. The company and its employees remain committed to continuous improvement and growth. This philosophy will ensure that the company is able to meet its vision of becoming the best company in the eyes of its customers, employees and shareholders, while remaining a strong partner in the successful commerce of London.

London & Midland General Insurance Co.

Progressive it was, progressive it still is.

London, 1947: The post-war era was a time to rebuild, a time to make a new start. The Progressive Insurance Company was one of many businesses begun in the spirit of optimism that marked the times. The name was indeed prophetic. Now called London & Midland General Insurance Co., the organization has seen many changes in the intervening years, but that enterprising nature, so integral to the success of a business, has never altered.

For the first decade the company struggled. In 1957, a group of prominent London businessmen purchased it. Reflecting their pride in their community and in this opportunity to invest in its future, the group renamed the company London and Midland (L&M) General Insurance Co.

Those entrepreneurs were: W.L. Duffield, Douglas B. Weldon, J.G. Thompson, Joseph Jeffery, R.M. Ivey, J.H. Moore, Col. Thomas Lawson, J.H. Stevens and R.E. Wilkins. Three non-Londoners also backed the business. They were publisher Roy Thomson of Edinburgh, Scotland, shipping executive Kenneth Powell of Winnipeg and E.W. Bickle of Toronto.

Five years later, it was purchased by Delta Acceptance Corp. Ltd., also a London, Ontario company. L&M proved to be one of Delta's best acquisitions with an unbroken record of profit to date.

In 1964, Delta merged with Avco Financial Services, the firm that owns L&M today.

Setting a pattern of innovative resourcefulness for the decades ahead, L&M identified a market and went after it. At that time providing insurance for high-risk drivers was not a profitable venture. L&M changed that. Their aggressive, gutsy approach paid off and by the '70s they had progressed to become one of the top 10 auto insurance companies in the country.

When the Ontario government created "Facility" to handle this high-risk insurance group, L&M decided to focus elsewhere.

In the early '80s they began to concentrate on specialty programs such as livestock, accidental disability and group personal lines insurance.

These programs didn't meet the income expectations of L&M and once again they showed their keen business acumen by replacing specialty programs with creditor insurance for financial institution customers, a service they were already providing for Avco customers.

"We see ourselves continuing to provide products and services to Canadian financial institutions," says Arthur J. Smith-Windsor Sr., V.P. and General Manager of L&M. "We've identified this as the area of greatest potential."

Today, L&M attributes much of its success to its "people first" attitude, in terms of both employees and customers.

"Our company philosophy centres on quality," says Anthony Miles, V.P. of Operations. "We pride ourselves on our outstanding customer service, our responsiveness, and our accuracy.

Our employees have suggested hundreds of ideas which we have implemented to improve customer service and L&M's efficiency," he adds, in explanation of the company's Quality Improvement Process.

Like the city whose name it bears, London and Midland will continue to grow, change, progress and prosper. "We've been a constant part of the fabric of the city," says Smith-Windsor. "We're proud of the role we've played in the business community."

Goliger's Travel

Goliger's Travel new location at 639 Southdale Road in Montgomery Plaza.

Goliger's new offices at the Montgomery Plaza location.

Over the years, Goliger's Travel has distinguished itself from other firms through its unique, progressive approach to travel service. By making its vision of the ideal vacation or business trip a reality to its clientele, Goliger's Travel has established itself as a leader in the travel industry.

Founded in Montreal in 1955, Goliger's Travel quickly flourished into a chain of agencies across Canada. Observing that the owner-operated company provides the best service for its clients, the firm made an important decision to expand the chain through franchising in 1979. The business has grown to approximately 80 agencies throughout the nation, providing the company with the buying power and technology of a chain, while retaining the highest degree of quality and services found only in an owner-operated business.

A progressive company, Goliger's Travel maintains its leadership in the travel industry with new technology, innovations and services. This was evident during 1991, when the Goliger's Travel chain affiliated itself with the two best travel companies in the United States, Hickery Travel Systems and International Tours. This affiliation has resulted in a network of over 1000 agencies servicing over 4.5 billion dollars annually, and has enabled the company to bring new, cost-saving computer technology and services to Canada that are unique to Goliger's Travel.

With a strict commitment to finding the best savings and the highest quality of service for its business and vacation clients, Goliger's Travel has been servicing such customers from its south London office for nearly a decade. In keeping with the firm's progressive vision, the agency relocated from Wellington Road to a larger office in the Montgomery Plaza on Southdale Road in 1991. 1991-92 also saw sales double over the previous year.

The firm excels in the management of travel expenses, in addition to the provision of travel services. The south London agency, owned by John Szustaczek, is a leader in the travel industry, providing business and vacation travellers across Ontario with the latest technology and services exclusive to Goliger's Travel in Canada. Another key to the success of any business is its staff, and the south London agency can attribute much of its success to its dedicated, knowledgable representatives.

Aside from providing travel services to vacationing clients and businesses of all sizes, the agency is proud to play an active role in the community, and involves itself with many charitable organizations in Ontario.

Canada Post

A tradition of growing with the community of London.

The post office and the London community have grown together for almost a hundred and seventy years.

London's first post office was actually located in London Township, in a general store at what is now the corner of Oxford Street and Sanatorium Road. The store's proprietor, Laurence Laurason, became London's first postmaster on April 6, 1825.

In these early days, mail was transported by horseback to isolated post offices across the region. Contractors hired to make the twice-weekly trips were paid seven and a half dollars for each journey, considered excellent pay at the time.

As the forks of the Thames grew as London's commercial centre, the decision was made to relocate the post office. Laurason lost his position in 1828 to Ira Schofield, who resided on a farm where Catholic Central High School is located today. That year also saw the beginning of stagecoach service to London, which carried passengers as well as mail.

Ira Schofield was stripped of the postmastership in 1830, when his daughter was accused of opening a letter addressed to a guest in their home. The position passed to George Jervis Goodhue, who opened a post office at the northeast corner of Dundas and Ridout streets. He served until 1852.

Reflecting London's growing stature as a regional centre, the London division was created in 1854 out of territory from the Toronto and Kingston divisions. Gilbert Griffin was appointed as the first inspector. A new post office also opened around this time, at the corner of Richmond and Queens Avenue.

Carrier service did not begin in London until April 1876, fifty-one years after the first post office opened. More than fifty people applied for the five positions.

A new, modern era for London's post office came with its relocation to the Dominion Public Building on Richmond Street in 1936. Modelled after New York City's Rockefeller Center and built at a cost of $1.25 million, the Dominion Public Building was and remains a masterpiece of the Art Deco style.

The building was opened on September 26, 1936. J.C. Elliot, Canada's postmaster general, turned a golden key in the building's front door as a man on the roof was signalled to raise the Canadian flag. The first letter was posted by G.A.P. Brickenden, a prominent Londoner, to his daughter in England.

In 1961, post office headquarters relocated to another new building, this one at 217 York Street, on the southeast corner of York and Clarence Streets. The office diversified in 1975, with sorting operations moving to a large complex on Highbury Avenue. Letter carriers continued to work out of the York Street building until it was sold in 1988.

The Highbury location is now headquarters for the southwestern Ontario area, renamed the Huron Division in the early 1980s. From London, mail is processed for the area from Windsor to Fort Erie to Collingwood.

The future of mail delivery lies in technology. By introducing innovations like electronic data interchange, the post office will continue a tradition begun almost a hundred and seventy years ago - a tradition of growing with the community of London.

MAIL ➤ POSTE

Canada Post Corporation / Société canadienne des postes

3M Canada Inc.

Innovation working for you

Oxford Park, the London 3M Canada manufacturing facility, is one of the largest in the 3M world under one roof.

3M Canada Inc. is the London-based Canadian subsidiary of the world wide 3M Company. With the Canadian headquarters and main plant here, the company markets and manufactures more than 60,000 products for industry, the professions, business, government and the consumer.

3M Canada also has two plants in Perth, Ontario. One manufactures "Scotch-Brite" products and the other, several types of tape. An operation in Havelock, Ontario produces coloured granules for the roofing industry as well as microspheres which are used in a variety of industrial products as lightweight fillers. A production facility in Simcoe, Ontario produces automotive trim and graphics and a custom "Post-it" Note production facility in Toronto serves the advertising specialty market. There are two operations in a plant in Morden, Manitoba producing epoxy resin powders and health care products.

The newest location in Brockville, Ontario, is a world class tape production facility designed for the growing export and domestic markets.

Although 3M Canada's formal existence dates back some forty years into London's history, 3M products have been manufactured and sold in Canada since 1930. Canadian Durex Abrasives, based in Brantford, Ontario was the Canadian arm of a consortium of companies headed by Minnesota Mining and Manufacturing (the 3M Company). When the Durex Corporation was dissolved 3M created its first international division by acquiring some of the assets of Durex and forming Minnesota Mining and Manufacturing of Canada Limited, later to become 3M Canada Inc. The new Canadian company manufactured abrasives, and coatings in a leas-ed portion of a former aircraft hangar in Brantford until a new plant facility was built in London.

The company was officially established on January 17, 1951 and on May 1 of that year the general administration office opened in London, followed the next day by offices in Halifax, Montreal, Toronto, Winnipeg and Vancouver.

The original plant, covering 145,000 square feet and containing new tape making, adhesive mixing and abrasive converting equipment, came to life on August 2, 1952. Over 200 employees relocated from Brantford and some 200 more were added that first year. Total sales reached $2.8 million.

At first, 3M Canada was an importer of 3M products; then it became a manufacturer. Later, through exports to the United States and other countries it began to enter the international scene. More recently it has become a rationalized manufacturer between Canada and the U.S. for several of the company's products. Abrasives, tapes, non-woven abrasives, better known as "Scotch-Brite" products, aerosol products and others are exported to upwards of 20 countries. These exports represent some twenty per cent of annual sales and over forty per cent of Canadian manufacturing capacity.

Sales growth over the years has been accompanied by physical changes in plant size and the construction of new plants to serve growing markets. Typically in 3M, as businesses grow, new business units, divisions and groups are formed to serve the growing customer base and to keep the company close to the customer.

The acquisition of Irvington Mica Insulator Company in 1955 necessitated

3M Canada's first expansion of 5,500 square metres to accommodate a new varnish coating tower and varnish house. Both are now long gone and replaced by more up-to-date products and production methods.

Subsequent additions to the plant and office areas of the London complex during the ensuing years have brought the covered floor area to well over 60,000 square metres as 3M reinvested its profits into more productive and efficient production equipment and technology. In a recent two-year period, for instance, more than $65 million was committed or spent to effect plant expansions, upgrades and new plant construction to meet the growing export and domestic production needs.

In 1976, to mark the 25th anniversary of the company, a recreation area and park was built at the London plant for employee use. The 5.5 hectare facility includes two baseball diamonds, a soccer pitch, four tennis courts, locker and shower facilities and a playground, picnic and fitness area.

In 1979 two 3M Centres were built to better serve the customer. One was in Calgary and the other Montreal.

In 1980, a new plant was built in Perth, Ontario to produce "Scotch-Brite" non-woven abrasives and the construction of a second at that location, to manufacture tape was also begun.

During that period a new laboratory was built combining technical, research and development facilities in one modern unit.

Research and development in 3M Canada functions as an integral part of the flow of technology and new products in the worldwide $13-billion 3M Company which employs some 89,000 people in 57 countries. While many products are conceived by the parent company, 3M Canada has a highly qualified staff of more than 100 scientists and technicians who custom tailor products to Canadian needs and contribute to the constant stream of new products. This on-going innovation helps ensure that 25% to 30% of annual sales derives from products that were not on the shelf five years before.

3M is not just a company that has a history of innovation, invention and growth. It is also a company that is an integral part of the communities in which it operates. It is a company that has had a world wide pollution control program in place for more than 15 years. This 3P (Pollution Prevention Pays) program is aimed at reducing pollution at source rather than adding end-of-pipe controls. It is done through reformulation, changes to the raw materials or the process to reduce or eliminate the source of pollution and by various other ways, such as reuse and recycling. The goal is to reduce such pollution by 90% by the year 2000 and to reach zero emissions in the next century.

3M also contributes in a major way to charitable organizations, the arts and cultural groups as well as to centres of learning. The 3M Teaching Fellowship "represents the only Canada-wide, interdisciplinary award for excellence in university teaching," according to the Society for Teaching and Learning in Higher Education. Bursaries and scholarships are also offered in more than 40 universities and colleges across the country.

Since Canada began rationalizing its manufacturing operations in the 1970s it has continued to concentrate its efforts on making a narrower line of products but for the entire North American market. This approach has earned 3M Canada manufacturing operations a reputation for quality and cost effectiveness in the 3M world.

The result has been a significant growth in the volume of our export business which has engendered new investment in expanded and increased manufacturing capability here.

As manufacturing is looked upon as a 3M "Centre of Excellence" in Canada, so too are many of the company's marketing, sales and administrative functions being established as "Centres of Excellence" in the North American marketplace. By focusing on those activities which it does best and making use of 3M Global resources, 3M Canada will continue to offer quality products and service to its Canadian customers in the emerging North American market.

Tartan Place London, headquarters for 3M Canada.

Central Park Lodges

"Canada's most trusted
name in retirement living"

*Enjoy the leisurely at-
mosphere of a suite.*

*Pleasant surroundings for
your enjoyment and
relaxation.*

Established in 1961, Central Park Lodges (CPL) founded the first chain of privately owned retirement and nursing homes in Canada. The vision of the founders was that the provision of care to the elderly should be based on the principles of dignity, privacy and a uniformly high level of service and care.

Our geographical base spans the Canadian provinces of Alberta, British Columbia, Manitoba, Ontario and Quebec and the American States of Florida, Pennsylvania and Texas.

Total resident capacity is approximately 9000.

With corporate headquarters in Toronto (Ontario, Canada) and divisional offices in Sarasota (Florida), Dallas (Texas) and Toronto (Ontario), CPL currently employs a full and part time staff of over 10,000 people.

Central Park Lodge - London has been serving the elderly in London and surrounding area for over 25 years. CPL London reflects the community we serve and our commitment is to quality and care. We provide a full compliment of service including convalescent and specialized care shown by our "continuim of care" approach.

CPL - London has all the conveniences of downtown living being only minutes from the main core.

CPL is proud to have played a vital role for many of London's elderly and looks forward to many more years of service to London and the community.

"The Central Park Lodge Team"
279 Horton Street,
London, Ontario N6B 1L3
(519) 434-4544

Catholic Education

Part of the spirit of London

When Lieutenant Governor John Graves Simcoe gazed across the forks of the Thames, envisioning the beginnings of a great city, Catholic Education was already gaining a foothold in this country. The great explorer Samuel De Champlain had been commissioned by the Catholic Monarchs of France to teach the native children and establish the Faith in Canada.

The Roman Catholic Separate School Board was operating in London as far back as 1858. The first Catholic settlers at the forks of the Thames were not far behind their Protestant neighbours in providing for their children as good an education as the primitive conditions would allow.

In the early 1840's the Upper Canada Legislature passed "The Common School Act", which helped lay the foundation of Separate Schools. It granted to Roman Catholics the right to establish Separate Schools, to appoint teachers of their own faith, and access to public moneys for the maintenance of the schools. In the early days, however, Separate School supporters were obliged to pay dual support to the "Common" (public) schools as well as to the Separate System. In 1853 an act was passed exempting Separate School supporters from "common" school taxes. This, along with the right to exist, was confirmed in 1863 and ratified by the British North America Act in 1867.

135 years later, the Catholic Schools of London and Middlesex County serve over 17,000 students in 33 elementary schools, 5 secondary schools, and an adult education centre, offering a quality education combined with the Catholic faith perspective. It has become an important part of the social, moral and economic fabric of London.

Thomas Darcy McGee, one of the

Fathers of Confederation, was among the first of many prominent supporters of the Catholic School System. In 1858, the Catholic Board's only school fell on hard times and was forced to close. McGee was instrumental in helping separate schools establish a permanent footing in London by making a sizable donation, allowing the school to reopen in September of that year.

Countless "famous" London citizens attended Catholic Schools. The Lombardo brothers were students at St. Peter's and for many years returned to maintain their lasting friendships. In May of 1954, Guy Lombardo donated a statue of the Blessed Virgin to the school in commemoration of his Mother.

Others include Bishop Henry, who attended CCH; former London Mayor Al Gleeson; City Councillor Pat O'Brien; former MP, Public Board Chair, and now Catholic trustee John Ferris; and NHL stars Jim Dorey, Rick Green and Brendan Shanahan. (Green's story is amusing. As a Grade 9 student at CCH, he was a preseason cut from the Crusaders Hockey team.)

The late Pete Howard attained athletic fame as a member of the Hamilton Ti-Cats of the CFL in the 50's and 60's. Actress Kate Nelligan attended the Catholic system, as did actress Lisa Howard, recently a star on a popular TV soap.

Other notables include Gord Wilson, President of the Ontario Federation of Labour; former Sarnia Mayor, MPP and one time interim PC Party leader, Andy Brandt; President of Parkwood Hospital, Michael Boucher; former City Councillor Bob Beccarea; and restauranteurs Eddie & Fred Escaf.

There are many others too numerous to mention, but who have made significant contributions to the success of Catholic Education.

Graduating class of 1942 from the catholic schools of London.

LONDON AND MIDDLESEX COUNTY
ROMAN CATHOLIC SCHOOL BOARD

CONSEIL DES ÉCOLES CATHOLIQUES
DE LONDON ET DU COMTÉ DE MIDDLESEX

The new John Paul II Catholic Secondary School which opened in September 1991.

Canada Trust

Helping London grow
for over 125 years

When 25 businessmen gathered above MacFie's store in downtown London in 1864, they couldn't have dreamed that the tiny Huron and Erie Savings and Loan Society they were creating would someday become Canada Trust - the nation's biggest trust company by a wide margin and one of the largest financial institutions in Canada.

The Huron and Erie was formed to offer an alternative source of funds to industrious individuals exploited by unconscionable money lenders. The founders recognized the vital relationship between the well-being of business and agriculture and the overall economic health of the community and set about to establish moderate interest rates. Response from area people was immediate. Within five years the company boasted assets exceeding one million dollars.

The growth had begun.

By June 1992 corporate and administered assets exceeded $131 billion and a staff of over 15,000 served several million Canadians from 354 financial, 133 real estate, and 23 trust services branches coast-to-coast.

Over the years more than 50 mortgage, loan, trust, and real estate companies have been brought together under the Canada Trust banner, with each adding geographic diversity and specific strengths. The most recent amalgamation was with the Canada Permanent Mortgage Corporation on January 1, 1986.

Mergers and growth brought several name changes through the years. In 1876 the original name was altered to the Huron and Erie Loan and Savings Company, and by 1915 the name was changed to the Huron and Erie Mortgage Corporation.

The Canada Trust name dates back

In the company's earliest days, letters were written by hand and copied in a letter-book by means of a hand press. By 1914 electric lighting, telephones, and typewriters had become integral to everyday operations at Huron and Erie's office.

Today Canada Trust's two towers at Dundas and Wellington boast the latest in technological innovation, electronically linking head office with over 500 financial services, real estate, and trust branches, coast-to-coast.

to the turn of the century. In 1899 the Huron and Erie acquired the charter of The General Trust Company of Calgary. Three years later the firm opened for business in London as the Canada Trust Company, in a well-timed move to fill a growing need for trust services.

In 1961 the registered name became Canada Trust-Huron and Erie, though the two component companies continued to operate separately. In 1976 the firm dropped the Huron and Erie name in favor of a name that reflected the nationwide scope of the firm and became known legally as Canada Trustco Mortgage Company, and to the general public, simply as Canada Trust.

Through the years corporate headquarters has moved several times in the heart of London's business district. The first company office was in the Crystal Block at Dundas and Richmond streets. In 1864 the young firm moved to a building on Talbot Street, then in 1866 took up operations in leased premises at 37 Dundas. By 1872 the company felt confident enough to construct its own building, on Richmond Street at Queens.

In the depths of the Great Depression, a new nine-storey office structure was built on Dundas Street at Clarence.

Today's Canada Trust Tower at Dundas and Wellington streets was constructed in 1973 as part of a city block redevelopment project that provided much-needed space for the expanding organization.

Guiding the company through mergers, continuous growth, name changes, and technological advances that have seen the introduction of telephones, electric lighting, typewriters, and, more recently, computers, has been a dedicated group of presidents: 1864-1866, Adam Hope; 1867-1870, Ellis W. Hyman; 1871-1874, John Birrell; 1875-1878, Charles Stead; 1879-1886, William Saunders; 1887, W.P. Street; 1888-1908, John W. Little; 1909-1924 and 1933-1941, Thomas G. Meredith; 1925-1932, Major Hume B. Cronyn; 1942-1956, Morley Aylsworth; 1957-1972, J. Allyn Taylor; 1973-1978, Arthur H. Mingay; 1978-1990, Mervyn L. Lahn; 1991-   , Peter C. Maurice.

With foresight, founding president Adam Hope and his associates determined to establish a firm committed to the principles of prudence, strict business morality, and the cultivation of trust. Time hasn't caused those tenets to waver. They continue to direct the day-to-day operations of today's Canada Trust — a leader in the financial services industry.

Staff of the predecessor Huron and Erie Loan and Savings Company, London, 1895.

Aboutown

Serving London's transportation needs since 1947!

Who is Aboutown?

Aboutown Transportation Limited started as Aboutown Cabs Limited in 1947. Current ownership by the Donnelly family took place in 1974. From thirty nine taxicabs in 1974, the company has since grown into a diversified transportation company. The name was changed in 1983 to more accurately reflect this diversification. Aboutown now includes not only taxis, but also limousines, school busing, paratransit services, minibus charters, shuttle services, airport services, highway busing, mechanical garage, body shop, car wash, propane fuel centre, and safety and training centre.

Aboutown Enterprises Inc. is the holding company which owns Aboutown Transportation Limited, Mitchell Air Cargo Services and London City Plymouth Chrysler Limited.

Community Players

Aboutown has always been and continues to be actively involved in the London community. It has sponsored many London community activities, such as Orchestra London, The Big Band Festival, The Corporate Challenge, Countdown London, Easter Seals, and

Our hot air balloon flying high over London. Lord Simcoe would have envied such a view of the fork of the Thames!

was instrumental in the start of the Annual London Balloon Fiesta. Always looking for an innovative and diversified approach to transportation, we purchased our own hot air balloon in 1985. You may have seen it flying over the City of London.

We're on a Mission!

Our mission is to be the premier supplier of small vehicle transportation in London in particular, and Southwest Ontario in general. We strive to be up to date in the latest developments in transportation and communication. It is improvements in these two areas that power our growth and allow us to provide quality transportation services to our customers.

Car 54 Where Are You?

Through our own in-house technology, in conjunction with our dispatch and driving staff, we have developed a computerized dispatch system that is designed to fill the niche for companies operating twenty to two hundred cars. The computer system automatically matches the appropriate vehicle to the customer phone call and

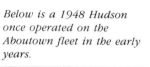

Below is a 1948 Hudson once operated on the Aboutown fleet in the early years.

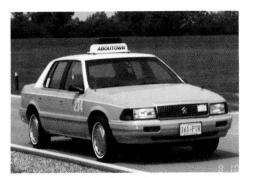

One of our 1992 Plymouth Acclaims. To cater to changing needs, these taxicabs are designated non-smoking.

sends that data to a screen located in each car. This system results in a faster, more efficient service to our customers. In addition, they are provided with a quiet ride, free from the incessant chatter of the traditional radio dispatch environment.

Safety First!

As our business expanded, so too did the need to have fulltime training staff and programs. A fully equipped on-site classroom was developed to augment hands-on training to ensure the safety and comfort of our customers. Safety and Training are long term priorities that continue to ensure high quality transportation services.

It's Not Easy Being Green

Although our colours are blue and white, Aboutown is green too. In the field of transportation, we, along with public transit, provide an alternative to the private car, the prime culprit in air pollution and ozone depletion. In addition, we helped pioneer the use of automotive propane in the London area. We started to convert our vehicles to propane in 1980 and we now have the vast majority of our 300 vehicles running on this clean burning, environmentally friendly fuel. We also recycle our office paper, pop cans, tires, oil, freon, car parts, metal, garage and body shop fluids, and use biodegradable soap to clean our vehicles.

Location, Location, Location

By our very nature, our vehicles go where the customers are. Our office location has changed over the years, but has always been fairly central to the downtown area. In 1974 Aboutown was located at 374 York Street across from the London Free Press. In 1980, we moved to the former McManus property at 24 Horton Street.

In 1985, we moved the first section of our operations to a newly renovated 1 and 2 Bathurst Street during the construction phase of the Horton Street bridge. The southeast corner of our building at 24 Horton was actually chopped off to permit the construction of the Horton Street extension. In 1988, our building beside the Thames River at 1 Bathurst was hit by lightning and had to be renovated again.

We have taken great steps to maintain the original Bathurst Street buildings that once included an ice house and repair facilities for the Grand Trunk Railway and later the London Street Railway. We are proud to be situated at the junction of the railway line and Thames river, the two major transportation routes over the last 200 years.

The Winds of Change

In 1985, the company took over the operation of Mitchell Air Cargo Services, a family run enterprise based at the London Airport that fit into our larger transportation family. To further diversify the group, while still keeping the focus in transportation, London City Plymouth Chrysler was added in 1990, on the site of the former Forest City Plymouth Chrysler in east London.

The company will continue to change and evolve as we move into the twenty-first century. Having just celebrated our 45th year in business, we are proud to be a part of London and help celebrate its bicentennial.

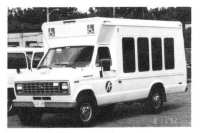

A closer look at one of our vans used to provide service for the physically challenged.

At the foot of the London Skyline is a view of our head office at 1 and 2 Bathurst Street and the parking lot for a "sea of vehicles", taken from the Horton Street bridge in 1992. The far corner is anchored by a flagpole flying the Canadian flag and the Aboutown insignia.

Beaver Foods Limited

Toward Outstanding
People and Service

President R.J. Henderson

Customers in Beaver Foods gourmet coffee shop at Fanshawe College.

Half a million meals a day! These are the impressive statistics that introduce you to the country's largest, all-Canadian contract catering company, based in London.

Beaver Foods serves these meals in more than 700 locations from Vancouver Island to Petty Harbour, Newfoundland and up to the Yukon. More than 6,000 Canadian employees meet the food service needs of business and industry, high schools, colleges, universities, hospitals, nursing homes, and remote camps.

Beaver is London-based, and is also London born. Founders Alex McIntosh and Jim O'Rourke began food service operations at Huron College in 1960. A trial at two London high schools in 1961 led to a contract for all London public high schools two years later. This early success blossomed over the years and made Beaver Foods the largest operator of secondary school cafeterias in Canada. Service is now provided to 400 schools, including the Public and Separate Boards of Education in the London area.

Beaver's involvement in the London community grew steadily to include several important local institutions which continue to be served to this day. In 1962, service began at Brescia College, followed by Fanshawe College (1972), Westminster College (1974), Canada Trust (1975) and the Public Utilities Commission (1987). At the same time, similar growth occurred across the country.

Exceptional contract service begins well before food is even purchased. A significant part of the Company's success must be attributed to the London Home Office personnel who have provided professional services over the past 30 years to cafeterias across Canada. A team of dietitians and nutritionists spend considerable time ensuring that menus promote healthier eating. Promotions experts develop programs that cater to all the customer's senses, while design personnel ensure facilities are attractive and deliver efficient service.

Along with the distinction of being the country's largest all-Canadian food service contractor, Beaver is arguably the most diverse, offering its employees considerable and interesting challenges. Whether providing residential or cafeteria services in a large institution such as Memorial University or Fanshawe College, or catering to thousands of the world's athletes, the press and spectators at the Calgary Olympics, Beaver employees respond to the specific needs and tastes of a varied clientele.

In January of 1991 a new chapter began in Beaver Foods' development. Cara Operations Limited, of Toronto, purchased all outstanding shares of the organization from its management owners. Cara provides Beaver Foods with concepts such as Harvey's Restaurants and Swiss Chalet to introduce in its large institutional accounts. These opportunities complement Beaver's own Roasters Gourmet Coffee Shops and franchise outlets such as Taco Bell. Both these concepts are enjoyed by the students, faculty and staff at Fanshawe College.

Pride in their service, honest and open relations with clients, and faith in and respect for their employees make up the cornerstone of all Beaver Foods operations. But, equally important has been the influence of the Company's roots in the London community, where its reputation among many valued clients fostered a history of expansion across the country.

Copp Builders' Supply Company Limited Since 1877

We are very proud to be a member of the London business community for 116 years and celebrating with our city their 200th birthday.

Our Company's roots were started, by Barnabus Skuse, in 1877 as a stone and lime kiln on Brick Street (now Commissioners Road) with an office at 95 York Street. From these locations we manufactured and sold bricks and blocks for a then growing City of London of some 20,000 persons. In 1908 William and Thomas Copp, who were commercial and residential home builders in London, purchased the business. The Company was incorporated in 1924 changing the name from Copp Bros. to Copp Builders' Supply Company Limited. In that year Stanley F. Copp, son of Thomas, joined the Company and four years later acquired the interest of his uncle William. Under Stanley the Company expanded into the supply of lumber and in 1951 built, at 85 York Street, the first modern showroom for building materials in the area.

In 1952 T. Brayl Copp, son of Stanley, joined the firm, and became President and owner in 1964. The present Head Office location at 45 York Street was constructed in 1966 and enlarged 10 years later to a warehouse/office complex of 65,000 square feet. In 1965 the first step to a multi-branch operation began with the opening of a new home centre known as Lumberland on Highway #22 near Hyde Park.

Further expansion took place with the purchase of the assets of London Lumber Ltd. in 1971, Kitchener Lumber Company in 1972, the opening of a Copp's Buildall in Sarnia in 1974, the purchase of Kernohan Lumber in 1979 and Hunt Lumber in 1981. A United States operation in Buffalo, N.Y., known as Crown Wholesale Lumber Limited,

was started in 1984 to serve industrial, commercial and residential building contractors in that area. In 1986 the Company acquired the Pittsburgh Paint distributorship for the greater London area. Currently the Company has four Buildall outlets and the Pittsburgh Paint Centre in London, one outlet in Buffalo, N.Y. and three franchised building material operations in the Kitchener, Ontario area.

John E. Sim, Executive Vice President joined the firm in 1977, and James M. Stewart, Vice President, Finance started in 1973. Both John and Jim have contributed much to the growth and success of the Company over the years. A fourth generation of the Copp family, Steven S. Copp, joined the firm in 1986 and recently became a shareholder and Vice President.

President, T. Brayl Copp, clearly believes the success of his Company, celebrating its 116th birthday along with London's 200th, is due in a large part to the support and dedication of all its loyal employees over the years.

James M. Stewart, Vice President, Finance; Steven S. Copp, Vice President; T. Brayl Copp, President; John E. Sim, Executive Vice President.

The Yes, We Wood® People®

Cuddy Food Products

Quality poultry
for healthy tastes

Today's turkey is enjoyed in a myriad of tastes and textures and chicken lends itself to countless choices of cuisine. However, for most of this century, poultry has been enjoyed in only one way: roasted as a whole body bird. If you ever wondered how we progressed from the regal roast turkey all the way to turkey as a deli meat classic, you need look no further than London, Ontario.

In fact, the further-processing of turkey into deli meats and boneless roasts in Canada was a long held vision of poultry pioneer A.M. (Mac) Cuddy. He was one of the first people to appreciate its versatility and potential. He felt strongly that turkey should become an everyday meat, not just part of a special occasion meal for holidays or weekends.

Finding new ways to serve turkey was a logical offshoot of his successful turkey breeding operation in Strathroy, Ontario. After all, this was the man who revolutionized the world-wide turkey

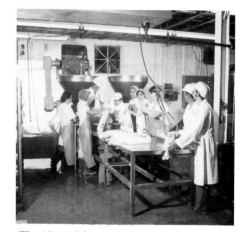

The idea of further-processed turkey was just getting off the ground in the 1970s. Above, production workers at the Cuddy Food Products' processing plant stuff blended white turkey meat into rolls, before cooking.

industry by developing the technology to breed turkeys all year round. So who better to pioneer the further-processing of this protein source?

So, the man who founded Cuddy Farms in 1950 made an early foray into the turkey processing business in the mid-1960s. Cuddy Farms already enjoyed a successful partnership with Riverside Poultry which had a primary processing plant on Trafalgar Street East in London. In 1967, A.M. Cuddy bought out the operation and expanded the live-receive facility to also bone and further-process the meat.

Unfortunately, the idea was ahead of its time. People still focused on whole body birds and neither consumers nor retailers could get used to purchasing "the king of the table" in any other way. So in 1970, A.M. Cuddy put his dream on hold for a few years.

During the early 1970s, there was more than enough to keep him occupied with the constant expansion of

In the mid-1950s, turkeys were sold to consumers only as whole body birds. Turkeys were inspected and graded before leaving the Riverside Poultry Plant, which was then part-owned by A.M. Cuddy. The Trafalgar Street operation was later bought out and became Cuddy Food Products.

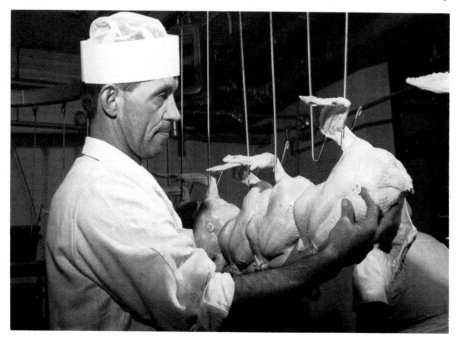

Cuddy Farms' operations. His oldest son, Bruce, after graduating from the University of Guelph, headed for North Carolina to establish Cuddy Farms, Inc. European markets opened up and turkey breeding operations in Strathroy were kept at peak capacity. The turkey hatchery and the surrounding turkey farms were constantly expanded to meet the increasing demand for quality hatching eggs and day-old poults (baby turkeys).

In 1974, A.M. Cuddy decided to take another grab at the brass ring, determined to fulfil his dream of further-processed turkey. At the time, turkey was still being sold as a commodity and prices reflected that mind-set. A.M. Cuddy continued to maintain: "We have to stop selling these turkeys like cord wood," and that's just what he did.

The new Cuddy Food Products operation got off to a bit of a false and faltering start. So in 1976, he gave his son, Robert, the mandate to revitalize the Trafalgar Street plant. Fresh from his business studies at the University of Western Ontario, Robert had his work cut out for him.

At the time, he had only one office employee and eight production people in the plant. As he found out, the challenge was actually more than just the technology to make the products: Cuddy had to actually change the whole mentality of the retailers and the customers.

The passage of time was of great benefit. By the late 1970s, consumers were more open to the idea of further-processed poultry. Family sizes were declining and more than ever, both parents were in the workforce. In such busy lives, convenience poultry meats could make inroads. Since few people had the time or the inclination to cook whole body birds, there was finally an opening for the healthy new alternative of further-processed turkey.

Even though consumers were finally ready, the real key to success this time was that Cuddy Food Products established a concentrated national sales force of its own. This move allowed the company to break into the lucrative foodservice and retail markets where it has thrived, grown and where it now holds a strong leadership position.

Another important turning point in the Cuddy Food Products history happened when Robert returned from a visit to Florida in 1979. He brought back with him a sample of a new product he had just seen and tasted: the McDonald's McChicken pattie sandwich. It was not yet available in Canada, but Robert was convinced it should be, and that his company could produce it better than anyone else.

For about 18 months, Robert pursued this dream, with the dogged determination he had learned from his father. Finally, a deal was struck: in November 1980, Cuddy Food Products in London, Ontario was named sole-supplier of the poultry needs for McDonald's Restaurants of Canada Limited. Cuddy started with the McChicken pattie and then began producing chicken McNuggets as well. This catapulted the turkey experts into the chicken business, and they have never looked back.

In fact, the introduction of these products in Canada virtually revolutionized the way poultry was sold and consumed. It opened doors for the constant expansion of processed poultry meats. Today, Cuddy Food Products employs about 1,000 people in the development, production and sale of quality poultry products for healthy tastes.

Not only are Cuddy products sold and enjoyed across Canada, but they have also put in gold-medal performances on the world stage. In 1992, 32 Cuddy poultry meat products were entered in international competition in Austria. World experts judged the Cuddy offerings alongside pork and red meat products from around the world. Cuddy is proud to say that 28 of the products submitted brought home medals to London, Ontario: 12 gold, 13 silver and three bronze.

On the strength of its quality-first agenda and entrepreneurial spirit, Cuddy Food Products now markets over 100 different chicken and turkey products with new ideas being developed every day. It is an obvious first choice for many leading institutional and retail customers across Canada and is currently stretching its wings towards the global marketplace.

Each of the Cuddy sons share key management roles within the Cuddy group of companies, founded by A.M. Cuddy in 1950. From left to right: Peter, Robert, Doug, A.M., Bruce and Brian Cuddy.

Cuddy Food Products offers poultry meats in a wide variety of tastes and textures. Cuddy supplies quality poultry for healthy tastes to restaurants, hotels, cafeterias, hospitals, grocery stores and delicatessens across Canada.

London Metal

Three generations of the Barnett family involved in the company: Seated (from left) are W.L. "Bill" Barnett, President; and Robert Barnett, Vice-President and Secretary. Standing (from left) are John Barnett, Office Manager; Alfred Barnett, Chairman; W.J. "Bill" Barnett, Sales Manager.

An established trade supply house serving the sheet metal and mechanical trades, London Metal Service stands upon sixty years of distributing sheet metal accessories and equipment for heating, ventilating, and air conditioning applications for both the residential and commercial markets.

Founded in 1933 by Bill Clifton, the company's potential was recognized by his first customer, Alfred Barnett, who was a sheet metal contractor with one shop in the old McClary Building, where the Galleria Mall now stands, and a second shop in St. Thomas. Barnett entered a partnership with Clifton in 1942, and by 1950 had acquired full ownership of the business. In the early years, the company set up warehouses on Carling Street, first in the old Perrin Building, and later in the Baldwin Building.

During the imposed rationing of the Second World War, Barnett earned the respect and goodwill of tradesmen in south western Ontario by distributing steel rations to this established accounts on an equitable basis, and consequently, kept many in business.

The present site of 675 York Street and the construction of the original warehouse in 1950 form the hub of a one-stop shop of supplies for the sheet-metal, heating, ventilating and air conditioning trades. Over three decades, from 1959 to 1989, the facilities underwent six plant additions and expansions, including in 1968, the purchase of the adjoining Imperial Oil property and the three-story, late-1800's warehouse — which is still in use. The latest addition, on the west side of the century warehouse, has brought the total building space to over 42,000 square feet on the 4.5 acre site, located in the geographic centre of the city.

Constant growth, however, has not been confined only to the structural development of the company, but also in the evolution of its inventory, from wood- and coal-fired units to energy-efficient furnaces; bi-metal thermostats to programmable, computerized energy management systems; hot-dipped steel to electroplated galvanized, and special coatings; hand tools and equipment to computer-driven plasma cutting systems. As a flat-rolled steel service centre and HVAC supply house, the firm maintains an inventory of over 10,000 items from over 300 leading manufacturers, and also offers complete semi-finishing steel processing services.

In 1971, Alfred's sons Bill and Bob assumed ownership as President and Vice-President respectively, and Alfred became Chairman of the Board. Under his sons' direction, London Metal Service entered the computer age in 1984, completely computerizing their operations by 1988. The firm continues to keep in step with the latest technological advancements with the constant upgrading of their computer system. In addition, the provision of lap-top computers has relieved the sales force of the burdens inherent with excessive amounts of hard copy.

A third generation of the Barnett family, John and Bill, continues the tradition of the family-run business, and the strength and stability of the company can also be attributed to a staff of 33 full time employees with an average service of over 14 years.

The President and Vice-President of the firm have remained committed to the continual advancement of their company and the industry by participating in national and international trade associations, which are involved with the latest developments to emerge in the HVAC and flat-rolled sheet metal industries.

O-Pee-Chee Company LIMITED

"Supplying Young Canada's
Favourites For Over 80 Years"

On February 23, 1911, the first package of Gipsy Gum rolled off the assembly line at the O-Pee-Chee Gum Company, owned and operated by the McDermid Brothers, John "J.K." McKinnon and Duncan Hugh, whose experience in the confectionery business extended to 1897.

An Indian word for "the robin," O-Pee-Chee appears in the Longfellow poem, "Song of Hiawatha," and was originally the name of the McDermid's summer cottage in Grand Bend. The name also reflects a favourite juvenile expression of the time, "Oh, peachy!"

In 1921 the firm was incorporated as a public company under the name of O-Pee-Chee Company Limited. At this time, sales reached $200,000 annually, profits quadrupled, and staff was expanded to 30 employees. O-Pee-Chee expanded its product line to include mints and several kinds of popcorn, such as the popular Krackley Nut brand. As a result of the continuing expansion of operations, the factory at 430 Adelaide Street was erected in 1928.

O-Pee-Chee survived the Depression by securing a Licensing Agreement with a Buffalo firm to produce and market a line of paraffin chewing gum and novelties in Canada, and export the products to the United Kingdom and Ireland. In 1934, J.K.'s son, John Gordon McDermid, joined the firm, as did Frank P. Leahy, who assumed the position of Sales Manager. O-Pee-Chee prevailed over the imposition of sugar rationing during the Second World War mainly through contracts to supply dried egg powder to Europe. Thrills Gum was the only confection that remained in production, and is still manufactured today.

During the war years, the two founding McDermid brothers passed away, and in 1945 the company reverted to private ownership. John Gordon McDermid presided over the business until his death in 1953, and was succeeded by Frank P. Leahy, who purchased the firm from the McDermid estate in 1961.

Under Leahy's management, O-Pee-Chee continued to flourish through Licensing

New plant and offices built in London East in 1989.

Agreements with two American firms, which provided O-Pee-Chee with the rights to manufacture and market their products in Canada. O-Pee-Chee took advantage of the 1960's phenomena of Beatlemania and card gum collecting by obtaining the rights to produce and market Beatle bubble gum cards in Canada. This was followed by a succession of collector cards from popular television shows such as Happy Days and Charlie's Angels, and from box-office smashes such as the Star Wars Trilogy, E.T., the Batman films, and Teen-Age Mutant Ninja Turtles. O-Pee-Chee responded similarly to hockey and baseball enthusiasts by producing collector cards, and has prospered in the recent exponential growth of sports

O-Pee-Chee gum being delivered in Brandon, Manitoba, July 25, 1913.

card collecting. 1992 marks O-Pee-Chee's twenty-fifth continuous year of manufacturing hockey cards.

In 1980, Frank Leahy died, and his son-in-law, Gary Koreen, who had been active in the business since 1968, became President and Owner of the Company. In 1989, Koreen amalgamated the manufacturing and distributing operations, and a staff of over 200 under one roof at the modern glass structure in London East.

Today, O-Pee-Chee enjoys the distinction of being one of the largest independent and privately-owned Confectionery Companies in Canada. From its new headquarters, O-Pee-Chee continues to maintain an active interest in the London community, and to appeal to its young market with such perennial favourites as Bazooka, SweeTARTS, Nerds, and Collector Cards.

St. Willibrord

Serving Southwestern Ontario Since 1951

St. Willibrord provides financial services to meet the needs of the entire community — including families, businesses and farm operations.

Located on Dundas Street East in London, St. Willibrord operates this and eight other branch offices across Southwestern Ontario.

St. Willibrord Community Credit Union was formed in 1951 by a group of Dutch Catholic immigrants. Making a new start in Canada was difficult for this group, who faced language barriers in addition to difficulty obtaining credit from other sources. Involved in the agricultural community of Southwestern Ontario, they recognized an opportunity among themselves to operate a financial co-operative by pooling their money together, and then lending it to each other.

The name "St. Willibrord" was chosen early in the credit union's history. To this founding group St. Willibrord symbolized their circumstances. The patron saint of Holland, St. Willibrord was an English person in a Dutch land — and the credit union members were of Dutch origin, living in an English-speaking country.

From these modest, yet solid beginnings, St. Willibrord Community Credit Union has undergone many changes and continual growth during over 40 years of operation in Southwestern Ontario. Originally, there were a few part-time "collection" points scattered across the area to serve a strictly Dutch membership. In two stages, first in 1977 and finally in 1983, St. Willibrord became a "community" credit union, meaning that anyone who lives or works in Middlesex or Lambton counties or in the City of Stratford or Town of Blenheim may join, or become a member of St. Willibrord Community Credit Union. Today, St. Willibrord operates with a network of nine branches in Arkona, Blenheim, London (3 branches), Sarnia, Stratford, Strathroy, and Watford.

In the early years, St. Willibrord offered its members the basic financial services of savings accounts, and small loans. Today, Credit Union members select from a full menu of services, including innovative savings and chequing accounts, investment and retirement products, mortgages, personal loans, commercial services and connections to a variety of international affiliates and networks.

Many people who are unfamiliar with credit unions in general or with St. Willibrord in particular wonder what makes St. Willibrord Community Credit Union unique among financial institutions. It is a modern, full-service financial institution. Everyone who does their banking at St. Willibrord is a <u>member</u> - each with an equal share investment and voting privilege in <u>their</u> credit union. Members use these votes to elect other volunteer members who control the credit union's direction.

As a financial co-operative, deposits are invested locally in the form of loans to other members. Profits on operations are reinvested in the future of the credit union, in the form of equity and reserves, and ongoing investment in service enhancements.

The credit union system, as a group, has pioneered several important innovations in the financial service industry, based on a well-deserved reputation of responsiveness to member needs. Some of the innovations include daily-interest chequing accounts, weekly mortgage payments, and automated banking services.

For a credit union with such a history of continual change and evolution, St. Willibrord has big plans for the future, as well. In 1993, the credit union will celebrate the opening of a new corporate office in London, and there are plans for upcoming branch expansions. The credit union will be keeping pace with ever-changing computer technology and member service enhancements.

St. Willibrord Community Credit Union is a forward-thinking organization, poised to meet future opportunities and challenges head-on.

London 200

CELEBRATE The Founding and the Future 1793 - 1993

London 200 is the year-long celebration focusing on our rich cultural and historic past. This celebration of two hundred years of remarkable achievement by London citizens, gives us the opportunity to revisit the past, revel in the present, and envision the future. A host of events will include world class sports, cultural arts, fireworks, and festivals.

The adventure begins December 31, 1992, and lasts throughout 1993.

We are celebrating more than the anniversary of the founding of London by Lt. Gov. John Graves Simcoe, we are honouring 200 years of history. Our objective is to cultivate heritage awareness and instill civic pride. Through London 200 activities, we hope to encourage and develop a positive and lasting effect on our community.

In order to know where we are going, we must understand where we have been. Therefore, London 200's history committee has spent months compiling a detailed chronology of our first 200 years. These efforts will contribute to a project that helps London's history come alive. A series of vignettes detailing unique events of our past are being produced for both broadcast and print media.

The London Boards of Education, the University of Western Ontario, and Fanshawe College agree that 1993 presents an outstanding opportunity to learn a great deal about London's past. London 200's education committee's arranging special appearances by a local actor who will represent our own John Graves Simcoe. These performances will bring this important historical figure to life. This and other activities are designed to inspire London's youth to understand and take pride in our heritage.

London 200 will provide countless reminders of how much we have to be thankful for.

Tourists and visiting friends will get an opportunity to see our great city at its best. Our guests will be sure to enjoy exceptional theatre, night life, restaurants, galleries, museums, parklands and world-class hotels.

In 1993, London 200 will leave a legacy to the future of our fair city. For example, we plan to help Grosvenor Lodge become a significant and integral part of London's heritage. London 200 is also spearheading a global conference on "Why It Pays To Be Green". Massive tree plantings are being encouraged as well. What better way to commemorate the Forest City's past and prepare for its future.

Two hundred years after John Graves Simcoe founded the City at the Forks of the Thames, Londoner's are celebrating a lasting legacy of progress in business, commerce, industry, and medical research. London can be very proud of its accomplishments. 1993 gives us the opportunity to rediscover our city. The future looks bright as we look forward to our next 200 years.

Lt. Gov. John Graves Simcoe as portrayed by Woody Lambe.

SPECIAL EVENTS

New Year's Eve, Founders' Day & Winter Carnival, Grand Military Re-Enactments, R.C.M.P. Musical Ride, Festival at the Forks, LPGA duMaurier Ltd. Classic, International Games Exchange, Benjamin Britton's War Requiem, Closing Ceremonies & Multi-Cultural Festival, Towards 2000, The Grand Theatre, The Simcoes, London Ringette Association, Arbour Day at the Forks, "Lily of the Valley" Debutante Ball, London Air Show, International Children's Festival, The London Classic on Ice, The Boris Brott Summer Music Festival, St. Paul's Cathedral, DeBeers Diamond Collection, Lazare Caplan Rainbow Collection, Western Ontario Lawn Bowling Championships, The Molson Light Balloon Fiesta, The London 200 Molson Light Balloon Glow, Western Fair Theme 200, Why It Pays to Be Green, London 200 Film Festival Contest.

LONDON 200

C A N A D A

Copyright The London Free Press
Photograph by Susan Bradnam

CHAIRMAN'S REMARKS

It was a mere 200 years ago that Lieutenant Governor John Graves Simcoe stood at the forks of the Thames River and proclaimed the location as the site for the capital of Upper Canada. Although London has not become the capital of Canada, it has emerged as the regional centre for business and culture in southwestern Ontario. In 1993, Londoners and their friends and visitors will celebrate London's founding, its history, its present and its future in a year long celebration known as London 200.

London 200 will not, however, be just a celebration. It will also be an opportunity to enjoy with Londoners, from all walks of life, the many attributes of our fine city. During the year, we will present a number of major events, many of which are unprecedented in our history, and will feature literally hundreds of community

Daniel R. Ross

and local events designed to highlight our rich cultural heritage. Whether it is the LPGA's du Maurier Classic to be held at the London Hunt and Country Club, the Festival at the Forks of the Thames or our Grand Military Re-enactment, we will be encouraging attendance and participation by all Londoners. The history of London will be featured in our schools, our theatres, in children's performances and in performances by our symphonies and choirs. We will celebrate the contributions of Londoners, be they large or small, and whether the authors of those contributions are famous or infamous.

It is our sincere hope that at the end of 1993, we will not only have an enriched sense of our history, but an equally enriched anticipation of our future.

On behalf of hundreds of committee members who have spent almost three years working towards this celebration, we encourage everyone to enjoy London - The Place To Be In '93!

The Royal Canadian Mounted Police Musical Ride and Tattoo Two Hundred.

STEERING COMMITTEE
Controller Jack O. Burghardt, E.W. (Ted) Eadinger, Robert V. Elsden, J. Etherington, Duncan D. Findlay, Janet Fridman, His Worship Mayor Thomas C. Gosnell, Michael A. Harris, William R. MacDougall, Angus L. McKenzie, Q.C., John C. Nash, Earl H. Orser, Nancy Poole, Daniel R. Ross, Kenneth W. Sadler, His Honour Judge John M. Seneshen, Robert G. Siskind, John Winston

MANAGEMENT COMMITTEE
Daniel R. Ross, Ted Eadinger, Louise McMillan, Del McLennan, Marjorie Millar, Arlene Kennedy, Hank VanderLaan, Tom Sabourin, Maureen Adlard, Gerald Fagan, Brenda Pilley, Nancy Poole, Natalie Knezic, Garth Williams, Doug Gordon, Duncan Findlay, Dawn Ralph, Diane Quinlan, Norm MacDougall, Cass Bayley

PROJECT MANAGER
Louise McMillan

ADMINISTRATIVE ASSISTANT
Heather Goddard

Representing the Organizing Committee are Maureen Adlard, Dan Ross, Ted Eadinger and Louise McMillan.

Patrons

The following individuals, companies and organizations have made a valuable commitment to the quality of this publication. The London Chamber of Commerce gratefully acknowledge their participation in London 200: An Illustrated History of London, Canada.

Aboutown Transportation Ltd.*
Accuride Canada Inc.
Avco Financial Services Canada Ltd.*
Beaver Foods Limited*
Bell Canada*
Blackburn Group Incorporated, The*
C.B.S. Equipment Ltd.*
Canada Post Corporation*
Canada Trust Company*
Central Park Lodge*
Charterhouse Printing Services
Copp Builders' Supply Company Ltd.*
Corporation City of London
Cuddy International*
Dawson, R.C. Co. Ltd.
Ernst & Young
Fanshawe College of Applied Arts & Technology*
Forest City Linen Supply*
Gallo Group Inc., The*
Goliger's Travel*
Howden, D.H. & Company Ltd.*
IBM Canada Ltd.
Kellogg Canada Incorporated*
Kime, Mills, Dunlop
Labatt, John Limited*
Labatt Breweries of Canada*

Lever Industrial Inc.
London Chamber of Commerce*
London & Middlesex Roman Catholic Separate School Board*
London Life Insurance Company*
London Metal Service Ltd., The*
London 200*
Matthews Group, The*
McCormick Canada Inc.*
McHardy Vacuum Ltd.
Microtronix Systems Ltd.*
O-Pee-Chee Company Ltd.*
Parkwood Hospital*
Peat Marwick Thorne
Quaker State Minit-Lube*
Reed Stenhouse Limited*
Sifton Properties Ltd.*
3M Canada Incorporated*
Sterling Marking Products Inc.
St. Willibrord Community Credit Union*
Thomas, James E. & Associates Inc.
University Hospital*
University of Western Ontario*
Victoria Hospital Corporation*
Wolverine Tube (Canada) Inc.*
Wright Lithographing Company Limited

*Corporate Profiles of London 200: An Illustrated History of London, Canada. The histories of these companies and organizations appear in Chapter 15, beginning on page 255.

Editorial Acknowledgements

Edward Phelps, Associate Editor

A year ago, in September 1991, the idea of a commemorative book marking 200 years of London history, came forth at a "London 200" committee meeting chaired by my good friend Nancy Poole, Director of the London Regional Art & Historical Museums (LRAHM). All major London histories were out-of-print; the time seemed ripe for a new book. Orlo Miller offered the text of *This Was London* (1988), and the London Chamber of Commerce sponsored the project as publisher. In March 1992, my dedicated colleagues Miriam Wright, as Editorial Assistant, and Glen C. Phillips, as Photo editor and researcher, commenced their task and have ensured the success of the final product. Orlo Miller and his energetic co-worker Maridon Miller offered many suggestions on additional source material which they had encountered in their sixty years of research, writing and publishing. I owe much to their patience and wise counsel.

Many persons gave freely of their experience and insight. The Chamber of Commerce editorial committee, including Jim Etherington, Jack Mann, Pat Bettridge, Kay McLaughlin, and Duncan Callam, read and reworked hundreds of pages of manuscript. At The London Free Press, Edythe Cusack, the now retired Librarian, was patient and tireless in her ability to provide data. Glen Curnoe and the staff of the London Room at the London Public Library, were very generous in providing assistance, as were Michael Baker and colleagues at LRAHM. Pegi Walden, Margaret Johnson, Olga Bishop, and Brenda Pilley provided assistance to Miriam Wright as she expanded the scope of the last 30 years of the history. Arthur D. Cartier, PUC member and former City controller, and old friend from Reunion London 1988 days, read the manuscript and offered many valued suggestions. My colleagues at the D.B. Weldon Library, including John H. Lutman, Guy St-Denis, Theresa Regnier, Alice Gibb and Stephen Harding were gracious in providing information and advice. I also thank Alan Noon of UWO and author of *East of Adelaide* for his constant help.

Words are inadequate to express my appreciation to my good friend and contemporary Daniel J. Brock, for his meticulous attention to detail and unfailing supply of advice throughout this project, from the concept stage, through the drafts of manuscript, and right up to the proofing of final pages, and his generous assistance to my co-workers Miriam Wright and Glen C. Phillips.

The enthusiasm and willing co-operation of a number of persons associated with the project have created a cordial and effective working atmosphere. I thank the many staff members at the London Chamber of Commerce who have been supportive and cheerful throughout; finally, the tireless, patient, and creative work of members of the Aylmer Express printing and publishing firm: Karen Hueston, John Hueston, Denise Ward, and many others of their staff for their unfailing warmth and courtesy.

If men could learn from history, what lessons it might teach us! But passion and party blind our eyes, and the light which experience gives is a lantern on the stern, which shines only on the waves behind dusk!
Samuel T. Coleridge
(1772-1834)

Readers of this volume will notice a number of spellings of early surnames which are at variance with those in many other writings on London. The surname spelling of our first resident Peter <u>MacGregor</u> is preferred by Orlo Miller, rather than "McGregor" which is more common. Miller's use of MacGregor is based on his researches into the genealogy of Scots Highlanders, where this spelling is the generally accepted spelling, the use of McGregor being considered an Irish derivation. Whilst the surviving signatures of Peter read "McGregor," certain descendants including his great-grandson Mahlon J. used the form MacGregor. In 1902 the London and Middlesex Historical Society erected its first commemorative plaque to Peter on a building at the southwest corner of Ridout and King Streets, now occupied by the Jenkins Seed House, and spelled his surname "MacGregor." Historians, however, have used the form "McGregor," as did Peter, including Goodspeed (1889), Bremner (1897), Campbell (1921), Seaborn (1944), and Armstrong (1986), and Brock, in *The North Talbot Road, Westminster Township,* (1986).

Two other names require mention; both Norfolk County men hanged at London for murder: Cornelius <u>Burleigh</u> and Henry <u>Sovereign</u>.

Cornelius' surname was spelled "Burley" by contemporaries, relatives, and later writers; in this case we are deprived of signatures since he was illiterate. Both spellings flourish in southwestern Ontario in 1992 in about equal numbers. The <u>Dictionary of Canadian Biography</u>, Vol. VI, 1987, uses "Burley".

In the case of Henry Sovereign, the use of "Sovereene" in the <u>D.C.B.</u>, VI, 1987, appears to be unique to Henry; only the spelling "Sovereign" (with a rare variant "Sovran") survives in the area.

Acknowledgement

Glen C. Phillips, Photo Editor/Researcher

I would like to thank the many people and institutions who made my task as this project's photo editor/researcher a true pleasure. Staff at the Ontario Archives, the Metropolitan Toronto Library, and the National Archives of Canada were all helpful. Guy St-Denis and Theresa Regnier at the Regional Collection, D.B. Weldon Library, U.W.O. were more than patient with my many requests. Mike Baker and Becky Gough of the London Regional Art and Historical Museums allowed me easy perusal of what may be the city's most fabulous, yet "undiscovered" collection of historical London images.

I further owe an incredible debt to the following private collectors who willingly offered their encouragement, as well as opening their collections to my eyes: Walter Eldridge, Bill Henshaw, Roy Kerr, Gene Lamont, Paul Miller, Chuck Riddick, Jack Riddick, J.M. Waters, John Whalen, and Don Whetstone. The contribution of several professional photographers is also recognized. Victor Aziz, Ron Nelson, Stephen Harding, and the indefatigable Alan Noon through their many talents added greatly to the quality of illustrations in this book.

Finally, I would like to thank Dan Brock for his helpful advice and suggestions, Miriam Wright for her patience, and Edward Phelps for his vision and counsel, as well as the members of the London 200 Book Committee, and Karen Hueston and Denise Ward of the Aylmer Express. Above all, I would like to tender a heartfelt thank you to my wife, Connie Stratton, whose loving support throughout this project was always an inspiration.

Titus Antonius Puis... His reign is marked by the rare advantage of furnishing very few materials for history; which is, indeed, little more than the register of the crimes, follies and misfortunes of mankind.

Edward Gibbon
(1737-1794)

Bibliography

I. BOOKS

Addington, Charles *A History of the London Police Force, 1855-1980* with an update to 1991 edited by Glen C. Phillips London, 1991.

Andreae, Christopher *The Industrial Heritage of London and Area* London, 1984.

Armstrong, Frederick H. *The Forest City: An Illustrated History of London, Canada* Northridge, California, Windsor Publications, 1986.

Barr, Murray, L. *A Century of Medicine at Western.* London, 1977.

Bremner, Archie *Illustrated London, Ontario, Canada* London, 1897.

Brock, Daniel J. *Best Wishes from London, Canada: Our Golden Age of Postcards 1903-1914* London, 1992.

Brock, Daniel J. *Dan Brock's Historical Almanack of London* London, 1975, 3 vols.

Buchanan, Edward V. *Roses in December, an Autobiography* London, 1986.

Cahn, Julius *Official Theatrical Guide, 1905-1906* New York, 1905.

Campbell, Clarence T. *Milestones 1826-1926* London, 1926.

Campbell, Clarence T. *Pioneer Days in London* London, 1921.

Carty, Arthur, C. *A Thousand Arrows: Biographical Memoir of the Hon. Henry Edward Dormer* London, 1970.

Carter, Francis, G. *The Middlesex Bench and Bar* London, 1969.

Connor, James T.H. *A Heritage of Healing: The London Health Association and Its Hospitals 1909-1987* London, 1990.

Conron, A. Brandon *The London Hunt and Country Club 1885-1985* London, 1985.

Corfield, William E. *To Alleviate Suffering, The Story of the Red Cross in London Canada 1900-1985* London, 1985.

Cronyn, Verschoyle P. *Other Days* London, 1976.

Crowfoot, A.H. *This Dreamer: Life of Isaac Hellmuth, second Bishop of Huron* Toronto, 1963.

Curnoe, W. Glen *Around London 1900-1950* London, 1973.

Drew, Benjamin, ed. *The Refuge: or the Narratives of Fugitive Slaves in Canada* Boston, 1856, facsimile ed., Toronto, 1972.

Getty, Ruth Dundass, ed. *Orchard Park Through The Years* London, 1983.

Gibb, Alice, and Pat Morden, ed. *Brackets & Bargeboards: Architectural Walks in London, Ontario* London, 1989.

Goodspeed, W.A. and C.L. *History of the County of Middlesex, Canada* Toronto, 1889 (reprint: Belleville, Ont., 1972)

Graham, Percy W. *Sir Adam Beck* London, 1925.

Gray, Leslie Robb, and C. Marguerite Gray *Proudfoot to Pepperbox to Posterity 1833-1983, the 150-Year History of New St. James Presbyterian Church* London, 1983.

Greenberg, Mark, and Edward Phelps *The Young Women's Christian Association of London, Ontario, Canada: A Century of Faith, Hope, and Good Works* London, 1989.

Guillet, Edwin C. *The Lives and Times of the Patriots* Toronto, 1938.

Gwynne-Timothy, John W.R. *Western's First Century* London, 1978.

Hamil, Fred Coyne *Lake Erie Baron: The Story of Colonel Thomas Talbot* Toronto, 1955.

Hamil, Fred Coyne *The Valley of the Lower Thames: 1640 to 1850* Toronto, 1951.

Hill, Daniel *The Freedom Seekers* Agincourt, Ont., 1981.

Hill, Pearl M. *Index to the London Free Press "Looking Over Western Ontario" pages,* Oct. 8, 1921 to Aug. 20, 1949. London, 1951.

Honey, Terrence W., ed. *London Heritage* London, 1972.

Innis, Mary Quayle, ed. *Mrs. Simcoe's Diary* Toronto, 1965.

Israels, Fred *Londoners Remember: A Collection of Reminiscences* London, 1989.

Kilbourne, William *The Firebrand* Toronto, 1956.

Landon, Fred *An Exile from Canada to VanDiemen's Land: being the Story of Elijah Woodman* Toronto, 1960.

Landon, Fred *Western Ontario and the American Frontier* Toronto, 1941.

The Local Council of Women *London Res Gestae Mulierum (Deeds of Women), 1893-1937* London, 1937.

Lutman, John H. *The Historic Heart of London* London, 1977.

Lutman, John H. and Christopher L. Hives *The North and East of London* London, 1982.

McDougall, Allan K. *John Robarts: His Life and Government* Toronto, 1986.

McTaggart, Kenneth D. *The Victoria Day Disaster,* ed. Les Bronson, Petrolia, Ont., 1978.

Miller, Orlo *This Was London, The First Two Centuries* Westport, Ont., 1988.

Miller, Orlo *A Century of Western Ontario* Toronto, 1949.

Miller, Orlo *Gargoyles and Gentlemen* Toronto, 1966.

Miller, Orlo *Twenty Mortal Murders* Toronto, 1978.

Miller, Orlo and A. Brandon Conron *The London Club: a century in light-hearted retrospect* London, 1980.

Mitchell, W.M. *The Underground Railroad* [reprint of 1860 edition] Westport, Conn., 1970.

Morden, Patricia A. *Putting Down Roots, A History of London's Parks and River* St. Catharines, Ont., 1988.

Nolan, Michael *Walter J. Blackburn, A Man for All Media* Toronto, 1989.

Noon, Alan *East of Adelaide: Photographs of Commercial, Industrial and Working Class Urban Ontario 1905-1930* London, 1989.

Paddon, Wayne *The Story of the Talbot Settlement, 1803-1840* St. Thomas, Ont., 1975.

Phelps, Edward, ed. *Middlesex Two Centuries* London, 1989.

Poole, Nancy Geddes *The Art of London 1830-1980* London, 1980.

Purdom, Thomas H. *London and Its Men of Affairs* London, 1915.

Read, Colin *The Rising in Western Upper Canada 1837-8* Toronto, 1982.

Rosser, Frederick T. *London Township Pioneers* Belleville, Ont., 1975.

Seaborn, Edwin *The March of Medicine in Western Ontario* Toronto, 1944.

Shawyer, Alisan J. *Broughdale: Looking for Its Past* London, 1981.

Shute, Evan *The Vitamin E Story: Medical Memoirs* Burlington, Ont., 1985.

Smith, Philip *The Trust-Builders: The Remarkable Rise of Canada Trust* Toronto, 1989.

Smith, Roger *From Golden Grain Grows A Mission, Commemorating the Fortieth Anniversary of Mission Services of London* London, 1991.

Spicer, Elizabeth *Descriptions of London and Its Environs, 1793-1847 Western Ontario History Nuggets,* 31, London, 1964.

St-Denis, Guy *Byron: Pioneer Days in Westminster Township* Lambeth, Ont., 1985.

Stephen, R. Alexander and L. Mackie Smith *The History of St. Joseph's Hospital: Faith and Caring* London, 1988.

Stiller, Calvin R. *Lifegifts: The Real Story of Organ Transplants* Toronto, 1990.

Stimson, Elam, MD. *The Cholera Beacon* Upper Canada, 1835. Reprinted in *Transactions of the London and Middlesex Historical Society,* part XV, 1937.

Stott, Glen *Witness to History: Tales of Southwestern Ontario* Arkona, Ont., 1985.

Sullivan, John R. and Norman R. Ball *Growing to Serve, A History of Victoria Hospital* London, 1985.

Talman, James J. and Ruth Davis Talman *Western 1878-1953* London, 1953.

Tausky, Nancy Z. and Lynne D. DiStefano *Victorian Architecture in London and Southwestern Ontario: Symbols of Aspiration* Toronto, 1986.

Tiffany, Orrin Edward *The Relations of the United States to the Canadian Rebellion of 1837-1838* Buffalo, N.Y., 1905.

United Way of Greater London *Listening to London: A Study of Our Community's Human Service Needs* London, 1990.

Warner, Quintin 1883-1955 *The Man and the Mission* ed. Edward Phelps, London, 1980.

II. PERIODICALS, ORIGINAL SOURCES, ETC.

Armstrong, Frederick H. and Daniel J. Brock "The Rise of London: A Study of Urban Evolution in Nineteenth-Century Southwestern Ontario" in F.H. Armstrong et al., ed. *Aspects of nineteenth century Ontario: essays presented to James J. Talman* Toronto, 1974, pp. 80-100.

Business Advocate (London Chamber of Commerce) vol. 1-6, 1987-1992.

Davis, W.L. *A History of the Early Labour Movement in London* M.A. Thesis, UWO, 1930.

Encounter (the weekly magazine of the London Free Fress) Sept. 1983-Dec. 1991.

"The Gallows Tree: Over Half a Century of Hangings in This City: The Culprits and Their Crimes" London *Free Press* (26 November 1885) pp 2-3.

Hessel, R.H. Manuscript Notes on London Labour History, ca. 1960 Regional Collection, UWO.

Kennedy, Joan *The London Local Council of Women and Harriet Anne Boomer* M.A. Thesis, UWO, 1989.

Landon, Fred "London and its vicinity 1837-38" *Ontario Historical Society, Papers and Records,* XXIV, (1927), pp. 410-438.

Local Council of Women, London, Minutes (microfilm) London Room, LPL.

London, Ont. City Clerk *The Municipal Handbook* London, ca. 1916-1991.

London, Ont. The Corporation of the City of London *Annual Report,* 1987-1991.

The London and Middlesex Historian, ed. Guy St-Denis, no. 1-2, 1990-1991 (Continues the London and Middlesex Historical Society's *Transactions,* v. 1-16, 1902-1966).

London Room, LPL. Historical Scrapbooks and Subject Files ca. 1900-1992.

Lord, Barry, "What London, Ontario has, that everywhere else needs," *Art in America* Sept/Oct. 1969, pp. 103-105.

Malone, Mary, "Imperial Beginnings" *London Magazine* (December 1986) pp. 115-118.

McFarlane, Alice, "Some Women in London's Past," (ms), (London Room), 1973.

Miller, Orlo, "The Bratton Kidnapping" *Canadian Science Digest,* 1,3 (April 1938), pp. 166-169.

Miller, Orlo "The History of the Newspaper Press in London, 1830-1875" *Ontario Historical Society, Papers and Records,* XXXII (1937), pp. 114-139.

Miller, Orlo "The Letters of Rebels and Loyalists" *Canadian Science Digest* 1,1 (January 1938), pp. 70-78.

Miller, Orlo "Topics of the Town," London *Free Press,* various issues, 1934. Scrapbook, Orlo Miller Papers, Regional Collection, UWO.

Miller, Orlo and Godfrey Ridout *The Saint — A Chamber Opera,* London, 1955, unpublished script, Orlo Miller Papers, Regional Collection, UWO.

Mould, Arthur Papers ca. 1920-50, Regional Collection, UWO.

Palmer, Bryan D. et al. "Labour History Project," manuscript, ca. 1974, Regional Collection, UWO.

Palmer, Bryan D., "Give us the road and we will run it," in *Essays in Canadian Working Class History,* Greg Kealey and Peter Warrian, eds. Toronto, 1976.

Proudfoot, William "The Proudfoot Papers, 1832-1848," London and Middlesex Historical Society, *Transactions,* various parts between 1915 and 1938, and other sources.

Railton, George "London in the Forties; Reminiscences" unpublished manuscript transcribed in the Edwin Seaborn Collection: Diaries, pp. 1074-1081, London Room, LPL.

Strong, George Templeton "The Panic of 1837" vol. 6 (1833-1840) *The Annals of America* Chicago, 1968.

Thorne, W.L. *Lady Aberdeen and the National Council of Women* M.A. Thesis, Queen's University, 1970.

Photograph and Visual Credits

In order to give this volume a wide exposure to the riches of previously little known or rarely used visual materials, both in the city of London and beyond, a number of public and private collections have been carefully searched for images. The author and editorial staff regret that they could utilize only a small portion of the unexpected quantity of superb material which became available. They are grateful to all those persons who in their professional or private capacity gave generously of their time and expertise in locating and documenting the reproductions in this book.

Credits are divided, owing to the book's format, into two sections: black-and-white and colour.

I. BLACK/WHITE IMAGES.

Public and private collections are listed separately; page numbers are given; where necessary the position on the page is indicated as U(upper), C(centre), L(Lower); the notation (2) indicates both pictures on a page come from the same source. Public collections are listed in the order of the size of their contribution; private sources are alphabetized.

London Regional Art & Historical Museums (LRAHM): 9, 18, 27, 29, 30, 41, 47, 65, 66, 73, 85, 97, 111, 117U, 123, 124, 127L, 129, 133, 136, 149, 154, 155(2), 156U, 157, 159, 162L, 165C, 167, 171, 175L, 179, 180U, 181U, 183, 188, 189, 193, 194, 206L, 240.

University of Western Ontario, The D.B. Weldon Library. REGIONAL COLLECTION: 21, 36, 37, 38, 57, 64, 68, 87, 95, 98, 100(2), 103, 104, 105, 106, 108, 112, 113, 114 (Canadian Illustrated News, 2 Dec. 1871), 117L, 122L, 131, 132, 138, 144, 147(2), 150, 152, 162U, 163, 168. SPECIAL COLLECTIONS: 56. MICROFORM COLLECTIONS (NEWSPAPERS): 40, 43, 51, 70, 75.

National Archives of Canada, Ottawa, Photography Collection. (NAC) (Page number, followed by the NAC reference number): 59 (C98836); 67 (C 7771); 71 (C128,313); 82 (C135,826); 146 (PA12239); 158 (PA135, 690); 165U (PA29542); 165L (PA31794); 166U (PA31803); 170U (PA74730; original from Alan Noon); 170L (PA24650); 174U (PA133,375); 174C (PA70970); 174L (PA31823); 175U (PA74689; original from Alan Noon); 175C (PA31998); 176 (PA84961); 177 (PA31788); 178 (PA31799); 180L (PA57418); 181C (PA43912); 181L (PA31797); 185 (PA67177); 192 (PA164,632).

Archives of Ontario (PAO) 4, 61, 89 109, 115, 116, 118, 122U, 127U, 134, 137, 139, 142, 156L, 206U, 215U. Metropolitan Toronto Library: viii (Simcoe); 90, 93, 160; City of London Economic Development Office: 195, 199, 239; Middlesex County Council: 22,

32; Canada Consumer & Corporate Affairs: 12; Elgin County Library: 62; Hamilton Public Library: 24; Ontario Ministry of Natural Resources (Surveyors Crown lands papers), 15; London Regional Childrens Museum, 231; Western News (Alan Noon photo), 250.

PRIVATE COLLECTIONS AND CORPORATE HOLDINGS

Victor Aziz Photography: 198, 201, 248, 249; Michael Baker: 252, 253; Graham Garrett: 54; Stephen Harding: 2, 246; William M. Henshaw: 180C, 187; Hugo & Caroline Messerhuber, 148; Orlo & Maridon Miller: 34, 77 (original of the Bishop Cronyn oil portrait is at Huron College), 130, 172; Ron Nelson Photography: 209, 210, 217, 228; Edward Phelps, 126 (1984 Historical Calendar), 143 (Dominion Illustrated News, 21 Sept. 1889), 151, 203, 238, 251L; Glen C. Phillips: 3, 119, 140(2), 143U, 153(2), 164U, 164L, 166L, 254 (business illustrations); Photographic Conservancy of Canada (Walter Eldridge): T.H. Orr Collection: 19, 52, 79, 121, 135, 141, 173; PCC: Keast Collection: 120; Charles Riddick, 164C; Jack Riddick: 200; A. Gordon Russell: 205; Erik Singer Photography (Orlo Miller portrait on jacket); John Tamblyn: 240 (courtesy of LRAHM); Merle R. TIngley ("Ting"): 226; J.M. Waters: 6; Donald Whetstone: 80, 161.

The London Free Press (LFP): 190, 196, 197(2), 202, 204, 206C, 208, 212, 213, 214, 215L, 216, 218, 219, 221, 222, 223, 224, 225, 230, 233(2), 234, 235, 237, 242 (George Blumsen photo), 243, 245, 251U (Morris Lamont photo).

II. COLOUR IMAGES

There are four colour sections, not separately paginated located between page numbers as indicated below. Pictures are itemized in the order of appearance.

Section "A" located between pages 70 and 71: Page 1. Both portraits from J.C. Dent, *Canadian Portrait Gallery*, 1885; page 2, Glen C. Phillips; page 3, Metropolitan Toronto Library (MTL), T15388; page 4, River Thames, National Archives of Canada (NAC) C13304; Our House, NAC C13301; page 5, from the River Thames, MTL T31488; from the bank of the Thames, NAC 13306; page 6, London 1842, MTL T15399; slide #1645; page 7, Barracks, by Henry Ainslie, NAC C542; Encampment, NAC C544; page 8, NAC C8782.

Section "B" located between pages 116 and 117: Page 1. Glen C. Phillips; page 2, London Regional Art & Historical Museums (LRAHM); page 3, Certificate, Lambton Heritage Museum; London from the Thames, MTL T15404, slide #1651; page 4, LRAHM.

Section "C" located between pages 186 and 187: Page 1, MTL T14466; page 2, "Jack Canuck," J.M. Waters; page 3, Labatt brewery

poster, Paul Miller; Queen Victoria, Valerie Anderson-Mann; page 4, Merrymaking, Glen C. Phillips; McCormick's, Gene Lamont; page 5, upper card, Glen C. Phillips; lower card, Donald Whetstone; page 6, Glen C. Phillips; page 7, Glen C. Phillips (2); page 8, Gene Lamont and John Whalen.

Section "D" located between pages 250 and 251: Page 1, Glen C. Phillips (2); pages 2-3, Victor Aziz Photography (4); page 4, Roy Kerr, used with the permission of the artist Ronald Nickles; page 5, LRAHM (2); page 6, City of London Economic Development Office; page 7, London International Children's Festival; page 8, The London Free Press (Sam McLeod photo, 1992).

Title page and jacket view of London: *Illustrated London News*, 1855.

Index